HOLLYWOOD'S REVOLUTIONARY DECADE

D0556371

HOLLYWOOD'S REVOLUTIONARY DECADE

Charles Champlin

reviews the movies

of the 1970s

JOHN DANIEL AND COMPANY · SANTA BARBARA · 1998

Published by John Daniel and Company
A division of Daniel and Daniel, Publishers, Inc.
Post Office Box 21922
Santa Barbara, CA 93121

Book design: Eric Larson
Cover Design: Frank Bucy/No Wave Press

"Shampoo" image used in front cover design
©1975 Vista Company. All rights reserved.
Courtesy of Columbia Pictures.

LIBRARY OF CONGRESS CATALOGING-IN-PUBLICATION DATA
Champlin, Charles, 1926–
    Hollywood's revolutionary decade : Charles Champlin reviews the movies of the
1970s.
    p. cm.
    A collectionof reviews first appearing in the Los Angeles Times.
    ISBN 1-880284-26-X (alk. paper)
    1. Motion pictures—Reviews.   I. Title
PN1995.C4437   1998
791.43'75—dc21   97-34608
                                                           CIP

For Peggy, again

ACKNOWLEDGEMENTS

These reviews all appeared originally in the *Los Angeles Times* and I am deeply grateful to the newspaper and its editor, Shelby Coffey III, for permission to reprint them here. I am also deeply appreciative of Mr. Coffey's predecessors, Nick B. Williams and William Thomas, and of my immediate editors over the years, including Leonard Riblett, Jim Bellows, Jean Sharley Taylor and Narda Zacchino, for the enthusiastic support and encouragement that made something more than a quarter-century of work so pleasant.

In the preparation of this book, I owe thanks to Judy Stangler and John Champlin for keyboarding the reviews for the computer and to my wife, Peggy, for leading me through the mysteries of that infernal device. And I extend great thanks and much admiration to John and Susan Daniel for embracing the idea of these remembrances of films past, and to Eric Larson for putting them together so handsomely.

CHARLES CHAMPLIN
SEPTEMBER 1997

Contents

Introduction

I BEGAN TO REVIEW MOVIES as the principal film critic of the *Los Angeles Times* in March 1967, on the retirement (mandatory at 65 in those days) of my predecessor Philip K. Scheuer. We both loved the movies, and he had come to Hollywood as a young man hoping to write for the silents, as he briefly did. It was clear to both of us that times were changing in the industry, primarily because of the devastating impact television was having on motion picture attendance. Yet neither of us, I think, could have confidently foreseen that the movies were at a junction in their long and raffish history that was second only to the coming of sound. They had reached a turning point that was not simply evolutionary but revolutionary in its dimensions.

Movie-going in America had reached an historic peak in 1946, when we bought 90 million-plus tickets every week. But for the last several years, in a total population some 90 million larger, ticket sales have been essentially flat at about 20 million admissions a week—a huge decline. Even by the 1950s, it was obvious that something had to happen to give theatrical motion pictures a more competitive stance against the upstart new medium. Three-D films and a greatly widened screen did not solve the crisis, nor did the big-budget so-called road show films, presented on a reserved-seat basis, by which Hollywood hoped to outscale television.

It seemed increasingly evident that the real solution lay in the area of content, showing and telling with an intensity denied (then) to television. In those distant days, television was still truly the living-room medium, its offerings tailored to all-family viewing. The networks had Continuity Acceptance or Standards and Practices staffs that oversaw the innocence of the home screen as rigorously as the Hays Code had policed the movie screen.

But along with urgencies of commerce to let the movies speak more plainly than television could, there was a compounding pressure from the creative community to lift the long-standing restrictions on what Holly-wood films could say and do and deal with. The Code, with its moral umbrella over the movies, had been in force with only minor modifications since 1934, and postwar America was a hugely different so-ciety from early Depression America. The first wave of postwar films from Europe—from Italy most particularly—had demonstrated forcefully that there was a quite different way of looking at life and reflecting social reality. "Open City" and "The Bicycle Thief" caught life among the ruins in a style closer to documentary than to fiction, and without the manda-tory happy or morally correct endings imposed by the Code. Ambitious American filmmakers were inspired by and impatient for that kind of cre-ative freedom.

Coincidentally, and fortuitously, the Code and the office which imple-mented it was on its last, tottering legs, its enforcing power gone. The major studios, which among them had owned many of the most impor-tant cinemas in the country, had agreed in 1934 to play no films that did not have the seal of the Production Code Administration. But starting in 1950 the studios were forced under antitrust consent decrees to sell off their cinemas. As early as 1956, Otto Preminger's "The Man with the Golden Arm," a drama about drug addiction (a forbidden subject under the Code), did well at the box office without the seal. The new exhibitors could show what they pleased.

Bowing to the inevitable, the industry, with production and exhibition joining hands, created the new system of film ratings that came into being in November, 1968. It was voluntary self-regulation, as the Hays Code and its ministrations had been, its real aim to ward off government cen-sorship by insisting that industry could police itself.

The ratings represented a fundamental philosophical change. Gone was the prior censorship, by which the PCA had evaluated and sometimes rejected scripts in whole or part even before the cameras turned. Gone was the presumption that *every* film had to be suitable for (or at least harmless to) every member of the audience, from moppets to octogenar-ians. In its place was an explicit acknowledgement that filmmakers had the right to make their films as they saw fit. The other side of the bargain, so to speak, was that parents were entitled to be alerted by the ratings that there would now be films unsuitable for younger viewers. For their part the theater-owners agreed, remarkably, to turn customers away from wholly or partly restricted films. The specifics governing the ratings have changed slightly since then. But what mattered in 1968 was that over night, almost literally, the movie screen was untethered as it had never been before in this country.

Brave times and heady stuff. And I quickly came to realize that I had acquired an aisle seat at a period of historic ferment in American films. Looking back thirty years later, it is abundantly clear to me, as to many critics, that the decade of the 70s was the richest and most significant in the last half of the twentieth century. The period—it was, I suppose, more precisely a dozen years—from "The Wild Bunch" and "Easy Rider" in 1969 through "Raging Bull" in 1980, by way of "The Godfather," "Chinatown," "Star Wars," and all the others—was unprecedented in its excitements and discoveries. Many of the films I reviewed have achieved the status of classics, benchmarks in the century-long growth of the art form, the films against which both past and future films are measured.

For the critic, it was a uniquely demanding time. The most interesting films were *about* something, as King Vidor's "The Crowd" and John Ford's "The Grapes of Wrath" and William Wyler's "The Best Years of Our Lives" had been about something. They had had a point of view about the society and about the times in which they arose. The difference now was that there were many more films examining the society, from often quite divergent points of view.

The relatively easy judgments on the form and aesthetics of film would no longer suffice. The critic had to look hard at what a film was saying and convey its point of view as carefully and insightfully as possible. We had a role to play, so I felt, as mediators between this new generation of movies and the filmgoers—there were many—who were occasionally shocked, put off and discouraged by what they encountered on the screen where once Fred and Ginger had danced.

I tried, unapologetically, to be an urger, even a teacher, hoping to persuade readers that a film might be austere or indeed a shocker, and the gritty naturalism or the acid-etched portraits unsettling, but that there could be much to be said for its revealing urgency. I felt, and said, that art has a transcendent power to illuminate even the darkest material and make it thrilling. Less easy to express was the idea that a film could proceed by indirection, examining abrasive relationships or dysfunctional families, for example, and in the end defining love by its absence and giving it a freshened savor, as Ingmar Bergman did in "Cries and Whispers" and as Mike Leigh did in 1996's "Secrets and Lies." The critic who spends his working life seeking excellence in the dark could only share the excitement of the filmmakers at the new possibilities open to them.

Criticism became more demanding in another way. Inevitably, the freer expression invited exploitation—and there was a lot of it going around. Watching all or pieces of 250 films a year as I did, it was easy to get the feeling that producers and directors were rushing to make up for all the years when language was cuss-free, bosoms were clothed and violence was bloodless. There was commercial value in the new explicitness, but in my more sanguine moments I hoped that a pent-up thirst—among audiences as well as producers—was being slaked and a happier time would follow. Fat chance. Audiences for exploitive fare simply became inured to the excesses and now receive (if they don't demand) ever-stronger doses.

It became clear soon enough that many in the audience had not abandoned their taste for action adventures and other popcorn pleasures. A number of good but hard-edged dramas of social realism ("Panic in Needle Park" one among them) did not do well. The movies were and are still primarily a medium of escape and diversion, entertainments that are, among other things, still the national date. It was just that now the sheer entertainments enjoyed the new latitudes of the screen, too, and the consequences could be appalling. But the best of the escape films had a new shine and sophistication. The first "Airport" in 1970 was an old-fashioned melodramatic thriller, but its up-to-date depiction of marital and extramarital relationships might well have been ruled out by the guardians of the Hays Code only a few years earlier.

There were letters and articles crying that the new ratings were ripping open "floodgates of filth" (a frequent phrase in the 70s) and, grimacing through the most gruesome of the new films, it was tempting to agree. Some films demanded judgment calls at a uniquely sensitive level: were the filmmaker's intentions honorably serious or merely exploitive? Was a film like Sam Peckinpah's "The Wild Bunch" in 1969 *about* violence or simply a strikingly brilliant display of violence for commercial purposes? I had no doubt the film was Peckinpah's sardonic personal commentary on our capacity not only to commit violence but to enjoy the doing of it. His point of view was unquestionably arguable but I admired the film and had no doubt Sam was in fact making a comment, as well as telling a fast, tough story, although you could certainly disagree with his point of view.

Was the Swedish film "I Am Curious (Yellow)" (1967)—a troubling *cause célèbre* early in my reviewing days—merely exploiting the then-unprecedented showing of male and female frontal nudity in a mainstream film? Or was it the seriously intended look at various aspects of Swedish life, including sexual mores, that it purposed to be? I granted it its seriousness, found the sexuality non-aphrodisiac in the extreme, and save for its minor and quick-fading shock value, thought the film boring. Not all judgment calls were so simple, or free of nagging doubts that you might have been harsh on a genuinely impassioned work, or forgiving of a cynical piece.

Again and again, it seemed to me, the critic was being asked to test a film against his sense of the reality the film was exploring. From time to time I was glad that I had come to film reviewing out of reporting and writing about politics and other disasters, rather than from the study of film aesthetics. (There were times, I do admit, when I have wished I knew more of film history and had seen more of the films of the past that I had missed growing up in a small town.) Yet in the 70s, when the reviewer was asked to be an incipient sociologist at least, I was glad in my days with *Time* and *Life* to have covered a mountain rescue, a race riot, strikes, a couple of murders, a bitter union election in Butte, Montana, a farm closing-out sale and a canoe outing for paraplegics, among many other adventures. I encountered the equivalents of many of them, sitting in the dark.

The new rating system alone does not explain the extraordinary succession of films that was to follow in the 70s. There were other forces at work. Film itself was continuing to evolve, and there had been breakthrough works even before the new rating system commenced: "In Cold Blood" (early in 1967), "Guess Who's Coming to Dinner" (1966) and "Who's Afraid of Virginia Woolf?" (1966), to cite only three. What they shared in common was a pushing against the norms that had been imposed by the Code.

Richard Brooks's dramatization of the slaughter of the Clutter family as told by Truman Capote had a gut-twisting realism seldom filmed before, and although the killers were executed and justice served, no one could listen to the sound track at the end of "In Cold Blood," silent except for the dying heartbeats of one of the killers, without pondering deeply the rightness of capital punishment.

Mixed marriage—"Miscegenation" in the formal language of the Code—was a forbidden subject. Stanley Kramer's treatment of it in "Guess Who's Coming to Dinner" in 1966 was sweetened by the presences of Spencer Tracy, Katharine Hepburn and Sidney Poitier (as a suitor-doctor who already seemed to have everything going for him except the Nobel Prize). But, however glamorous the casting, the theme still confronted an upper middle-class white couple with the prospect of their daughter (Katharine Houghton) wishing to marry a black man. Tracy's speech giving the parents' blessing to the couple is almost unbearably moving to watch now, not least because he was expressing his love to Hepburn (art echoing reality) and because he died less than a month after the production finished and before the film was released. It says something of Kramer's careful handling—and of the country's changing attitudes—that the film played without incident across the South and with only one incident in the industrial North.

"Who's Afraid of Virginia Woolf?," produced and adapted by Ernest Lehman and directed by Mike Nichols, with its "hump the hostess" language intact from Edward Albee's play, was so in advance of the existing Hollywood usage that Jack Warner himself insisted the ads say "Suggested for Mature Audiences," two years before M became one of the new ratings (later to be GP and still later PG, which a cynic said meant "Pretty Gory"). The film was its own landmark in the depiction of human relationships. In the case of George and Martha (Richard Burton and Elizabeth Taylor), a surpassing love had been transmuted by its own frustrations into unprecedented and lacerating screaming matches, which somehow suggested paradoxically that love was still present.

It was also true that as the decade began, there were new filmmakers appearing or coming to maturity. The film schools, especially USC (George Lucas), UCLA (Francis Coppola) and NYU (Martin Scorsese), were graduating a new generation of independent-minded and innovative talents.

And while the basic grammar of films had not significantly changed since D.W. Griffith began to invent it just after the turn of the century, new technologies—faster film, lighter and quieter cameras, all the wizard apparatuses of special effects—gave the new visionaries a palette to go along with their platform, and their predecessors could only have envied both.

There had also been a series of court decisions, one involving Louis Malle's sexually explicit "The Lovers," that widened the legally permissible latitudes of the screen, just as comparable decisions (involving the novels *Ulysses* and *Lady Chatterley's Lover*) had unbound the novel.

U.S. Customs continued, but less frequently, to "arrest" foreign films as obscene objects and to send them to trial. I remember being invited, as a potential expert witness, to attend a screening of "Quiet Days in Clichy," adapted from a Henry Miller novel. The film was about two young Paris layabouts who pick up a beautiful young girl. She seems to be a dream of easy availability until the lads realize she is retarded and needs their protection more than their caresses. The sexiest scene, as I remember, was of them bathing rather innocently in an old-fashioned zinc tub. But the scene I remember most vividly was of the great expatriate jazz man, Ben Webster, sitting in a corner and noodling away, marvelously, on his tenor sax. I don't recall the motivation for the scene, and it hardly mattered. I was never called to testify, but when the film went to trial, the judge reluctantly dismissed the obscenity charge on the grounds that he could not prove the film was *not* artistically intended. It did not prosper in release, possibly because it was neither sexy enough nor artful enough to command attention.

Rereading reviews written a quarter-century ago or more, and sometimes under extreme deadline pressure, has been a nervous but, in most cases, relieving experience. The critic for a daily newspaper is in practice a consumerist, giving readers enough information about a movie to enable them to decide whether to go see it (and then to compare their opinion of it with the critic's). But you have to hope that your verdict on a film will not embarrass you a month, a year, five years or a quarter-century later.

I once wrote that criticism was undoubtedly a kind of dangling participle of an art, dependent on the art it was criticizing. Yet I felt strongly that criticism must aspire to be art. The aspiration to be art was in fact the respect that the critic pays to the art of others. I had not been reviewing long when a reader sent me a clipping about criticism from a journal in Los Angeles called *Manas*. The piece was unsigned but it spoke so directly to my own feelings that I have carried a copy ever since, and have wanted to thank the author.

"Consider a work of criticism," the article said. "It is art or literary criticism [or film criticism, I add].

"The writer may begin with descriptions....He gives you a setting of some sort. But there is no tingle of fresh meaning until he creates something of his own. Until, in other words, art generates art. Criticism which fails to be art is hardly worth reading. Understanding a work of art means finding parallel resonances of meaning in yourself, experiencing its contagion of discovery. Unless this happens, somehow, in a work of criticism, it amounts to nothing but the technique of telling about technique."

I was often asked if I ever changed my opinion about a film, as Joseph Morgenstern reversed his judgment on "Bonnie and Clyde" (from blast to rave) in successive issues of *Newsweek*. My answer (true so far as I can remember) is that I never did a 180-degree turnabout, but that I have often fretted about the shadings of a review. I was too forgiving of an obstreperous and ill-matched subplot in Stanley Donen's "Two for the Road," with its ingenious handling of time and its abrasive hero in Albert Finney. I think I undervalued Jean-Luc Godard's "Weekend," falling into one of the critic's pitfalls and responding emotionally to his cynical pessimism, which I did not share, and taking out my anger on the film's form. I would probably not be as hard now as I was on "Rosemary's Baby" at the time. I admired its sleek skills but complained that Roman Polanski had loaded the dice in favor of the devil. Mia Farrow as God's defender did not represent a level playing field. I could see it with a little less high seriousness today.

The films which I've come to think I probably admired excessively (not many, despite my reputation as a kind critic) are embarrassing to read about again, and I wince for the customers I may have led astray. Most of the protests I received complained that I had not warned readers adequately about the intensity of the violence they would see, and more than once the complaint struck home. Critics can become inured to violence, too. And if a film is seriously intended and the violence organic rather than gratuitous, even a critic sensitive to violence may accept it. But many filmgoers have no such tolerance, and some of them have dropped out of the audience permanently, thinking movies no longer have anything to say that they want to hear.

Violence was always the most difficult element of a film to think about and write about. Blood bags to simulate bullet wounds and graphic makeup that would sicken an emergency room surgeon grew commonplace after 1968, and the make-believe violence of earlier years now demanded to be believed and shuddered at. Was it necessary? Was it for thrills? Was it true to context? You couldn't always be sure, you could only warn the customers that it was coming, and once in a while the forewarnings fell short.

I wrote at least 125 reviews a year, two and sometimes three a week, across the whole range of movies from Ingmar Bergman to Mel Brooks, Disney (the old Disney) to David Lean. I saw most of the movies once, and most at large press screenings. If a film was notably subtle and demanding, and there was time, I saw it more than once (Bergman's "Cries and Whispers" three times to note all its nuances). If I thought I should have admired a film more than I did, I tried to see it again. "They Shoot Horses, Don't They?" was such an earnestly intended movie from such a fine novel that I was almost angry with myself for thinking it didn't work. But I saw it again and felt even more strongly than before that for me, at least, it really didn't work. The actors always looked like actors acting; you saw the scaffolding, not the edifice.

For me, films work or they don't work. When they do, acting ceases to look like acting; even familiar actors disappear into the characters they're playing. Movies are an illusion of course, made possible by the phenomenon of persistence of vision. But our awareness of this falls away when a movie gets hold of our emotions—when it works.

Critics are thought to have a dreadful and killing power, but I think the power of the film critic is much overrated, and where it does exist it is far more likely to be positive than negative. If the critic is right and a film truly doesn't work, the first viewers will agree and word of mouth will kill it swiftly. The critics work their collective and positive influence most effectively on deserving foreign films, independent films, offbeat films that have limited advertising budgets. These are also the films whose potential viewers pay most attention to what the critics have to say. Occasionally the critics will rescue a film its distributor has abandoned, as the New York critics rescued "Sunday, Bloody Sunday" with rave notices of a film United Artists had no hope for. (It was never going to be a blockbuster, but at least it was enabled to find its audience.) The almost unanimous critical endorsements in 1996 of "The English Patient" and "Secrets and Lies," neither likely to have been a mass audience favorite, were enormously helpful in keeping the films in view for the awards they rightly received.

I've never known a film critic who wasn't passionately in love with the movies. And I've often said that the critic lives in the constant hope of the resurrection, hoping that the next film will lift him out of his seat with joy. As dark as many of the best films of the 70s were, it was a time of frequent joy for those of us lucky enough to be writing about what we saw.

In selecting the reviews for this book, the problem was not which to include but which would have to be left out for reasons of space. I've done only the most minor editing, to remove the housekeeping details of where and when they were opening. With great self-control, I've resisted the temptation to make hindsight look like foresight. This is what I wrote at the time, and I hope that now and again I found the eloquence the films deserved. It really was an extraordinary period for movies, and I hope this collection will revive memories—or send you off to the video store with a want list—or both.

CHARLES CHAMPLIN
LOS ANGELES, SPRING 1998

HOLLYWOOD'S REVOLUTIONARY DECADE

1969

The Wild Bunch

Sam Peckinpah's essay on the urge to violence in the human soul was one of the decade's most controversial films in its theme and its execution (a series of violent firsts, including blood spurting from a fresh-cut throat). Using the freedoms of the new rating system, it broke away from the older conventions of screen violence (bloodless and often comfortably accepted as make-believe), which was never to be the same again.

ON ITS OWN TERMS Sam Peckinpah's "The Wild Bunch" *ought* to be every bit as controversial as "I Am Curious (Yellow)" and it may come to be. But I rather doubt it. It is by several thousand red gallons the most graphically violent western ever made, and one of the most violent movies of any kind.

But we still don't get as uptight about violence as we do about sex. And ironically enough our comparative responses sort of second the moral of Peckinpah's movie, which is about violence and not simply gratuitously violent.

Violent it is, however. "The Wild Bunch" is in fact not so much a movie as a blood bath. We see the bodies flinch and the bullet holes appear and the blood explode from the exit wounds. Death is blood-drenched, disfiguring, ugly. Bodies jolt and fall and writhe and die quite literally by the dozens. There was one moment which even I watched squint-eyed, as if to dim the horror.

The squeamish, the weak-hearted or the simply tenderhearted are quite seriously warned away. Those who go will see a wondrously made, thought-provoking movie.

Peckinpah's argument, if I understand him, is that violence is a primal instinct in each of us—man and boy, mother and child. And he suggests, in his gory dramatic terms, that we have not merely a capacity

23

for violence but a joy in violence, a blood lust.

"The Wild Bunch" begins and ends with two of the most detailed and extended gun battles ever made outside a war epic, I should think. And these flank a good deal of lesser violence in the middle, but at that there are 35 more minutes of violence on the cutting room floor at Warner Bros., excised when audiences fled in quantity from two sneak previews. (In Kansas City, I understand, the theater where the sneak was held was picketed the next day.)

Whatever it is, it isn't "Heidi."

The bunch, led by William Holden (in an excellent performance, better than any he has given in years), are a half-dozen border ruffians operating in South Texas and Mexico circa 1913. Nemesis is represented by an even raunchier bunch led by a former pal of Holden's (Robert Ryan, also excellent) who has been blackmailed into working for law and order as the price of not going back to jail.

There are also *federales* and Villa's rebels and *bandidos*—and absolutely no one, so far as I remember, sworn to nonviolence.

A lot of the plot elements and some of the secondary ideas are dead familiar. Everyone wants to make one last killing (so to say) and get the hell out. What is different is the strong evidence Peckinpah provides that they don't *really*, and that in the choice between retreat and bloody confrontation, it's hardly a contest at all.

Amongst the secondary concerns are a fair amount of talk about man-to-man loyalty (real honor among real thieves) and a sardonic look at law and order in its capacity to be more corrupt than corruption. Along with the dark view of violence is a rather Hemingway-esque celebration of courage and of competence at whatever you do on whichever side of the law.

But violence is the major theme. We watch children watching the gun-play more in fascination and envy than in horror. And we see them dancing gleefully around and on a man being tortured to death. Early on, we have seen the happy children setting tarantulas to do battle with killer ants and then incinerating the lot.

In a curious way, only those who totally reject Peckinpah's dark view of the human soul can totally reject his picture (he was coauthor as well as director). Otherwise, Peckinpah has it both ways. Those who revel in the spectacular violence (and many will) prove his contention. Those who finally reach a benumbed horror at the slaughter share the horror I think he is saying he feels himself. And if we are finally unable to react at all—and this kind of satiety does set in—he is proving, as Lee Pogostin did in "Hard Contract," that we can, and perhaps have, become dangerously accustomed to the killing pace in Peckinpah's make-believe world and in our own.

It seems inappropriate to talk of "The Wild Bunch" as a beautiful film. But in fact it is beautifully made and full of spectacular visual images: a desert rainstorm, men and horses stumbling down a sand dune, a line of horsemen galloping into the lens, the four survivors of the wild bunch walking confidently (joyously?) into a suicidal shoot-down with several dozen *federales*.

"The Wild Bunch" is quite overlong, the result of an infatuation with some of those beautiful images. (It is by now the nonviolence, including an interminable coda, which could safely be swiftened.)

Peckinpah's statement is not in itself profound. It is in fact quite simplistic, like the notions of bravery and competence and the relativity of goodness. It is all framed within the comfortingly familiar conventions of the classic western, including, I would say, the characterizing of Mexicans as childlike simple, whether good (poor, exploited but rebellious), bad (*bandidos* or Army) or indifferent (fun-loving *señoritas*).

But his statement has implications deliberately wider than his story, in a day in which many of us are wondering how indelible the stain of violence upon us is.

Ernest Borgnine, as another of the bunch, has one of his best recent roles. Edmond O'Brien is superb as a grizzled old-timer. Warren Oates, Jaime Sanchez and Ben Johnson are fine in lesser roles, and indeed there's a high degree of professionalism all the way.

Lucien Ballard's cinematography is, as I have implied, often breathtaking in its beauty. In the nature of things, I'd guess that the second unit direction of Buzz Henry was especially vital in so active a film as this. The titles—film to freeze-frames to graphics to film again—are exceptionally interesting.

Peckinpah, a notably individualistic director whom Hollywood has not always found it easy or comfortable to cope with, seems to me to prove here that the studio's pains are surely worth it. He makes movies which are real movies and which ripple with power and crackle with energy. This one does not quite achieve the express-train momentum he aimed for but it does not miss by much. And the power in the most powerful moments will be too much for some viewers.

Further questions can be asked. Does Peckinpah mean to be saying something about the reality or unreality of movie violence, for example? Is there a comment implied about the healing or purgative value of watching violence, for another example? I can't be sure, but as I've noted, I think that Peckinpah's concern has been with violence directly and not with the shadow-play of violence.

Whether the urge to violence is as universally planted in us as his events insist I also can't be sure. (It raises Hobbes with our romantic view of man in nature, if I remember freshman philosophy correctly.) The instinct may, if we are lucky, be more defensive than aggressive. But it also seems true that reason and nonviolence are learned responses—the veneer civilization imposes on the real us. "The Wild Bunch" is set in a time and place in which the veneer had only begun to form.

Peckinpah would remind us, I believe, that the veneer has not yet become *that* durable anywhere.

Midnight Cowboy

When it was re-released on its 25th anniversary, John Schlesinger's impressionistic portrait of two losers in the underbelly of Manhattan looked amazingly contemporary, ahead of its time in its images, its editing and, of course, in the prophetic wisdom of its casting of Hoffman and Voight. It remains Schlesinger's masterpiece, and one of film's.

WHAT OUGHT TO BE SAID right away, because it's easy to forget it after the fact, is how radically "Midnight Cowboy" differs from a certain set of expectations we might have had for it.

The story of a good-looking blond buck from Texas fired with simple-minded dreams of making it as a stud hustler in Manhattan could easily have become another of the gamy sexual permutations which the screen is so earnestly examining for us these days.

But John Schlesinger's film is instead an invariably moving study of unlikely (and unsexual) friendship and of collaboration for survival in the sad and gritty shadows cast by the bright lights of Times Square.

It evokes Manhattan's lower (if not its lowest) depths with a fidelity which recalls George Orwell's *Down and Out in Paris and London,* a world of grifters, drifters, pawn shops and of all-night coffee counters whiter and colder than icebergs.

It is a world whose Everyman needs a shave and soles for his shoes and is grateful if he can swipe a packet of crackers. It is a place of kinky and furtive encounters, where unlikely dreams have long since eroded into twenty-four-hour nightmares of failure and loneliness.

It sounds unbelievably grim, which does not prepare you for the raucous and ribald humor of "Midnight Cowboy," or for its astonishing tenderness and sensitivity and its defiant hope, whose tragedy is at last not so much of place as of personality and the pursuit of bad dreams.

Dustin Hoffman as Ratso, a gimpy Bronx Italian who could hardly be further away from the world of "The Graduate," creates a character so whole, so convincing, so singular, that it takes no little effort to remind ourselves that the same actor was also the collegian in pursuit of Katharine Ross and Mrs. Robinson.

Newcomer Jon Voight as Joe Buck, the refugee dishwasher from a Texas beanery, is so powerfully persuasive in his high-pitched drawl and cowboy costume that you read with disbelief he is a product of Yonkers, and a Texan only for Schlesinger's purposes. Voight is in fact a major addition to the family of important American actors and his portrayal of a good-hearted lunk whom life has kicked around pretty good and who tries to create one myth so as to pursue another, is damned near perfect. He is sensitive and insensitive, childlike and all too adult, comical and pathetic.

The success of their collaboration, as actors, has few parallels that I can recall in recent times. It seems clear that Voight and Hoffman discovered their characters together, and revealed them through speech which often has a just-found, improvisational quality. Their relationship as characters—the penny-ante street grifter and the stud hustler trying with desperation to find anybody who wants to be hustled at a price—moves with unwavering credibility from trickery to rage to tolerance, to concern, to loss.

(The postlude, so to speak, seems to me to suggest a grenade with the pin pulled. No small part of the skill of Schlesinger and Waldo Salt, who did the brilliant script, is that we are left at last to imagine the final playing out of a desperate biography.)

As an exercise in filmmaking, "Midnight Cowboy" is dazzling; indeed, once in a while it seems almost too dazzling for its own good. Schlesinger has, for instance, made extensive use of subliminal flashbacks, a device which is not exactly new-hat at this time. Yet the logical way in which these flashbacks are triggered by events in present time struck me as the best use of the technique since, perhaps, "The Pawnbroker."

Then, too, the flashbacks are fragmentary, almost inchoate (and frequently very difficult for the watcher to decipher until he can at last assemble the whole mosaic in his own mind). As such they seemed to me to be a far truer simulation of an actual stream of consciousness (or subconsciousness) than the flashback usually provides. In story terms, they sketch the life-path which led Joe to New York—sluttish mother, vanishing father, young and oversexed grandma with lots of visitors, a gang rape which caught both Joe and a girl he loved. If the bio is arguably expendable, I counter-argue that it is invaluably illuminating.

Other grandeurs of technique work not so well, or rather they work fairly well but in some violation of the naturalism of the rest of the movie. These include a funny set-piece with a kaleidoscopic television set while Joe romps in bed with a lady he thinks he has hustled, and a fantasy sequence for Ratso which quickly comes to seem a writer's invention, not his.

"Midnight Cowboy" is overwhelmingly a two-character story in which nobody else matters much, yet the excellence of its subsidiary casting is another of the satisfactions of the picture. Among the most impressive of the supporting roles are Jonathan Kramer as a guilt-haunted middle-aged homosexual, John McGiver as a religious screwball, Sylvia Miles as the faded blond lady in bed and Brenda Vaccaro (excellent as the secretary in "Where It's At") here wryly and prettily amusing as the one legit customer Joe Buck finds. Ruth White is splendid as Joe's grandmother, and Jennifer Salt does extremely well in the highly emotional role as his girl. Bob Balaban is excellent as a young homosexual.

As Schlesinger proved abundantly in "Darling," he is a careful and perceptive witness to the world we live in. In "Midnight Cowboy," the suspicion is that he has, as an Englishman, seen these special sectors of the American milieu with a visitor's freshness and clarity of sight and insight: the real as against the mythic Texas, the real as against the (tall) storied Manhattan. On a limited scale he has also found and showed us the folk faces which lent such a seamed fascination to his "Far From the Madding Crowd."

There is, I must say, a long psychedelic party in the Village, an event I hope we can hereafter regard as sufficiently documented by the movies. But I must also say that Viva, Ultra Violet and International Velvet helped make Schlesinger's party as successful as any such party is ever likely to be.

John Barry is credited as musical supervisor, which I take to mean that in addition to his own contributions he oversaw the pastiche of pop sounds which place "Midnight Cowboy" so accurately, if jarringly, in our time. Toots Thielemans plays lonely harmonica, singularly right for a picture with so much to say and show about loneliness.

The excellent photography is by Adam Holender, and in a story in which sound has a special importance (Joe Buck's security blanket is a portable radio), special mention is due the team of Jack Fitzstephens, Vincent Connelly and Dick Vorisek.

Jerome Hellman produced, and has overseen a strong and important film. "Midnight Cowboy" discovers an unattractive slice of our lives, and it is unquestionably not a family film. Yet beyond the specifics of circumstance (or out of the press of circumstances) it also discovers compassion, self-sacrifice and a kind of stubbled nobility among men who themselves discover it only in time to realize what might have been.

Easy Rider

All movies take their place in cultural history; but "Easy Rider" was instant history, blurring the lines between art and the strident, divisive realities of the 60s. The film's shocking finale and despairing pessimism, and the low-budget, documentary-like way it was made suggested the birth of an American neo-realism. Its power remains unique and unequalled.

THE WHOLE CYCLE of cycle pictures, "Wild Angels," "Hell's Angels on Wheels" and all the others, have had at their best a raw, brute vitality, a gaudy urgency, a message of social alienation and deep discontent which kept transcending the exploitational formulas, the melodramatics, the distorting simplifications of character and event.

On the face of it, "Easy Rider" is a cycle picture. But it is to what has gone before as calculus is to third-grade arithmetic.

From its deceptively amusing beginnings to its swift and terrible end, "Easy Rider" is an astonishing work of art and an overpowering motion picture experience. It is also a social document which is poignant, potent, disturbing and important.

The central difference (though there are several) between "Easy Rider" and the earlier bike pictures is perhaps simply that the earlier riders (for purposes of drama as much as anything else) were cast as men of violence or at least as men quick to meet with violence the violence they triggered around them. But Peter Fonda (who also produced the film), Dennis Hopper (who also directed it) and their newfound co-rider Jack Nicholson are nonconforming but also unassertive men of peace adrift in a society they find conformist in its violent fear-hatred of their easy, shaggy unorthodoxy.

The script, which Fonda and Hopper wrote in collaboration with

Terry Southern, conveys (with an unnerving, understated veracity) a society deeply divided and mistrustful, its confidence gone, reduced to an ugly and intolerant defense of what it takes to be the status quo.

But the story does not make the easy suggestion that a picaresque new generation of on-the-roaders has found the way and the light. The talk is spare throughout, and a terse sentence of Fonda's near the end of their adventure, "We blew it," is heavy with implications of his own dawning apprehensions that opting-out is an inadequate response. Existentialism has to take place somewhere, presumably, but to what extent can that somewhere be left wholly to its own devices?

Fonda and Hopper tool into Mexico and make a big cocaine buy from a grinning local entrepreneur named Jesus. They return to Los Angeles and, beneath the roaring glide path to International, sell the buy to a dealer in a chauffeured Rolls (composer-producer Phil Spector in a funny, wordless characterization).

With dollars beyond their dreams hidden in their gas tanks, they take off on their chromy, high-barred bikes for the Mardi Gras at New Orleans—a tawdry reward if there ever was one, which is part of the point. They toss away their watches, a ceremonial celebration of the end of earthly concerns.

They stop for lunch with an Arizona rancher, his Mexican wife and their numerous brood. The confrontation is initially tense but is at last warm and moving, and Fonda's wistful admiration becomes an early indication "Easy Rider" is something special.

A hitchhiker leads them to a hippie commune which is trying to scratch out a new life-on-the-land near Navajo Mountain. Again, Fonda views the enterprise with a kind of wistful respect.

Arrested in a small town (for being who they are), they share a cell with an alcoholic local lawyer, Jack Nicholson, who joins them for the pilgrimage to Mardi Gras. Nicholson's performance, creating a man who reeks of bourbon and failure but who is also richly funny and endlessly sympathetic, is one of the consummate pieces of screen acting. He has engendered an individual who will haunt all of us who have seen the picture.

In a small town café, this time in Louisiana, the riders sit out a taunting ugliness, a siege of stage-whispered hatred, which is one of the most dramatic and stomach-knotting sequences I've seen in a long time.

The Mardi Gras sequences, shot in 16mm during the actual event, contain a frighteningly authentic representation of a mescalin trip which is a savage revelation, not a joyride. The performances here, by Tony Basil and Karen Black, are, like all the others, desperately fine.

It all ends with sudden and shattering casualness, and we are left in the darkness with an uncommon and overwhelming sense that we haven't been told a story, we've heard a cry of anguish and alarm. Its truths seem not so much perceived intellectually as felt bone-and-gut-deep and expressed not in tidy sentences but in fragments and phrases wrenched from real experience, the chaos of living and intense personal feeling.

The music, which has been brilliantly edited to the film and vice versa, is the music of this time. It includes, among other titles, Steppenwolf's "The Pusher" and "Born to Be Wild," The Byrds' "Wasn't Born to Follow," Jimi Hendrix's "If Six Was Nine," the Electric Prunes' "Kyrie Eleison" (eerily appropriate to its place in the movie) and Roger McGuinn's "Ballad of Easy Rider."

Fonda and Hopper, it should by this time go without saying, give immense performances: Hopper as the more traditional "Hey, man" rider, impatient, self-indulgent, fearful of anything that looks like commitment; Fonda as something more of a bridge figure, sensitive and perceptive, hung up on his awareness that neither road nor establishment have all the answers, or all the problems. He is at least unambiguously tragic, discovering and experiencing the truth that the freedom of the road may well only be another kind of evasion and captivity.

With all else it does, "Easy Rider" confirms the revolutionary new day in motion-picture making. It was made for the unbelievably low cost of $340,000 and was financed privately by executive producer Bert Schneider. It has now been bought for distribution by Columbia, but was made before the distribution deal was set, assuring that much more initial creative freedom for Fonda and Hopper.

It was filmed entirely on location and made extensive use of non-actors discovered on the spot. The café customers were all Louisiana locals, as were two farmers who become agrarian angels of death. The gains in speed and economy were, of course, enormous. The café scene, shot in an afternoon, could have taken days on a sound stage.

But it is the gain in authenticity which matters to the moviegoer, and this gain, too, was enormous. "Easy Rider" is a work of fiction, an act of creation, but it derives its remarkable power and conviction from the reality of the faces and the face of the American Southwest and South. There is a shock of recognition, sometimes a reassuring one, more often not so reassuring; indeed a pressing reminder that forebearance is a part of the American Dream, too, and that some acts of reconciliation are required.

Not insignificantly, Fonda is called Wyatt and Hopper is Billy. At one point Hopper introduces them as Captain America and Billy. They do in a latter-day way catch two lines in the American genealogy: the true dropout who outlaws himself from society and the man who in a volatile society could go either way but whose instincts are right.

Among many contributions worthy of high praise, I would cite the cinematography of Laszlo Kovacs, which is central to the intentions of the movie, and is stunning. Among the cameo roles, Luana Anders and Sabrina Scharf as ladies of the commune and Robert Walker as its leader, Luke Askew as a hitchhiker and Warren Finnerty as the rancher, are memorable.

If there is an American New Wave, film historians may well one day cite "Easy Rider" as early evidence of it.

Bob & Carol & Ted & Alice

In a sense this was a transitional film, talking about sex with a new candor and flirting with the then-newsy business of wife-swapping but ending up as pure as Will Hays himself might have wished. Then again, this witty romantic comedy was about a transitional generation, caught between the old playing rules and the new.

"CONSIDER THE POSSIBILITIES," the copy hints slyly. I suppose that all's fair in ads and war. But when the movie is titled "Bob & Carol & Ted & Alice," the ads prepare you for an exploitation film about wife-swapping. In this case the ads are misleading and could turn you away from a scintillating social comedy and a movie which have more to say to you about you than any flick you'll see this year. True enough, Bob and Carol and Ted and Alice ultimately find themselves in a wide-screen bed in Las Vegas, miserable with rediscovered modesty and a reassuringly traditional chagrin.

But "Bob, etc." is only symptomatically about wife-swapping, threatened or actual. It is, as a friend of mine who felt the shock of recognition pointed out, one of the few movies thus far to be concerned with the generation *in* the gap: the awkward-age generation who are too old for acid and too young for Geritol, the affluent misfits who are After Ella but Before Beatles.

This was the Eisenhower Generation celebrated in sweet college years as the inert generation which wanted security and no waves.

Security they got; by now they've got it made. Their primary problems have all been solved, thus creating a vacuum which, like any other vacuum, Nature abhors. So it is that "Bob, etc." is not about wife-swapping but about what affluence does for an encore. This is the stuff of which psychiatrists' notebooks once were made, and which now provide the meat of encounter groups, sensitivity sessions, group therapies, and institutes poised on the rocky cliffs of Big Sur.

The story starts in fact at an institute like Esalen, where hot baths help soak free a grime of inhibition. Bob (Robert Culp) and Carol (Natalie Wood) seek to know themselves, and having found themselves shed tears of honesty and forgiveness. Ted (Elliott Gould) and Alice (Dyan Cannon) are they of little faith in this voyage of unsparing self-revelation.

The movie was coauthored by Paul Mazursky and Larry Tucker, and Tucker also produced and Mazursky also directed (exceptionally well). As they proved in "I Love You, Alice B. Toklas," which they also coauthored, they know how to construct comedy from the sights, sounds and stresses of contemporary society.

"Bob & Carol" is a situation comedy, brilliantly contrived, structured as carefully as a Hope monologue or a Sid Caesar skit. But just as a statue sculpted in marble remains marble, so a comedy rooted in truthful observation remains truthful however ornate the sculpting gets. Indeed, "Bob & Carol" risks what only a solidly based comedy can risk: to be quite serious and quite moving. The long, establishing sequence at the institute tests that thin line beyond which deeply earnest people are seen to be ludicrous. There is humor, but essentially what we have here is an assortment of people who have failed to communicate and are seeking to repair the lines. They may be incipiently funny, even foolish, but they are in fact sympathetic and all too identifiable in their concern.

What flows thereafter from one couple's weekend encounter session is not so much a madcap flight of invention as a merely modest extension of what could well have been. The two couples exist in a world in which keeping up with the Joneses financially has lost its savor and its urgency. What the couples discover is a new set of sexual ground rules in their affluent society—or, more to the point, discovering whether those ground rules indeed exist.

Mazursky has evoked four entirely remarkable performances. Dyan Cannon has a long scene with a psychiatrist (Donald F. Muhich) which is a classic cinematic set-piece, a definitive comic comment on the psychiatrist-patient confrontation.

Elliott Gould plays a young lawyer, evidently successful although you get the impression he is really not equipped to defend anybody against a meter violation. Gould creates and sustains a marvelously funny character, larger than life but never unlifelike. He and Miss Cannon have a bedroom scene which manages to be ribaldly amusing but also, simultaneously, a dire commentary on what our couplings have come to.

The jokes throughout, like all artful etchings, are done with acid. Miss Wood is the wide-eyed and desperately sincere catalyst who puts the permutations in motion, and she is very, very good. Robert Culp as a TV documentarian acts with a restraint which enables him to be amusing and yet to remain more dimensional than a caricature. He reminds us, to coin a phrase, that any of us is culpable. The quartet dominates the screen, but there are superior supporting performances by Horst Ebersberg as a tennis pro who goes courting with Miss Wood and Gregg Mullavey as the leader of the encounter group on the coast. K.T. Stevens is good in a small role as one of the groupies.

Inevitably when a movie works close to the unvarnished truth, it can slip. It is emphatically adult all the way, but once or twice the comedy gets too broad and seems like titillation for its own sake. It can be argued (has been) that the resolution of the movie is too pat and reassuring and lets the creators have things both ways, at once undercover and aboveboard, you might say. Unquestionably, after all the possibilities have been considered, the movie ends up as pro-tradition and anti-modernity as, let's say, "Goodbye Mr. Chips." Yet I for one didn't feel we were getting a kind of marriage-bed repentance. Indeed the point of view struck me as consistent and consistently incisive all the way through.

Quincy Jones did the score, and it's one of his best efforts.

1970

M*A*S*H

---

*It's interesting in retrospect how late Robert Altman enters the review. The film was his launch-pad to major work, after one excellent low-budget studio film, "Countdown," about a moon landing before there had been one. Abandoned by Warners, it played (he said later) only on second-rate cruise ships. But like "M*A*S*H" it predicted almost everything about Altman's unique filmmaking—speed, irreverence, the feeling of improvisation, the sure hand, the evoking of great performances. And, of course, the film begat television's finest series.*

"M*A*S*H" ARRIVES preceded by the same kind of shock-waves of acclaim, the shouting word of mouth, which "Easy Rider" had. In a gloomy time, "M*A*S*H" is the picture which Hollywood has been clamoring to see (and for all its cynicism, Hollywood as an industry town really does thrill to an extraordinary film).

The clamor and the acclaim make all good sense. "M*A*S*H" is a rough, unique and stunning work, a black comedy on the absurdity of war (and much else) which is both the most gruesomely gory film since "The Wild Bunch" and the funniest film since I'm not sure which. You are torn between nausea and hysterical laughter most of the time. There has been comical surgery before, of course, like the operation in "Candy" which sickened a lot of viewers even though it was manifestly a spoof. What is awesome is that the surgery in "M*A*S*H" is—to coin a dreadful phrase —painstakingly accurate. It is so real as to put your stomach in a permanent clench. And it couldn't be otherwise, because the absurdity is a mask for rage, and the shattered bodies we see are the measure of the rage.

"M*A*S*H" stands for Mobile Army Surgical Hospital, a Korean War phenomenon. Our heroes, Donald Sutherland and Elliott Gould principally, are in fact surgeons drafted into the war in Korea, living in battlefront conditions and working over the remnants of GIs on around-the-clock shifts. To keep sane amidst the insane carnage, the medics behave off duty with a fierce, mad, saving irreverence. The incidence of lovemaking between the doctors and the nurses is high and exhilarating. The Korean tent-boy makes frosty martinis. There are practical jokes which make "Mr. Roberts" look like an afternoon at a Cub Scout camp-out. It is Sgt. Bilko rated X. (Technically, R for Restricted.)

In one unforgettable scene, the officers align themselves in a living tableau which precisely imitates *The Last Supper* to the last gesture. The occasion is a mock-farewell to the unit's dentist (John Schuck), who lies in a coffin before them, eager for suicide. He is an indefatigable stud who has let one failure become the specter of latent homosexuality.

Irreverent at least, maybe blasphemous. The chaplain is a nice, affable sort to whom nobody pays any attention. It's a new message—that there's no one *but* atheists in foxholes—and not wholly convincing. But the whole sense of the film is humanist and, if you will, secular, insisting that everything be looked at unadorned by tradition, form or ceremonious duty, with no overlays of sentiment or slogan.

The superb script is by Ring Lardner, Jr. Robert Altman was the director, and the handful of people (mostly on airplanes) who saw his "Countdown" knew then that Altman knows how to put stories on film. Here Altman starts with and sustains a breathtaking pace and an improvisational and documentary feeling. He shot most often with long lenses so that the actors, the marvelous actors, were always working to each other and not to the camera. The gloss, and the one-liners, of comedy are gloriously absent.

"M*A*S*H" seems to have a life of its own. You sense that someone got it going but that thereafter things just happened. Even when the events are obviously quite structured, they retain a kind of authenticity. What is most remarkable at last is the extraordinarily complex response the film sets up. It is very nearly able to induce a manic-depressive state in its audiences. We laugh loudest and longest when we are nearest to despair.

The shattered bodies and the spurting blood give the campy goings-on their meaning. And finally we, too, laugh at the chunks of flesh dropping into a white enamel basin beneath the operating table, because sanity will abide no other reaction.

Elliott Gould extends the triumph he made in "Bob & Carol" and Donald Sutherland, who was enormously touching as the dying aristocrat in "Joanna," shows again what a strong and versatile actor he is. Tom Skerritt is excellent as a third surgeon. Robert Duvall is impressive once again as a humorless Bible-quoting major who cracks up out of his inability to crack wise. Sally Kellerman is nicely amusing as a chilly head nurse with concealed fires. Jo Ann Pflug is another nurse who registers handsomely. René Auberjonois is the chaplain and Roger Bowen the brassy idiot who runs the hospital. With all else, there's an extended football game sequence which is marvelously executed and very funny.

"M°A°S°H" will disturb the squeamish and offend those with a low tolerance for irreverence. Yet what one remembers and will be haunted by is not the crudity or the brutality of "M°A°S°H" but its abiding compassion and its horror of death and suffering.

With "Easy Rider" it shares a gift of anger, as well as the acclaim, but "M°A°S°H" is more professional, if less personal. It, too, will prove to be unforgettable.

Woodstock

The unifying characteristic of the Hollywood films of the 1970s was boldness. Sometimes, oftentimes, it was a boldness with a cynical eye to profits. In other and more enduring instances, it was artistic boldness—daring to do what had not been done before on the same scale or with the same candor and depth. "Woodstock," with its twenty cameramen deployed to record an epic musical gathering, became itself an epic.

THE WOODSTOCK ROCK FESTIVAL of August 1969, started out to be a nice, simple, king-sized money-making weekend. It ended up as an historic togetherness of crisis proportions.

More than 400,000 young people showed up on 600 rural acres of Sullivan County, New York, creating one of the most glorious traffic jams ever seen and causing monumental shortages of food, water, shelter, plumbing and mobility. But from all accounts it was peaceful, joyous and altogether a resounding tribute to a lifestyle (wholly unlike the disastrous festival at Altamount in Northern California only a few months later).

The Woodstock gathering has now been recorded in what I think is an historic piece of film, "Woodstock: Three Days of Peace and Music." It is a rousing three-hour account of a three-day weekend of music, distilled from 315,000 feet of film shot by twenty cameramen and from eighty-one hours of eight-track sound. It was directed by twenty-nine-year-old Michael Wadleigh, previously known for a well-received independent film called "No Vietnamese Ever Called Me Nigger."

Wadleigh and his platoon of film editors have made superb use of the split screen—have in fact made clear that the split screen is an urgent part of the grammar of film and not an amusing gimmick. The reverberations of the electronically driven music find their shimmering images on the screen; a guitarist faces a mirror image of himself, and his two images flank a third image of a drummer, perspiring and intent. Sounds and images echo. Sometimes there are two disparate but related images; a song of children and children in the crowd. It is all ebullient and astonishing.

The use of film technique is conscious and artful, but there is no sense of technique for its own sake, as a plaything. The multiple images, the wild sound tracks, the faces gone lavender or green under the floodlights in the dark night, the sometimes deafening music, all come as close as film can to recapture the essence of a unique and remarkable moment in time.

"Woodstock" is a record, not an analysis. There is no narration and no real attempt to examine society or a generation of musical history or of American affluence, to learn how it was that nearly a half-million young people showed up, stayed through three cloudbursts in three days and cheerfully endured hardships that would have evoked instant mutiny in any army camp on earth.

Let the analysis come later. This is source material, brilliantly compiled. It is aimed primarily at the audience that was there—or would have been there if it had been humanly possible to get there.

Music is the principal commodity and there are great, satisfying segments of Richie Havens, Joan Baez, Arlo Guthrie, Crosby, Stills and Nash, Joe Cocker, Ten Years After, Sly and the Family Stone, John Sebastian, Country Joe and the Fish, Jimi Hendrix and the enormously powerful Santana group.

It is a scene which may unsettle anybody on the far side of the generation gap who happens by, for pot and more ominous drugs were much in evidence; the language was invariably brisk and to the point and there was a good deal of exposing of the body beautiful (and otherwise).

Still, the genuinely unsettling questions are posed not by short words or unabashed bareness but by the sight of those tens and tens of thousands of young people arrayed on the sloping hillsides as far as the helicoptered camera can see, and drawn by what emptiness elsewhere into this unprecedented ceremony of identification and assertion.

Michael Wadleigh's stunning film, produced by Bob Maurice and financed by Warners to the tune of a reported $600,000, raises true concerns about how responsive our society is to this generation. Yet in its affable optimism, "Woodstock" also suggests that we're not without a considerable and defiant hope.

Five Easy Pieces

More than the new ratings, it was the post-television film audience, which was now several audiences, some of them eager to discover art-house sensibilities in mainstream films, that made a subtle film like "Five Easy Pieces" commercially viable on a modest scale. Jack Nicholson's unrooted, dissatisfied dropout, unforgettably demanding an order of toast, was in his way a film landmark.

AS A YEAR FOR MOVIES, 1970 has until now been thin and disappointing, and an honest connoisseur would have had trouble compiling a Best Three list he could live with the day after tomorrow. But, all in a rush, things are looking up.

"Five Easy Pieces" is a fine-grained, raucous, saddening, flawless piece of contemporary American portraiture which can in the best sense of the term be called this year's "Easy Rider."

It stars Jack Nicholson, who was unforgettable as the drunken, doomed Southern lawyer in "Easy Rider," and it also involves Bert Schneider, who produced both; Laszlo Kovacs, who photographed both (beautifully); and Bob Rafelson, who was co-producer of "Easy Rider" and who has directed "Five Easy Pieces."

Among all the things it was about, "Easy Rider" was about three men who could not discover a comfortable place for themselves in their society. Whether the fault was theirs or society's depended on who was watching the movie.

Now Nicholson is on the road again, and again he is a sensitive, charming, well-educated, intellectually upper-class dropout from his origins and expectations in American life. Unable to find any other permanent niche for himself, he is on the run from self-indulgence to self-indulgence with (it seems a fair guess) self-destruction lurking just around one of the next several bends in the road.

"I'm always getting away from situations that get bad if I stay," he tells his father. The father, now paralyzed and speechless after a stroke, was evidently a famous conductor. Nicholson ("Robert Eroica Dupea") and his sister were trained as concert pianists, their brother (middle-named Fidelio) as a violinist.

But Nicholson, when we meet him, is working as an oil field rough-neck in the Southwest and is shacked up with a waitress who speaks like molasses tastes and who would rather be Tammy Wynette than anybody. She is played by Karen Black, whose performance as a sweet, stupid broad is as exciting in this context as Nicholson's own was in "Rider." Sad-eyed and sexy, the captive of all the second-rate plastic dreams, she is magnificently funny and immeasurably touching.

The themes of dissatisfaction and rootlessness link the two movies. But the two are considerably different in other ways. "Five Easy Pieces" is not the powerful personal statement which the presence and participa-tion of Dennis Hopper and Peter Fonda made "Easy Rider," and it does not have the same raw urgency and crude melodrama. It is not the angry, both-barrels indictment of a fearful society.

"Five Easy Pieces" is, on the other hand, a far more subtle, consid-ered and complicated work of the movie-making arts. It is cooler and more detached and it is far more genuinely and outrageously funny. It moves with absolutely no loss of accuracy or detail from its beer, bowling and broads working-class world, small-city, Southwest-style, to the overrefined, febrile, cerebral world of the arts (here positioned on a foggy island oasis in the Pacific Northwest). Musically the worlds are character-ized on the first-rate sound track by Tammy Wynette ("Don't Touch Me If You Don't Love Me, Sweetheart") and by Chopin, Bach and Mozart pi-ano pieces, performed by Pearl Kaufman.

Nicholson has again given a portrayal which is exhilarating to watch. He's the charming wastrel, glad to be tender so long as he is not pressed to make a lasting commitment, witty, amusing, eager to bounce in and out of lives, anything to avoid looking in mirrors or confronting himself.

At first, leading a kind of "Saturday Night and Sunday Morning" life in the oil field, Nicholson and his cacklin' drawl suggest a man who quit school in the fifth grade and has been bummin' around happily ever since. It's Nicholson acting, but it's also the Nicholson pianist character acting, blending chameleon-like into the scenery to avoid being who he is. Later, home for a visit, Nicholson is the trained pianist, who can play Chopin af-fectingly and weep for his father, but who has also gone coarse and sour.

It is a complex, full-range portrait of a man we can be amused and entertained by, can begin to understand and to pity but cannot, I think, really sympathize with. Ultimately, in fact, it stays unclear quite why he has opted out. He reveals not so much a society which has destroyed him (as the easy riders were destroyed) but a society which has allowed him the luxury of destroying himself, if at last he is going to.

Bobby Dupea's problems seem mostly his own, private though certainly not uncommon. He is not a nice guy: he abandons the girl he has got pregnant, and tries to seduce his brother's fiancée. Yet he seems, for all that, too inert to be called a real antihero. He is a case history, not a class action, but he is so thoroughly credible and recognizable as to be worth worrying about. Perhaps the problem is that his aspirations were designed for him and thrust upon him. Possibly failure seemed preferable to the possibility of failure. Maybe the society appeared no longer capable of generating idealism or motivating excellence (although the story offers hints in both of Dupea's worlds that this is not so). Perhaps the carry-over message from "Easy Rider" is that despair, *not* hope, is eternal.

Whatever the read-out, "Five Easy Pieces" is an extraordinarily skillful and involving movie. The title, I guess, ironically links the worlds of fine pianos and swell girls.

As in "Easy Rider," the real world of oil fields, mobile homes, motels, a recording studio and an old family mansion on a Pacific island have been used and captured on film. They are the settings for the work of a little-known but incredibly good ensemble of actors.

Billy (Green) Bush is an oil field buddy of Nicholson's, with a giggling laugh you are not likely to forget soon. There is a dazzling sequence involving a pair of lesbians hitchhiking to Alaska. One of them (Helena Kallianiotes) delivers a slashing, deadpan, vile-tongued monologue on filth and corruption which is in the show-stopper class. Susan Anspach is cool and intelligent as the brother's fiancée, and Lois Smith is good as his sister. Ralph Waite is the pompous, faintly unctuous brother, William Challee the silenced but eloquent father.

A special bow to Sally Ann Struthers, who, playing a bowling alley pickup, broke my heart with a story about the dimple in her chin. Marlena MacGuire is nifty as her vivid blond pal.

The script of "Five Easy Pieces" is by Adrien Joyce (real name: Carol Eastman), who coauthored the original story with the director, Bob Rafelson. Line for line, it contains the best dialogue—accurate, revealing, funny—that I have listened to in a very long time. It is the screen equivalent of the John O'Hara ear at its most precise.

The words are said, with the force of life itself, by Nicholson and the astonishing Miss Black, who was one of the New Orleans prostitutes in "Easy Rider."

The 1970 vintage may yet be worth remembering.

Little Big Man

The traditional Western had been all but done in by television (there were something like two dozen Western series on in one season in the 50s). But the genre was waiting to be redefined, never more movingly than in Arthur Penn's masterful commentary on the full tragedy of the collision of white and Indian, told in a film that is both massive and intimate, comic and dark.

THE OLD MAN IS A FREAK: 121 years of age by his own reckoning but still alert and even cantankerous and claiming to be the only white survivor of Custer's Last Stand. He is being tape-recorded by a supercilious young jackanapes of a historian who's got it all wrong.

The sad, faded eyes squint into history and the reedy but decisive old voice snaps, "Turn the damned thing on; this is how it was." Suddenly he's a child being taken off by the Cheyenne from the guttering ruins of a wagon train, and "Little Big Man" is under way.

"Little Big Man" is Arthur Penn's seventh and most ambitious film: a densely packed, episodic, daring, uneven but unrepentant gallop through the winning of the West. It shifts from high drama to low slapstick to bloody violence, to quiet tragedy and bitter social commentary.

Great hunks of the movie could be hacked away without weakening the surging narrative thrust. It's no matter.

What Penn—and Calder Willingham, who wrote the script from Thomas Berger's expansive and picaresque novel—have not been guilty of is the anthropological solemnity of other recent films about the Indians. And in the end, by seeing the Indians as men and women and children rather than as a Culture or a Historical Force, Penn's "Little Big Man" states the tragedy of the confrontation more eloquently and powerfully than any of the other recent films, and more effectively indeed than any film I can remember seeing.

For Penn, "Little Big Man" follows "Alice's Restaurant" and "Bonnie and Clyde," a sequence which makes its own eloquent point that the work of few directors in the world reveals a wider-ranging intellectual curiosity and concern.

Penn always seems simultaneously to be exploring the world and also the medium of film. The single constant in his work has been his ability to extract performances of extraordinary sensitivity and rightness.

Here he has done it again, but now within the context of visual effects which in their size and complexity are on a post-DeMillean scale. It is a fascinating achievement which may miss an icy and total perfection but which might, on the other hand, have lost something of sprawling energy and urgency if it had been a whit more controlled and less indulgent.

Dustin Hoffman is the Little Big Man, creating a character different from any he has done before, in a performance which could have been blindingly vivid and showy (and which now and again is), but which in the crucial quiet moments has a almost self-effacing quality which is perfect.

He ricochets from the white world of his parents to the Indians who raise and name him, is reclaimed by the whites, suffers with an overwrought preacher (Thayer David) and his oversexed wife (Faye Dunaway), shills for a frontier con man (Martin Balsam) who is a kind of cynical Greek chorus for the film, returns to the Indians and is later dragooned back into the white world he now, with reason, despises.

As a reluctant emissary between the two cultures, Hoffman gives the audience a fresh and unique perspective on each of the cultures, and he also newly informs and heightens our feelings of horror at the brutality of the confrontation.

Chief Dan George plays Hoffman's Indian mentor, and has a salty dignity which is very impressive to watch. Amy Eccles is Hoffman's Indian wife, and her combination of gentle beauty plus a mischievous charm is enchanting. Jeff Corey has a fine brief outing as Wild Bill Hickock, and Richard Mulligan makes General Custer a posturing psychotic fool.

Miss Dunaway, wearing a thick Southern drawl and abandoning her husband to work in a brothel, is the comedy relief and, however unlikely her role may be in the total context of the picture, she gives her scenes great flair.

1971

Carnal Knowledge

This, more than any film in the early days of the new ratings, tested the limits of the unfenced latitudes. The raw language, the sexual goings-on, the encompassing theme of male-female relationships in changing times were all sensational, not to say incendiary. Yet the pervasive tone of disillusion and despair was dampening as a cold shower and whatever the film was, it failed of eroticism and could be acquitted of exploitation.

"CARNAL KNOWLEDGE," which Mike Nichols has directed from an original script by Jules Feiffer, is the iciest, most merciless and most repellent (and seriously intended) motion picture in a very long time.

Its theme is sex and its concern is obsessive. It is an indictment of the sexual patterns of a whole generation—Nichols's and Feiffer's own. But the indictment also means to cover the whole middle-class American society of which the distorted sex is a symptom. Only the very young, who have been wise enough to reject their parents' ethic, have apparently been exempted from the indictment. But only apparently; Nichols and Feiffer are profoundly pessimistic.

In the end, in fact, the revelations may reveal more about the revealers than about the larger society. The question raised by "Carnal Knowledge" is indeed whether the indictment can be sustained, whether we can accept the pathological case history the authors give us as representative of the larger society or simply see them as aberrational extremes. That there is truth in the characters is, I think, beyond doubt; that they wholly reflect their own generation, let alone a whole society, I find gravely doubtful. Finally only the viewer can verify or reject for himself the vision of ourselves as Nichols and Feiffer see us. The critic can only do a bit of forewarning about that vision.

Quantitatively, the candor of word and deed in "Carnal Knowledge" outreaches anything we have yet had in a mainstream commercial American movie. The language is so incessantly crude as to become more than characterization. It is a kind of act of violence against the human spirit.

Nichols and Feiffer are a generation of men obsessed with sex, and with women as sexual objects to be exploited but not trusted because women will emasculate you if you give them half a chance (and maybe even if you don't). Bad sex and love cannot coexist, they seem to be saying, but then again love is so elusive it may not exist at all.

We meet Jack Nicholson and Arthur Garfunkel as freshman roommates at Amherst, virginal but talking a fast game and hot for conquests. (Nicholson is manifestly too mature to be a beginning collegian and it is one of the few lapses in a notably well-executed movie that so little attempt was made to de-age him. The point is not minor, because he is left so little room to convey a change or a hardening. He is old, cynical and doomed at 17.)

We leave them until something like 20 years later. By then Garfunkel, a doctor with at least one failed marriage behind him, is now making it with a barefoot teenaged flower child who he says is teaching him what love is. (Whether it is love or simply sex without obligation is rendered ambiguous by the author's pervasive despair. Love means not having to say a damned thing.)

Nicholson, a well-heeled tax accountant with one unavoidable marriage behind him, is now reduced to fetishist encounters with a prostitute who turns him on by murmuring about the weak wickedness of women and the glorious avenging power of men. He lives in an ongoing nightmare of vanishing virility.

It is some indictment. Yet the Nicholson figure is never comprehensible as anything but a clinical study, although the study offers no clues to how he got that way. His only glimpse of love seems to have been mostly a quest for steady-state sex. The Garfunkel figure has had a rounder awareness of love and his hangup is considerably more affecting because he has presumably tried and failed to put sex and love together. "Maybe you're not suppose to like it with someone you love," he says wistfully.

As he always does, Nichols evokes excellent performances. Although he is too foul-mouthed and obsessive a conception to earn even our pity after a while, Nicholson turns in some powerful moments. He keeps us believing, which is the neatest trick of all. Garfunkel, in a first-rate performance, projects a sweet, baffled concern; indeed he seems more perceptive than the script lets him be. (What is hard to know is what he ever saw in his palship with Nicholson.)

Nichols has also gotten outstanding characterizations from Ann-Margret and Candice Bergen, Ann-Margret very sympathetic indeed as a blowsy, overripe tomato tired of being squeezed and desperate to be wed, Miss Bergen as the boys' first conquest and then Garfunkel's wife. (The story drops her abruptly and evades any real examination of why the marriage failed.) Cynthia O'Neal as Garfunkel's cool but avariciously sexy mistress also has some vivid appearances.

The story on the face of it confirms that there is an American male terror of tenderness as being an eroder of vitality. So confirming, it seems also to confirm the darkest charges of the women's liberationists: that women everywhere are treated only as exploitable sexual objects.

Yet the authors (if not the characters) also seem to be indicting the ladies for, of all things, sexual permissiveness, as if the surrender of love to sex was all their idea, and that they do their emasculating not by clinging but by refusing to be docile and faithful. It is at last a curious indictment, arbitrary, personal and limited, and to the extent that there was truth in it, more than a little outdated.

"Carnal Knowledge" is streaked with harsh humor. And although the movie's cold cruelty and pessimism make it, I believe, an uncomfortable sit for almost everyone, its steamy invasions of the bedroom will have the usual voyeuristic appeal and a young audience may well be glad to accept the unqualified charges against a generation of parents.

Panic in Needle Park

Not until "Trainspotting" in 1996 would the sordid world of the narcotics addict be depicted with such ruthless accuracy. The Scots film had a leavening of humor; "Panic in Needle Park" never let up. A joke of the time said its high concept was "Romeo and Juliet on junk." Its sense of hopelessness was its strength— and its weakness—at the box office and as a social document.

"PANIC IN NEEDLE PARK" is the latest of the drug scene movies. It is also, I think, the best of them. But if it's a peak, it's also a dead end. That is, it both defines and exhausts the possibilities of the movie which contents itself with describing (however, accurately and horrifyingly) the drug milieu, but does not choose to go beyond surfaces to causes.

Given its self-imposed limits, "Panic" is a very nearly perfect piece of movie making. It can be admired as a piece of art whose theme matter is almost incidentally drugs. The leading performances by Al Pacino and Kitty Winn as a smack-doomed couple in Manhattan are dismayingly authentic and sympathetic, ranking with the best performances of the year.

The script, by Joan Didion and her husband John Gregory Dunne, catches the frenzied connivings, the noddy incoherences, the camaraderies and the treasons of the addict world with the fidelity of tape recordings but with the shaping selectivity of art. The observing eyes are cool and the voices are free of rhetoric: no psychedelic highs, no yellow journalism lows.

After the incessant camera trickery of "Puzzle of a Downfall Child," director Jerry Schatzberg handles this material with a self-effacing austerity, achieving a documentary-like earnestness in which the personality of the creator remains entirely unobtrusive.

The plot is really only a downward progression. A middle-class Midwestern girl bounces from a bad love affair and an abortion into the arms of a Needle Park hustler still able to convince himself that he's only "chipping"—e.g., using heroin, but not addicted.

But he's soon strung out and the girl deliberately joins him on the hook and begins her own spiral into ego-shredding scuffling, including two-bit prostitution, to keep the habit fed. She even allows herself to be blackmailed by a narcotics detective into informing on her own man, and in the cynical despair of that world, he understands all too well.

The movie does not so much end as stop. The couple, together for worse and worse yet, seem to have nothing ahead but more grief and then surcease by overdose or some other misadventure.

It is all harrowing in its unflinching look at the addict world. There's hardly a moment which does not ring true. The Dunnes drew their script from reportage by James Mills of *Life* about life in the Needle Park area of Manhattan's West Side.

The supporting performances are more convincing than the appearances by presumably real street people recruited in the recent "Dusty and Sweets Magee." (One of the interesting things about the two films is that "Dusty," with greater claims to authenticity, seems ultimately less persuasive and terrifying than "Panic," whose figures are fictional.)

Alan Vint as the entrapping narc; Richard Bright as the boy's burglar brother; Kiel Martin, Michael McClanathan, Warren Finnerty, Marcia Jean Kurtz and Vic Ramano as addicts and pushers are all first-rate.

Yet for all it is possible to admire the accuracy and the artistry of "Panic in Needle Park" and to feel that the ultimate horror of addiction—

the total destruction of the personality—has perhaps never been better conveyed, there remains a lingering dissatisfaction.

At this point, it seems insufficient merely to cope with the immediate scene, however well. The nagging question is, what are the frustrations and furies in the straight world which make addiction a preferable alternative?

Miss Winn makes me believe in Helen as a credible individual, bright and sophisticated, aware of the dangers of the addict world. Indeed, the true horror of "Panic in Needle Park" is that hers is not the accidental fall of an innocent but a deliberate act which can be interpreted as suicidal.

Is it, subconsciously, a delayed suicide? Is Indianapolis really that ghastly? Were her parents that ogre-ish? Is a failed love that traumatic? Is the only way to share Bobby's life to join him in an unrelenting, untouching stupor? Maybe so; in fact, I guess, probably so. I'm prepared to believe almost anything the Dunnes want to tell me, but I wish they told me something, or at least laid in a few glinting clues. Otherwise we're left with a horror story for which there is no evident prevention or cure and which is seen to be beyond any comprehending.

It is true that addiction is the most intractable social problem in our society, but by now we've been adequately reminded of the bleakness of it all (never more impressively than here). The next insights will have to deal with the whys.

McCabe and Mrs. Miller

Robert Altman, riding to fame on M*A*S*H after a long wait for an important film, has proved in the last quarter-century to be idiosyncratic, unpredictable, irreverent, unorthodox in his mastery of technique, and ever-watchable. His wildly off-trail Western, existential and demythologizing, with Warren Beatty as his doomed antihero, divided the audience between love and hate, as Altman usually does, but it stays vividly in memory.

THERE ARE SEVERAL THINGS TO BE SAID about Robert Altman as a movie maker, and the most important of them is that he is not shy or timid. Lulling audiences to sleep is obviously his idea of nothing to do.

Audiences exist to be impressed, affected, startled, stunned, awed, delighted, to be confronted, confounded and if necessary wrestled to the floor. Altman seems to be rather more interested than Robert Aldrich in the ideas which stories can carry, and he has somewhat more self-control than Ken Russell; but he is like them in the bravado of his approach to movie-making and in his command of the medium, born of a long and fairly frustrating apprenticeship.

He is probably incapable of making an uninteresting movie. What he does do, as both M°A°S°H and "Brewster McCloud" have indicated, is make movies which audiences despise or delight in, in almost equal numbers.

Altman's newest movie, "McCabe and Mrs. Miller," is yet another highly individual work about which you can feel virtually anything except indifference. I wouldn't have missed it, even though it is as uneven as the stare of a cheap mirror.

What's best about it—including the photography by Vilmos Zsigmond, Julie Christie's performance and an atmosphere as believable as a hangnail—is powerfully good, and an exciting reminder of the way a movie can get to you by its sheer vigor.

"McCabe" is also self-consciously stylized and artful, conscientiously crude and so coolly cynical in its life-view that we're finally unable to give much of a damn whether the characters live or die. (It is not that the characters themselves are bad or unpleasant—they're all bad, although most of them are pleasant—it's just that the cynicism is so thorough-going that we realize how manipulative it all is, how fictional the creations are.)

Altman built a whole forlorn zinc-mining town, vintage 1900, in the rain-sogged, snow-chilled wilds of British Columbia. The raw weather is so evident that you're grateful for every glimpse of a pot-bellied stove.

Warren Beatty as McCabe is a dudish card-player who plods into town in a pelting shower on a spent horse. Where he's been or what he's after is unclear. You don't know if he's shark or bait or neither. It is the movie's style to tell you very little and leave you unsure about even that little. The opening sequences, dark and cacophonous, are nearly impossible to decipher and Altman, I think, pushes the audience's tolerance about as far as it can go. He conveys the aromas of primitive and miserable living; then style begins to draw attention to itself.

Beatty, black-bearded and sustaining himself with a raw egg dropped in a glass of neat bourbon, opens a saloon and imports three tarnished belles for a three-tent brothel. Miss Christie shows up uninvited, a Midlands whore with visions of corporate grandeur. With Beatty's capital, she launches a backwoods bagnio with real class and a bathhouse besides.

The pair are soon so prosperous that the emissaries from a gigantic and ruthless mining syndicate come to buy them out. The biggies won't take no for an answer, and send in three hired killers when Beatty stalls. That sets up the movie's long but suspenseful final stalk-down, shot during the cottony silences and ironically innocent whiteness of a real blizzard.

Altman gives you a touch of everything from superplain sex to the crazy local preacher who doesn't talk at all, from a bucket brigade to a steam tractor and the coldblooded murder of an easygoing cowboy (Keith Carradine), from Miss Christie relaxing with an opium pipe to a giggling squad of prostitutes who really look like mine-camp hookers and not starlets with their clothes off.

For whatever reason, the star parts are equally entertaining but not equally solid. Miss Christie, hair done up in a cheap frizzle, gives one of the best performances of her career, creating a character who is tough and cautious and too aware of the cruelties and costs of the real world to be your traditional harlot with a heart of gold. There's tenderness there, or a brusque affection, but it's guarded by years of scar tissue. The charm of her playing is that she lets us see the sensitivity which the character has to conceal.

The Beatty portrayal is colorful—cigar-chomping, egg-gulping, teeth-baring, squinting, lurching—but it has a lot less consistency than Miss Christie's. He's an antihero, of course, drawn into a showdown because there's no escape. But it's not ever clear whether he's clever enough to be a con man or dumb enough to be a nice guy, and the trouble is that even McCabe doesn't seem to know. That would be fair enough, but it's his creators who don't seem to know.

The initial intention of "McCabe and Mrs. Miller" appears to have been to prove that you could demythologize a certain hunk of the Western past and still entertain, still sketch in the beginnings of a romance, in fact.

And the demything carries a fair way. Presbyterian Church, the name of the camp, is hell upside down, with chilblains instead of blisters. It looks bleak and miserable and the life within it looks crude, raw, dumb, forlorn and hopeless. And Miss Christie's co-workers are a far cry from the dance hall girls of the mythic (Hollywood) past with the strapless tutus of gold brocade and their peaches-and-cream complexions.

But more is blurred than Beatty's character. The destruction of myth has been very selective. The shoot-down preserves the most enduring myth (or convention, if myth is too grand a word) of them all. The teaming of antihero and antiheroine is admittedly recent, if not new; but the ruthless, faceless syndicate, the urbane assassin and his pathological sidekicks have jogged our way before. The politically ambitious young lawyer (William Devane) who is eager to make a martyr out of McCabe is a contemporary figure, though the movie reduces him to a cameo.

What I'm saying is that there is less here than meets the eye, although what meets the eye is generally entertaining, often vivid—and looks to have been gruelingly hard to get on film.

It becomes a star vehicle, and the charm of its principals obscures the sardonic and corrective view of the past which, if I'm right, the movie had been intended to take.

Interesting is a dead word. Train wrecks, tall blondes and chicken pox can all be interesting, one way and another. But "McCabe and Mrs. Miller" is an interesting film. Very interesting, if that helps any.

There are a number of fine supporting performances: René Auberjonois as a rival innkeeper, Hugh Millais as the towering assassin, Shelley Duvall (from "Brewster McCloud") as a young widow converting to the oldest profession, Corey Fischer as the preacher, Manfred Shulz as a teenage killer.

Leonard Cohen wrote, and performs, songs which along with some lonesome fiddle playing constitute the movie's music. It's a welcome change from the symphony, though for my taste it's just a mite too austere and artful.

David Foster and Mitchell Brower were the producers.

The Last Picture Show

Peter Bogdanovich, who began as a film journalist, was one of the generation of new talents emerging in the 70s. His study of Hawks and other masters paid off. "The Last Picture Show" is beautifully directed and becomes an homage not only to the role the movies played in our small-town lives but to the men who made them and the way they shaped reality for us. The film's now-permissible nudity was curiously wrong, pretty but inappropriate to the period, on- or off-screen.

IN THE OLDEN, GOLDEN DAYS Hollywood occasionally turned the camera on itself and discovered romance, comedy and melodrama in the stars and the making of movies.

But it was make-believe about make-believe, and the movies rarely if ever looked at themselves outside Hollywood, never (so far as I know) tried to see themselves as the immense cultural phenomenon they were, shaping the speech, tastes, goals, ideals and notions of reality of everyone who watched them.

It would have been the kind of movie they didn't much make then, at that.

It's only now, as the Golden Age fades like a fast dissolve, that the movies have begun to see the movies in perspective, as a powerfully shaping part of the past for us all (and not powerless yet, by any means). There seem to be more and more allusions to movies within movies.

Jean Simmons, as the wife in "The Happy Ending," sits half-sloshed and bored watching Bogart in "Casablanca" and says, "Here's lookin' at you, kid," in a conscious, bitter tribute to the kind of romantic idealism she can't discover in her own life. The teenagers in "Summer of '42," in another kind of irony, watch Bette Davis and Paul Henreid in a suave romantic tragedy worlds apart from—but inspirational to—the clutchings in the back row.

And now comes Peter Bogdanovich's "The Last Picture Show," the most considered, craftsmanlike and elaborate tribute we have yet had to what the movies were and how they figured in our lives.

Bogdanovich is a young film critic and film historian who has done books on Allan Dwan (the pioneer Hollywood director who did many of the Shirley Temple films), Fritz Lang and John Ford. He recently completed a two-hour documentary on Ford and his work.

Bogdanovich's earlier feature, "Targets," also reflected a film buff's fascination with the movies. It starred Boris Karloff (in his last appearance) as an aging horror film star, and its climactic scenes were at a drive-in.

The opening shot of "The Last Picture Show" is a very, very slow panning shot around the wide, deserted main street of a small Texas town early on a blustery, dusty fall morning. And the first enterprise we see is the Royal Theater, playing Spencer Tracy and Elizabeth Taylor in "Father of the Bride."

The year is 1951, and Bogdanovich has made his movie in black and white, a presently daring but absolutely correct choice, because (as he obviously feels) there is a kind of previous reality which simply can't be captured (or recaptured) in color because we perceived it in black-and-white. But also, the use of black-and-white is part of Bogdanovich's tribute to the filmmakers of the Golden Age who created in black-and-white images of such richness, density and subtlety across an infinite scale from deep black to chalky white that color could hardly have been more eloquent.

The director is honoring also the traditions of the well-made film. In a time of hand-held footages, jump cuts, wipes, zooms, elisions and non sequiturs and of technique deliberately degraded for the sake of impact, "The Last Picture Show" has a stately, deliberate, well-joined control which celebrates the immaculate surfaces of the great Hollywood movies and their makers.

Bogdanovich's script (coauthored with Larry McMurtry whose novel is the source) introduces us to a town's-worth of characters large enough to repopulate King's Row and the west side of Peyton Place.

The key figures are two high school pals, Jeff Bridges and Timothy Bottoms, whom we meet the morning after they've played badly in a big football game. "The Last Picture Show" is essentially about their coming of age in the waning days of the movies and in the waning days of the settled, relatively isolated world of small-town America.

Others in the gallery are a sweet, mute, retarded boy (Sam Bottoms), a philosophical pool hall proprietor (Ben Johnson), the high school's cool, rich blond teaser (Cybill Shepherd), her oversexed mother (Ellen Burstyn), the high school coach (Bill Thurman), the coach's frustrated wife (Cloris Leachman), the salty gal who runs the diner (Eileen Brennan), a rich, fat kid from the next town (Randy Quaid), a bosomy high school girl (Sharon Taggart) who is called, I'm afraid, Marlene Duggs. Plus assorted kids, truck drivers, town louts, sheriffs and deputies.

The performances range from awfully good on up to spectacularly good. It is a movie of set-pieces, of long takes in which the camera sits unobtrusively at rest and lets the actors do their stuff, which they do indeed. Both Johnson and Miss Burstyn have soliloquies at opposite ends of the movie about the love (their own) which got away. They are moving to watch whether you are believing a word of it or only admiring really fine actors at work. The same is true of a long, tremulous scene between Miss Leachman and a lost young love, Bottoms, as she acknowledges that she has turned a hard corner into middle age. It is a fine piece of acting, an elegy for lost dreams which is the theme of the movie.

Love dies, a boy dies, the Royal closes. (Bogdanovich gives us bits of early television, mostly vile, leaving no doubt of his own contempt for the medicine show which killed the palace of dreams.)

At the conscious, intellectual level of tribute to the medium, to the movie makers and their visual styles and to the kind of middle-American environment in which the movies had their greatest authority, "The Last Picture Show" is extremely impressive, the work of a well-versed, disciplined, imaginative and important young director.

But it is perhaps the ironic confirmation of everything Bogdanovich is saying that "The Last Picture Show" seems to evoke so little gut-level emotional response. We watch—I watched—with cool admiration a very cool intelligence at work. The events are hot but have an icy remoteness about them.

What Bogdanovich has done, deliberately I'm sure, is not so much to try to recapture small-town life as to reconstitute a vision of small-town life (usually steamy) as American movies gave it to us under 10,000 place names in 10,000 crises.

The hungering wives, the leching husbands, the unshaven saints and the doomed children, the loss of innocence and the finding of wisdom, the cuckoldings and the confrontations all have their origins in real life. But what we find in "The Last Picture Show" is another aspect of Bogdanovich's summoning of the movies that once we saw, the trans-muted view of life which perhaps began by mirroring us but ended by shaping us (in the sense that we consciously or unconsciously sought to model ourselves on the characters we saw on the screen).

Part of Bogdanovich's elegy is for a simpler society in which we could respond openly and fully to the larger-than-life events of the silver screen, could cry on cue for the sweet child killed. We can still cry but we are harder to beguile, or so we seem. And in a fairly complicated way, if we are moved by "The Last Picture Show" it is by our memory of how once we were moved.

As if he were also measuring a change in the movies, Bogdanovich in-cludes a lot of love-play and a fair amount of nudity. Some of it is handled humorously but most of it is self-conscious and the heaviest of it jars with the rest of the movie by failing to be convincing as either the real past or the cinematic past. It smacks a bit of having it both ways, as comment and as the thing commented on.

The music is primarily the chart sound of the time, and it is certain to evoke many a memory. "The Last Picture Show" is an exceptional and original work, not so much a movie-movie as a film buff's film, an exercise in regret and a reminder of various losses.

Not least among the losses are the glories of black and white, el-egantly used here by Bogdanovich and the veteran cameraman, Robert Surtees.

Stephen Friedman produced for Bert Schneider's BBS Productions, the firm which gave us those prime symbols of the post-Golden Age (or of a new age), "Easy Rider" and "Five Easy Pieces."

A Clockwork Orange

Is "A Clockwork Orange" an American film? It was made in Britain from a British novel with a British cast. But, like Kubrick's earlier "2001: A Space Odyssey," it is the work of America's pre-eminent director-in-exile (nothing to do with the blacklist) and was largely financed by Hollywood's Warner Brothers. By now the ever-eclectic Kubrick seems curiously stateless, undefinable geographically, following ideas wherever they take him in time and place. In its dark vision of a drug-warped, violent tomorrow, "Clockwork" became one of the more disturbing landmarks of the 70s.

STANLEY KUBRICK is the most consistently interesting director now working in English. He is adamantly independent, living almost reclusively on a country estate outside London where he has offices and editing rooms and from which he oversees every aspect of his films, including advertising and the shape of the theaters in which they play.

He has an enormously wide-ranging curiosity and a horror of repeating himself. He undertakes any project which strikes him as important, no matter how forbidding the technical problems seem to be, because he has no peers as a problem-solving and innovating cinematic technologist. He is one of the least collaborative men in a collaborative medium, and films as dissimilar in handling as "Paths of Glory," "Lolita," "Dr. Strangelove," "Space Odyssey" and now "A Clockwork Orange" confirm his singular vision.

Few men would have ventured to translate Anthony Burgess's darkly brilliant satire on a future (but only slightly future) Britain which is being terrorized by violent, drugged teenagers who speak a strange private slang of their own. The reader of the novel could infer that Britain had been under Russian domination in one form or another, and the language, which the teeners call nadsat, is a mixture of Cockney rhyming slang and Russian derivatives. "Horrorshow," meaning wonderful in Burgess's Britain, stems, with ingenious irony, from the Russian word for wonderful.

What links "A Clockwork Orange" to earlier Kubrick films is not only its cinematic challenge but its harsh and pessimistic view of humankind as dominated and/or endangered by weak and nasty fools. Even the machines were nasty in "Space Odyssey," and the cryptic, distant optimism Kubrick hinted at in the end lay not only over the rainbow but through a space-warp.

Kubrick's "Clockwork Orange" is violent, crude, cold, profoundly gloomy, now and again blackly funny and as a piece of movie-making, alternately dazzling and curiously static and overlong.

Burgess's narrator, and Kubrick's, is a bored teenager (well-played by Malcolm McDowell) who with his droogs or pals hangs around the Korova Milkbar, where they spike the milk with vollocet, synthemesc or drencrom and other hallucinogenics, some of which whet the appetite for ultra-violence. The hero, Alex, is a sadist, murderer, rapist, but also a lover of classical music, especially Beethoven and Mozart. He's adrift in a new world not only of available drugs but of instant sex and strident sensuality used as consolation prizes by the intimidated adults. Burgess envisioned a kind of new Dark Ages in which what survived of literacy cowered in secret behind locked doors.

Alex, jailed for the brutal murder of a neurotic lady who kept cats (Miriam Karlin), is brainwashed under an experimental new program, into a conditioned revulsion at violence. He becomes a handy ploy for unscrupulous politicians who set up an outcry to have him reconditioned back into his old hedonistic self. Significantly, the end of Burgess's novel found the old Alex challenging his old values and beginning to yearn for even older values—health, home, wife and children. Kubrick's Alex seems to prefer a compromise: Beethoven's Ninth, but bosomy slave girls feeding him grapes.

Kubrick's future shock, that is, looks even blacker than Burgess's. His adaptation of the novel is impressively faithful, but with revealing additions. Kubrick's vision seems more apocalyptic. The sexuality, including very explicit phallic artifacts, is more obsessive relative to the violence than in the novel.

Using no sound stages and building only two sets, including the milkbar, Kubrick impressively conveys tomorrow's world, with its concert halls abandoned and decaying like Greek ruins, vandalized by sex- and blood-thirsty gangs. There are passages of awesome power—the beating of a literate, despairing old wino, the rape of a wife (Adrienne Corri) while her helpless husband (Patrick Magee) is forced to look on. Fun stuff, all observed with chilly clinical detachment by Kubrick.

Like "Carnal Knowledge," "A Clockwork Orange" is an intensely personal picture (it is finally Kubrick's social vision, not Burgess's), and one which inevitably sets up an intensely personal response. One admires its uncompromising singularity and its great if intermittent technical achievements. You accept that its over-length and perhaps its overexplicitness are the costs of an unconsulting autonomy—and at that preferable to a safer, majority vote conventionality.

But you also, I think, are led to question whether this is the form the nightmare takes and whether the unrelieved hopelessness of Kubrick's prophecy is more perceptive than Burgess's insistence that in the end free choice will lead men to sanity and not away from it. I'm afraid I found "A Clockwork Orange" brilliant but disappointing, its moments of power offset by an overwrought stridency, and its message overbalanced by the medium. It is a remote work, icy and abstract, strangely shy of the echoes of real human voices. But it is also genuinely thought-provoking and uncompromising.

1972

The Godfather

Much as I admired Coppola's film, confidently predicting its box office success, I still underestimated the phenomenon it would become. It is to Coppola what "Citizen Kane" was to Welles, except that "Godfather II" was to extend the triumph and create a whole that was greater than its parts.

THE MOST REVEALING THING I CAN TELL YOU about "The Godfather" is that it cost $6 million and has already brought in more than twice that—$13 million in advance payments from exhibitors eager to play what they're betting will be a walloping great hit. And they're absolutely, 100% right. Mario Puzo's novel was an irresistible, eventful, easy-to-digest, hard-to-put-down best seller (a half-million hardbacks, 10 million paperbacks) and Puzo and director Francis Ford Coppola, who coauthored the script, have delivered the novel just about as faithfully as a novel can be delivered.

You liked the side action upstairs in the bedroom during the wedding? You got it. Liked the horse-head bit? You got it. The restaurant caper with the crooked police captain? You got it, you got it.

A slam-bang novel with boundless energy and the spicy suggestion that all sorts of secrets are being told under thin disguises has become a rousing movie (a *movie*-movie, as they say) which seems to me to succeed perfectly at what it set out to do. It is marvelously well cast and acted. It evokes a fairly nondescript period in American life—the mid- to late-40s—with unerring fidelity and interest. It is swift and theatrical, probably the fastest three-hour movie in history. It is incessantly and explicitly violent, but saves on emotional wear and tear by having the bad guys kill off the bad guys, so that what's to care? As I remember, the only innocent who gets it is the nice Sicilian wife who goes to pieces in the car, but that only sets you up for the massive counterblows back home. And at that, the whole extravagant operation is so Little Caesarean that to respond to it anywhere near the threshold of pain is like reading Harold Robbins for symbols. It misses the object of the enterprise.

"The Godfather" is an entertainment, not a documentary, however close it may come to some of the realities behind the headlines. But because it generates an aura of considerable believability, it is a saving grace of the movie that it keeps its balance. If, that is, we develop a kind of admiration for Don Corleone and then his son as protectors of their family, "The Godfather" reminds us—brutally—that they are corrupt and merciless murderers, pimps, peddlers and thieves. The wistful talk about going respectable precedes the further assassinations. Unlike Bonnie and Clyde in Arthur Penn's movie, the Corleones have not been absolved by being explained in a social context, but like Bonnie and Clyde they have been humanized.

Marlon Brando, his voice a reedy whisper, his jowls stuffed to a patriarchal sag, his body stiffened with years, his hair etched with gray, gives a performance which is at once a tour de force and so economical that it seems to be understated. He does not so much appear to act as to establish and exist as a presence, a strength. The picture opens with a whiny supplicant pleading to the camera. The camera edges sideways, making us aware of a bulky silhouetted listener. The speaker verges toward tears. The listener raises a hand, makes a small, imperial, beckoning gesture. Someone noiselessly fetches the speaker a steadying drink. After the long, theatrical buildup, the camera pulls back, confirming what we knew and were impatient to see for ourselves, that the listener was Brando as Don Corleone. It is one of those moments special to the movies, reminding you what tingling power a star can transmit from the screen—and what a potent star actor Brando is when the material is to his measure.

Toward the end of "The Godfather," Brando as an old man in semi-retirement plays with his grandson in the garden. The sequence seems in part to have been improvised. It is so natural, so charming, so totally the character, rather than the actor acting, that you can only be astonished and grateful to watch such a talent. It is a moment of affecting power such as I've not seen him equal since his classroom soliloquy in "Reflections in a Golden Eye." His Don Corleone is a portrayal which reveals more than pages of dialogue could hope to convey.

Hardly less persuasive is Al Pacino, who was first-rate as the young addict in "Panic in Needle Park" and who as the don's son, Michael, drawn reluctantly into the family affairs, seems to change from within, even as we watch him, from the nice normal guy to an ice-hearted and methodical murderer who can impassively serve as godfather at a christening while his rivals are being systematically gunned down in at least two states. Pacino makes Michael an even nastier piece of business than his father had been, colder and, once committed, less touched by a common humanity. (Simply because it is a movie, with a movie's impact, "The Godfather" here seems to offer less forgiveness, less hope of amelioration or change in the Mafia—the word is never used—than I remember in the book.)

The supporting gallery is large and terrifically effective. James Caan is excellent, again, as the don's hot-tempered son, Sonny. Robert Duvall is very strong (tough but capable of feeling) as the adopted son who is the family's lawyer. Richard Castellano, from "Lovers and Other Strangers," is undemonstratively solid as a henchman, and professional wrestler Lenny Montana is very persuasive as another. Sterling Hayden and John Marley have what amount to cameos as a crooked cop and a studio boss respectively and both are fine. Two offbeat castings work very well: singers Morgana King as Brando's wife and Al Martino as the Sinatra-like figure Brando helps. Diane Keaton, in her first film, is authentic as Pacino's WASPish New England wife. Simonetta Stefanelli has a charming innocence as his luckless Sicilian wife. Richard Conte as a rival chieftain and Al Lettieri as a traitorous henchman, Gianni Russo as a traitorous son-in-law and Talia Shire as his wife are all vivid. John Cazale is a weak brother and Alex Rocco a Las Vegas hotelier, both impressive in a large and admirable company.

The technical aspects of "The Godfather" all struck me as upholding the best traditions of the form. The production design by Dean Tavoularis, the art direction by Warren Clymer, the set decoration by Philip Smith, and Anna Hill Johnstone's costumes all conspire to evoke a kind of awkward age too different to be the present but too close to be the colorful past.

The music by Nino Rota (who also did "8½") is remarkable for its grace and its unobtrusiveness. It is nicely understated. Gordon Willis did the photography, which seemed to me to vary to fit the time and the mood. The earliest scenes have a reddish tone that suggests garish early screen color. The wedding exteriors have the squinty, overbright look of home films. Sicily shimmers under the island's dazzling white sunlight, and so on. William Reynolds and Peter Zinner edited.

Francis Ford Coppola on this evidence can cope with the spectacle film both as writer and as director. The pleasure of the film is that the performances by Brando and Pacino, strong and vivid as they are, do not overweigh the work of the ensemble. The consistency of texture is an index of Coppola's skillful control. He has indeed brought off an assured and richly detailed piece of movie storytelling on a massive scale. The violence, I had better repeat, is *violent* and graphic, and it is part of the movie's considered and considerable lure. We are back in the tradition of the gangster film, if in a much tonier neighborhood. Albert S. Ruddy produced for Paramount.

"The Godfather" becomes an instant classic.

Cabaret

The movie musical is probably the most bemoaned casualty of the post-television age, with the cadres that created the musicals at MGM and elsewhere long since dispersed. "Cabaret" is not only one of the best films of any decade, it is at once a kind of syncopated last hurrah to the musical that was, and a teasing taste of the musical that would evolve if musicals continued to be made. A few have been made, reflecting their own times. Bob Fosse's film stands alone in his dramatic integration of music and story and its portrait of a feverish, ominous time and place.

"CABARET" IS AN EXQUISITELY SCULPTED MILESTONE in the history of the film musical. It extends to the musical the coming of age of the movies as an art form. It may not be the best musical ever made—I couldn't say—but it is the most thrilling I have ever seen, the most adult, the most intelligent, the most surpassingly artful in its joining of cinema, drama and music to evoke the mood and events of a turning point (and turning place) in history.

The movie musical had made explorations beyond the sequined splendors of the early frolics. There had been "Pal Joey" with its amoral protagonists and its cynically amused view of life, "Oklahoma" with its glimpse of malevolence amidst the romantic tradition, "West Side Story" with its matchless success at transmuting raucous street events into high tragedy. "Cabaret" consolidates and extends those gains in a work which brings insight, candor and compassion to flawed creatures in an ominous society, and so doing provokes thought about what the later goings-on in the cabaret will be.

Looking at the Berlin of 1930, "Cabaret" creates the equivalent not (like "West Side Story") of "Romeo and Juliet," but of the tradition of brutally satiric drawings by Hogarth, Daumier and most specifically

George Grosz who, like "Cabaret" itself, looked at a decadent, self-indulgent, feverishly creative, divided society, unhappy and restless, fatefully beginning to listen to the Nazi siren song.

The cabaret, smoky and garish, with Joel Grey sleek-haired and rouged as the master of ceremonies, could well be a way station on one of Dante's descending circles of hell. The dancers, masked in mascara, and the blowsy all-crone band in straw hats, give the place a hallucinatory quality that is evilly fascinating.

Director Bob Fosse, who filled the movie version of "Sweet Charity" with wondrous things but who could not at last overcome the thin uncertainties of the basic material, here proves what an extraordinarily inventive filmmaker he is. "Cabaret" never once stops for a musical number. In ways that I am eager to watch again, "Cabaret" moves in and out of music, in and out of exposition, each enhancing, explaining, motivating, exemplifying the other, with a cohesion that is just plain awesome to see.

Liza Minnelli is the star, and she most authentically is. As Sally Bowles, the expatriate American girl performing in the cabaret, she has both the waiflike vulnerability and the steely, reckoning ambition of the character. We sense what you might call an intermittently repentant amorality, a drive which has by no means lost the ability to feel. I suspect that Miss Minnelli is a good deal more professional performer than the Sally Bowles of Christopher Isherwood's originating Berlin stories. And, ripping through the superb John Kander-Fred Ebb score, she is terrific. But she is also, in her cloche-cropped hair, her green eye shadow and her bee-sting lipstick, Isherwood's Sally Bowles beyond question. She's the virgin courtesan, and oddly contemporary as a girl both rejected by and rejecting the niceties of the distracted, polite, middle-class world in which she began.

Michael York is the struggling young English writer who falls in love with Sally. He is probably in part the surrogate for Isherwood himself, witness more than protagonist and finally repelled by all he sees in the society around him. York suggests charmingly the duality within the writer, although the role is the least rewarding in the film, existing as it does principally to illuminate the other characters. These include Marisa Berenson as a Jewish girl who reads the future all too clearly; Fritz Wepper as the boy who loves her; Helmut Griem as the aristocrat who loves both Sally and the writer and who continues to think the Nazis can be controlled.

The performances are all first-rate, and so is the gallery of faces—glimpsed through the cigarette haze of the cabaret, on the streets and in the shops—which Fosse has assembled. Geoffrey Unsworth's cinematography, especially inside the cabaret and during the numbers, is immensely fluid and atmospheric. The sense of period has been sustained in fine detail through the production design of Rolf Zehetbauer, the art direction of Jurgen Kiebach and the costumes of Charlotte Flemming. Sally's boarding house is a particular triumph and the costumes run a gamut from cool elegance to a sweaty, gartery tawdriness.

Jay Allen's script follows ably on the successive labors of Isherwood, the late John van Druten (who turned the stories into "I Am a Camera") and Joe Masteroff, who derived the stage "Cabaret" from the play. He opens up the play and accommodates a re-division of emphasis between Grey as Master of Ceremonies and Miss Minnelli as Sally.

But I think it is important to the film, and important to say, that while Miss Minnelli gives a remarkable star turn, "Cabaret" becomes an all-star vehicle, whose principal star is Fosse. Indeed, the impact of Grey's performance as the emcee, a kind of wing-collar Greek chorus commenting on all the follies and weeping for all the inhumanities of humankind, is still central to the success of "Cabaret" as a hellish glimpse of the world in miniature.

The ending of "Cabaret" is the measure of its daring and its strength. We've come out of the tumults. Now there is another, anticipatory drum roll. It simply stops. The screen is black, empty, silent. The effect is unsettling, overwhelming. We're left with our own anticipations—for those characters, for ourselves, in their cabaret, in our own. I trust Fosse and his cast and crew understand that the continuing silence is the richest applause of all. Engrossing and uncompromising, a work which is as electrifying as high art must always be, "Cabaret" is the kind of achievement— at once singular and collaborative—which the musical movie will have to be measured against hereafter.

Deliverance

For all the reservations I had about "Deliverance," and wrote about, the film has a still-haunting emotional power; its ominous suspense and the feeling that civilization has been left behind in every sense still grip the innards.

AT THE LEVEL OF BRUTE PHYSICAL ACTION—men against a malevolent river—John Boorman's "Deliverance" is an absolutely first-rate piece of movie-making. Jon Voight, Burt Reynolds, Ned Beatty and Ronny Cox, riding their rocketing, frail canoes down the wicked white water of the Chattahooche in the rugged north Georgia mountains, are so manifestly enduring what we see them enduring that you can taste the fear and hear the hammering hearts. The location looks as primitive and foreboding as it must have been, and Boorman and cinematographer Vilmos Zsigmond keep us so close to the action that we feel all the aches—and the exhilaration.

Bracketing this dousing, rousing action, not unlike a set of bookends, is another movie which could, I suppose, be called "James Dickey's 'Deliverance,'" and in which the confrontation with the wilderness river is established and concluded as a very heavy parable. Dickey is a preeminent modern American poet, a rare one who is also a man of action, an outdoorsman who hunts with bow and arrow and celebrates masculinity. The movie seems to be raising questions about nature (is it benign or malignant?), about some need in modern man to assert himself in nature, and about whether man in his natural state is benign or savage.

For me, "Deliverance" is least successful when it is trying to be most thoughtful. There is, in particular, a long, trailing denouement which is so mannered and so anticlimactic that it compromises the impact achieved by such heroic efforts earlier. By some kind of irony, it also seems that Boorman's exposition is cloudiest and most awkward when the poet's philosophical concerns are being laid in.

The four explorers are all city men, led by Reynolds (in a fine and credible performance) as an obsessive believer in self-reliance who sees nature as the greatest adversary of them all, to be outwitted but never defeated. His presence is easily accounted for (the author allows him to know himself perhaps more clearly than such a compulsive woodsman might really be expected to). The coming together of these four men is not so easily accounted for, and while their uncertainty about each other sets up an early mood of uneasiness which is useful to the drama, the gap in story logic is also a kind of needless reminder that what we have here is a symbolic drama in which men and events are to be manipulated by the poet-philosopher's hand.

Yet after an initial shakiness, Boorman plunges us into a wonderfully affecting sequence. The gentlest of the four (Ronny Cox), a guitar-strumming and reflective man, finds a strange, silent boy picking at a banjo on a porch in the dying hamlet near the river. The boy has odd eyes and a misshapen head, as if his family had inbred a few times too often. Man and boy exchange musical phrases and suddenly play an extraordinary hoedown duet. Then, as suddenly, the moment is over and the boy will not speak, presuming he can. It is a rich moment cinematically, full of energy but then ominous, suggesting the presence of ignorance and potential trouble amongst people living primitively in primitive country.

The feeling of menace grows as Reynolds negotiates with hill men to drive the cars back down to the river's end. And, in quick time, the city men are to confront not only the primitive gorge but some brutish types who wrest a mean living beside it. There is a rape, ghastly and protracted, and there are two killings, swift and shocking. But the course of events is anything but clear-cut—nothing so straightforward as Peckinpah's rites of passage to manhood through adversity and the uses of violence.

Part of the minor dissatisfaction I feel about the movie is that—if you follow me—it is not clear enough soon enough that the events are in fact fatefully ambiguous, and that Dickey's poetic sensibility is worrying over the difficulty of sorting out what seems from what is, and the danger of acting before you are sure.

Amidst the terrifying credibility of the river-running there is another action sequence (Voight scaling a sheer cliff) which by contrast rings untrue (however difficult it may actually have been to do and to shoot) and which is marked by some quite confusing exposition. As with any very good motion picture, the flaws loom large because they measure the distance to the masterpiece the film just missed being. "Deliverance" is an engrossing adventure, a demonstrable labor of love whose pains have largely paid off in making us empathize with stirring deeds in a setting of cruel beauty.

Reynolds suggests that given the right material he is more than just another pretty hand and Voight, in the most substantial role he has had since "Midnight Cowboy," proves again what a versatile actor he is. Ned Beatty and Ronny Cox are excellent in the briefer roles as the other voyagers. Billy McKinney and Herbert Coward are the very believable villains. Author Dickey himself makes an appearance as a sheriff who can surmise but not prove what happened up river. He emerges out of some of the movie's confusing exposition, and on the whole I think another casting would have been wiser because his flat and deadpan delivery muffles the power of the moment.

This is probably an appropriate moment to say that I haven't read Dickey's novel. I cherish the principle that a movie has to be judged on its own terms as a movie, (it's what's up front that counts). The practical truth is, however, that the more familiar you are with the source material the more difficult it is to judge a movie purely as movie. You may admire the adaptive skill, as in "A Clockwork Orange," or deplore the inadequacy of it, as with "Portnoy's Complaint." But you are not likely to be neutral.

In this case, however, the movie is all I have to go on, and I can only suspect that there was more to "Deliverance" on paper than meets the eye.
And what I can't be sure is whose input the movie could have used more
of, Dickey's or Boorman's. I have no doubt that, whatever its flaws, "Deliverance" is an uncommonly ambitious and admirable undertaking. Tom
Priestly did the editing.

Sounder

*Significantly or ironically, the most successful of the first 70s
non-exploitive films about the black experience was produced and
directed by whites, although from a fine script by the black play-
wright Lonnie Elder III. The early vogue of the black film was
damaged by its own excesses, but the way led (slowly as usual) to
more black technicians, more black directors and more black
stars (no longer limited to "black" stories). Down the road
awaited both "The Color Purple" and Spike Lee.*

THE NEW FILM PHENOMENON is, of course, the discovery of a
large and eager audience (principally but by no means entirely black) for
movies starring, about—and increasingly made by—blacks.

Beginning approximately with "Cotton Comes to Harlem" in 1970
(directed by the black actor Ossie Davis)—the dimensions of whose box
office astonished everyone including the producers—and carried forward
through "Shaft" and sequels and imitations, the black-for-blacks movie
has become a genre as well as a source of controversy. As the movies have
grown more gaudy and assertive, the black community has begun to de-
bate whether the movies are a legitimate spur to racial pride, identity and
achievement, or whether they're just an updated form of exploitation,
with new black stereotypes (notably the ruthless superstud hero) just as
demeaning in their way as the servile shufflers out of the old Hollywood.

Generally urban and crime-centered, the new movies are escapist
fare, with dream-heroes as much larger than life as any in what must now
be identified as the white movies of the past. But escape begins at home,
and these new black movies have strength and appeal because they tell it
like the black audience knows it, portraying a city life of tension and violence, The Man, hustle and heroin, despair and defiance, in which often

only crime seems to pay. The vision is uncomfortable but it isn't unreal, and heroes are found within it, if not within the law.

The tastes of this audience for black pictures will be put to a sharply different test by "Sounder," a superb and deeply affecting new film about another kind of black experience.

The year is 1933, the place backwoods Louisiana, the protagonists a sharecropping black family—father (Paul Winfield), mother (Cicely Tyson), daughter (Yvonne Jarrell), older son (Kevin Hooks), through whose perceptions the story is seen and told, and younger son (Eric Hooks). "Sounder" (the name of the family dog) was adapted by Lonnie Elder III from the book by William H. Armstrong, which won the Newbery prize for children's fiction.

As produced by Robert Radnitz and directed by Martin Ritt, that time and that feudal place, with its economic slavery replacing the political slavery, is recaptured with a fidelity and a sensitivity which is both heartbreaking and heartwarming. "Sounder" is, in fact, that rarest of things, an adult family film, with unembarrassed claims on the attention of the entire audience and with none of the softening of reality or the glazing over of hard truth which usually goes with the family form. It is almost impossible to watch the film without being moved to tears.

It begins with a marvelously photographed raccoon hunt by lantern light through the piney woods. (John Alonzo was the cinematographer.) The raccoon gets away, because the father is not larger than life-sized but a real man with a capacity for experiencing bad luck as well as good (and, being black in Louisiana, a fair amount more of bad than good).

The bare bones of the story are primer-thin. The father is arrested for stealing food and given a cruelly disproportionate sentence. The family carries on. The boy makes a long pilgrimage to visit his father at a sawmill labor camp and encounters en route a thoughtful and life-changing teacher (Janet McLachlan) at a country school. But the plot lines are fleshed out with the whole remembered texture of the life: a ballgame in a pasture after church, music as diversion and as restorative (composer-performer Taj Mahal proves a powerful actor and also did the film's spare, eloquent score); the clustered, powerless black community whose preacher cannot even make the dreams of glory and golden stairs sound convincingly consoling amidst the indignities of earth; the sympathetic white woman (Carmen Matthews) whose helpfulness has to be clandestine even though she's a pillar of the community; the establishment whites—the storekeeper/landowner (Teddy Airhart), the sheriff (James Best)—whose frightfulness lies not necessarily in malice but in the confident serenity of their assumption that a white God made them superior and put them in charge of the world.

Ultimately "Sounder" offers a thin and guarded hope that, through education and escape, there would be a better chance for the next generation. But the movie, to its immense credit, does not back off from reality. Even the hope begins in the pain of separation, and we cannot escape our own awareness as audience that "Super Fly" is as credible a sequel to "Sounder" as was the presence of Ralph Bunche at the UN.

At the same time, "Sounder" is an extraordinarily touching testament to man's resistance to all the forces that deny his dignity and his worth, and a warming witness to the ability of warmth itself, humor and solicitude to endure amidst the most threatening and demoralizing conditions. In that sense, "Sounder" speaks to all men everywhere about all men everywhere.

Martin Ritt's movies have almost all, from the beginning, revealed his strong social awareness. None has shown the sensitivity, the gentleness, the sure and subtle control of "Sounder."

The performances are uniformly fine and engaging, strong and credible. Winfield as the father is tender, sexy, angry, ashamed, rascally, proud and dignified, a full, flawed man, not a contrived hero figure. Miss Tyson as the mother is a fighter, strong-willed, scared but defiant, a survivor against odds, and the portrayal is inspiring to watch. Kevin Hooks as the boy thrust toward manhood *is* the boy, not an actor.

Radnitz, who has produced an honorable string of family films, positive and sentimental, has here produced his finest work, a film which finds its positive human values in an adversity seen unblinkingly.

You have to hope that "Sounder" finds the audiences, black and white alike, it deserves, because it is an entertainment in the best sense, engrossing but also working to the ends of social amelioration, exploring a different part of the black experience in a different way from "Shaft" *et seq.* And if there is room for the exploitation flicks, there is urgent need for the compassionate insights of movies like "Sounder." I urge you to have a look.

Fat City

Hollywood has always loved boxing—a crisis in every round and more in the dressing room. Huston's film placed the fight game right in the middle of the downside of small-city America. It is a piece of social realism enpowered by the newly liberal ratings but even now seldom matched for its sad honesty. Too much honesty, it may be. Despite producer Ray Stark's valiant attempt to resuscitate a film he loved, audiences stayed away again, missing one of a great director's finest films.

JOHN HUSTON'S CAREER has had more episodes than "The African Queen." He has gone from the early triumphs of "The Maltese Falcon" and "The Treasure of the Sierra Madre" to so eccentric and freaked-out a masterwork as "Beat the Devil" to the glorious "Queen" herself, and forward to so admirable if unavailing an enterprise as "Reflections in a Golden Eye" and a piece of competent hackwork like "The Kremlin Letter."

In recent times it has been only too easy to believe that some of the acting roles, vivid but trivial, and some of the directing assignments were accepted without hope or enthusiasm, just to keep the horses groomed and the foxhounds fed in Ireland. Huston jumped, or fell or was pushed from "The Last Run" when it became perfectly clear that the power and the artistic say-so lay with the star, George C. Scott, and not with Huston himself. A mournful day, if you happen to have enjoyed "The Maltese Falcon."

Through it all, and despite the riding to hounds abroad, Huston has remained a prototypically early American director, with the kind of equal affection for pirates and princes that I would have expected to find in Mark Twain as well.

Out of his own early meanderings Huston knows grifters, hustlers, losers, soiled ladies, small towns, side streets, the smells of dust, sweat, fear and failure and the metallic taste of your last thin dime. That information, so to speak, and the acts of charity and valor which survive despite it, gave "The Maltese Falcon" and "The Treasure of the Sierra Madre" a particular richness, showed up a continent away in the Bogart character in "The African Queen" and can be traced in the mood and feel of the best of his other works.

The good news for those who have admired Huston's truest work (or for those who couldn't care less but who like engrossing movies) is that in

"Fat City" Huston has confronted a piece of material and a milieu perfectly suited to his insights and his talents. The result is his best film in years, and one of the best he has ever done: a lean, compassionate, detailed, raucous, sad, strong look at some losers and survivors on the side streets of small-city Middle America.

Leonard Gardner did the script from his own lean, hard-muscled novel about a pair of boxers in Stockton, one of whom is having a side fight with the bottle but who thinks he can make a comeback in both rings, the other who still hopes, this late in time, that boxing is a way out of having to pick walnuts or top onions for a living.

Stacy Keach is the older fighter, not bad enough to quit, not good enough to go places, caught in the limbo between and surviving on cheap wine, self-fooling lies and farm labor (rolling onto the buses in the predawn darkness, hacking and moaning). It's a very, very fine and affecting performance. Keach creates a man who is not bright but not dumb, charming in an easy, barroom way, sympathetic even when he rages because the rage is triggered by his unavoidable glimpses of his own defeat.

Jeff Bridges is the kid, and he makes him not the brightest, but attractive and nice, not a winner in or out of the ring, but not a total loser either. Losing, Gardner seems to be saying, is a relative thing. Sometimes it's worse than others. Bridges conveys a tenderness, an awareness of the need to be gentle with those who are losing even harder than you are, and a strong if passive will to survive that is an effective complement to Keach's.

There is in "Fat City" a third dazzling performance by a New York actress named Susan Tyrrell as a blowsy, whining, self-dramatizing barfly who takes up with Keach after her own man (played with competence and cool dignity by fighter Curtis Cokes) leaves for a short-term engagement in jail. Miss Tyrrell, her voice a maudlin rasp, betrayals by all mankind worn like bruises on her pale skin, is extravagantly histrionic, but you feel that the performance is part of the character, rather than a way of impersonating the character. She gives an enormous vitality to the movie.

The characters, of course, move within a milieu—of fringe streets, shacky houses with weed-grown yards, roach-ridden hotels in which the management's instructions are hand-lettered in pencil, the agribusiness orchards, the worn saloons and the coffeebars as whitely sanitary as mausoleums.

Huston and his photographer, Conrad Hall, have caught all this (and more) with a kind of undramatizing accuracy which becomes the more impressive by not drawing conspicuous attention to the camerawork. The eloquence lies in letting a particular world reveal itself.

Before he made it to Hollywood as a writer (first screen credit forty years ago), Huston had himself been a boxer, fighting in tank arenas in middle California. What surprised him, and surprises us as watchers, is the persistence of that special subculture; the clammy-walled dressing rooms crowded under the stands in the small, smoky halls, the fighters riding buses to save money, the bookers and the managers and the rituals of the gym, rhythmical and reassuring, spartan and oddly pure in contrast to the sleazy world outside.

It is all there, not with the melodramatics of "Champion" or the cynicism of "Requiem for a Heavyweight" but with a kind of everyday casualness which puts a ceiling on the hopes without really cushioning the despairs by way of consolation.

Huston recruited his supporting cast within the boxing world present and immediately past, and skillfully avoided the self-consciousness which often goes with that kind of casting. Art Aragon, the golden boy now a bail bondsman, is among those most prominently on view.

Candy Clark plays Bridges's girlfriend, a small but accurately observed part which reveals how much life imitates postures from popular art. She is very good.

Kris Kristofferson did the wistful score, which catches exactly the mood of lives whose principal accompaniment is from jukeboxes (which is in no way to put down the quality of Kristofferson's music).

Ray Stark produced, with evident affection.

"Fat City" (a gambling term for green pastures, or being in clover) is not a big picture. It's a slice of life, looked at closely and sympathetically. Its losers lose, or break even, with a kind of innate dignity, and make only small ripples.

"Chief among its virtues, if it has any at all," Huston wryly said after the showing of "Fat City" at the Cannes Festival, "is its modesty." That's true. What is also true is that although Huston and Leonard Gardner are dealing with somber materials, their film is finally ennobling, partly because there is that will to survive running through all the despairs, and partly because high artistry is always inspiring.

1973

Save the Tiger

One of the ongoing ironies about major studio activities in Holly-
wood is that it is easier to get a fifty-million-dollar film financed
than one costing less than one million. "Save the Tiger" cost less
than a million and, after a two-year struggle, got made finally be-
cause the star worked for nothing and Martin Ransohoff of
Filmways came aboard. The gambles paid off. Lemmon got the
Oscar he'd earned and the film, now a classic, returned its costs.

IN RECENT YEARS a tight handful of films, each markedly different
from the others, has made strong impressions on American audiences because, like lightning rods catching thunderbolts out of the uneasy air, they
have isolated and given voice to ideas, questionings, anxieties that were
abroad in the society and waiting to be said.

"The Graduate," farcically particularizing a new generation's restless
dissatisfaction with the material goals of the parent generation, was one
of those films. Another was "Easy Rider," with its inchoate but impassioned look at the hatreds crevassing the country but also with its dawning perception that you can't opt out of all responsibility. "Five Easy
Pieces" and its dropped-out hero, who seems to prefer not trying to trying and failing, caught a larger, later uncertainty about goals. On the
other side, part of the success of "Love Story" can be explained by its
wistful insistence, endorsed by its audiences, that we are really still romantic idealists at heart.

To this small company of movies which have found their time can
now be added Steve Shagan's "Save the Tiger," a profoundly unsettling
portrait of an early-middle-age American businessman, simultaneously
compassionate and corrupted, likable and full of self-loathing, moved in a
day of crisis to wonder where have all the values gone and what became
of the nice guy he was. In its study of disillusion and the erosion of

values, Shagan's story, which he wrote and produced, becomes in a sense an extension of "The Graduate," brushed with sardonic humor but closer to tragedy. The point of view now belongs to the graduate's father and his contemporaries, whose certitudes about plastics and the good life at poolside have unexpectedly and bafflingly crumbled.

Harry Stoner grew up on the 1939 Brooklyn Dodgers and Bunny Berigan, radio and the movies and the great boxers. He was drafted and fought at Anzio and would have said he did well. He came back confidently to pursue the American dream of the good life. When we meet him he has made it, at a price. He lives in Beverly Hills splendor and is partner in a dress firm in the Los Angeles garment district. It costs him, he reckons, $250 a day to get out of bed. The firm has had a catastrophic season; his partner has had to cook its books to stay afloat. The nice guy from Anzio pimps for important buyers and is negotiating with an arsonist for insurance money to get the firm into one more season.

Unattractive, all of it. What gives the film its power and its disturbing ability to touch those a world away from Stoner's demoralized life is the extraordinarily affecting and sensitive portrayal of Stoner by Jack Lemmon. It is much the best thing Lemmon has ever done, which is saying a great deal if you remember only "The Apartment" and "Days of Wine and Roses." The tenderness, the intelligence, the likability, the distraught innocence—which have been denied to Lemmon in "The Out-of-Towners" and "Avanti!" and were supplanted by an unattractive and abrasive clangor—are all restored here and they are crucial. It is not necessary, not possible, to admire the man Harry Stoner has become, but it is urgent to understand him and to realize that his disillusion and his captivity within aspirations that once seemed reasonable and even admirable are not his alone.

"If we were making missiles and got in this kind of trouble," says his partner, played with dour and sympathetic naturalism by Jack Gilford, "the government would write us a check. But we make dresses."

Everybody fiddles with taxes; computers have removed the human element, and the possibility of compassion, from everyday life. The virtues and the values began to go, and how does a man know where to stop the changed world and get off, assuming he can? The partner stops at falsifying the books (only the impersonal government is victimized). Lemmon stops at borrowing from the mob, although that's self-preservation, not morality. The only refuge for Harry is the past, the seemingly simpler past of Harry Walker and Cookie Lavagetto, Marcel Cerdan and the Goodman Sextet. The recollected past gives the movie its texture and its sadness, because the past fails as refuge and its echoes merely confirm

Harry's awareness of irretrievable loss.

John Avildsen, who directed "Joe," was the director here, and he again demonstrates his considerable ability to get social reality on film. "Save the Tiger" was shot in sequence and entirely on locations: in a garment loft, a Malibu beachhouse, a Chinatown restaurant, in a downtown sexploitation movie house where Harry talks terms with the cool arsonist ("It's technology, not morality, boy"). The difference is that "Save the Tiger" is as quiet and internalized as "Joe" was shocking and melodramatic.

Shagan, translating a state of mind and a point of view into story terms, has built his structure carefully and the devices sometimes reveal themselves as devices. A long coincidence brings Lemmon together twice with a hitchhiking hippie chick (Laurie Heineman) who is too neatly prototypical of a later generation lost in its own way without ever having had, as Shagan says, the chance to be innocent. What saves the sequence is that it achieves its ends of illuminating more of the Stoner character and of the beguiling Miss Heineman's times.

Similarly, an old Jewish pattern-cutter in the factory is almost too neatly symbolic of a still older generation which has held on to traditional, simpler values of love and work. The sequence comes off, again, because of the careful and affecting playing of Lemmon and William Hansen as the old man. The delicate problem of avoiding any inference of anti-Semitism Shagan has handled, effectively, by his considered balancing of Gilford's indignant rectitude against Lemmon's reluctant criminality and again by the inclusion of the chiding old cutter.

It remains possible to argue that Shagan's indictment of the times is too harsh and that the American middle class does not universally share Harry Stoner's disenchantment nor his corrupted willingness to hang on to what he has by any means. And yet Harry's litany of laments about a world whose values have been misplaced and whose capacity for human contact has been grievously reduced is all too obviously not his alone. But, if it seems too late for Stoner to reassess his own aspirations and set some new rules for his life, Shagan suggests that there is still hope for a younger generation who can learn from both the past and the present without being captives of limited goals, or the lack of any goals.

Like the earlier touchstone films, "Save the Tiger" is a small and intensely personal work, carrying the concerns of Shagan (who fought for two years to get it financed), Lemmon (who did it for no salary) and Avildsen (whose sympathetic response to the material is evident in every frame).

The performances are uniformly stunning, centering inevitably on

Lemmon's and Gilford's but including as well Miss Heineman in the difficult role of the girl, Norman Burton as the lecherous visiting buyer, Patricia Smith as Lemmon's weary wife, Thayer David as the confident arsonist, and William Hansen as the old man. Harvey Jason is the firm's waspish designer and Lara Parker is a call girl and both take their roles beyond the clichés.

Marvin Hamlisch's excellent score also incorporates a good deal of actual Big Band-era sounds, and Berigan's "I Can't Get Started," which closes the film, is not less than heartbreaking.

Ed Feldman was executive producer.

In the force and conviction of its social commentary, "Save the Tiger" stands alone among current American films. My guess is that we will see no more controversial movie this year, for like it or not, Shagan has caught some currents from the present uneasy air.

Last Tango in Paris

A French-Italian-American co-production, directed by Bernardo Bertolucci in Paris, "Last Tango in Paris" was nevertheless one of the most significant films of the American 70s. It used and validated the screen's new-won freedom to deal graphically and emotionally with human sexuality. The role was Marlon Brando's most revealingly personal and gives the film most of its unprecedented power. It is still an unsurpassed proof of a film's ability to plumb the soul.

THE TROUBLE IS THAT by now it is very nearly impossible to *see* "Last Tango in Paris." So much has already been written in extravagant praise and even more extravagant damnation of the movie, and so much has been reported on the making of the movie (covers on both *Time* and *Newsweek*), about what Marlon did and didn't do, would and wouldn't do, about the heroine and her incessant private life and the director and his politics and his intentions real or postdated, that "Last Tango" is not a movie any longer, it is a tourist attraction like Pigalle or North Beach.

I am one of the culprits, self-confessed, and I am not really trying to lay off the blame onto those who have written so inflammatorily about a movie they have not seen or who unfairly represented a movie they had seen. But the sad fact is that it is now monstrously difficult to watch "Last Tango" calmly, on its own terms, without taking sides from the start on the grave question of whether it is the greatest landmark since Stravinsky's *Rite of Spring,* as Pauline Kael has said, or whether it is only a "Deep Throat" for intellectuals, as the most waspish of the Eastern critics has charged. (It would be hard to think of another movie which needs to be defended quite so urgently from both its enemies and its friends.) What would be useful would be to clear the dance floor just for a minute and then start all over again, refreshed and cleansed, trying to see the film as it is.

The tone is established during the titles themselves, which are illuminated, as it were, by some of the famous and tortured paintings of the English artist Francis Bacon, with their distended faces which resemble spoiled meat or melted plastic and which suggest decadence, disintegration and despair. "Last Tango" is a film of decay and despair, in which the activities of the adults are time-serving rituals on the edges of an empty and pointless center, and in which the young seem already to be infatuated with their own pasts for lack of a future or of a present which contains anything more than casual sexual contacts.

As he did previously in "The Conformist," Bernardo Bertolucci finds sexual behavior symptomatic of the situation of society. In "The Conformist," sexual anxieties and frustrations seemed to be the makings of a Fascist. In "Last Tango," a kind of sexual abandonment seems to characterize lives (or at least a life) which have ceased to have real meaning.

How far the readout from the particular lives in "Last Tango" is to be taken is left finally to the viewer. What must be kept clear, I think, is that sexual behavior is being examined and commented upon in "Last Tango" and not—in the film itself—exploited. Bertolucci's film is remarkably beautiful to watch. The aura, most often, is somehow autumnal, golden but thin and unwarming, with the city seen most often at night or at the end of the day in the partial light of dawn or dusk and with the interiors murky beneath dim lamps or shuttered against the sun.

We first see Brando walking zombie-like beneath an elevated tramline. He is unshaven, red-eyed, weeping; except for the expensive camel's-hair coat he could be a wino, a drifter. (The plot has now been summarized so often that it is easy to forget how catching and how mystifying Bertolucci's exposition is. The sense of discovery, the gradual revelation of character, is one of the strong points of the film.)

A young girl in a floppy hat and long coat and boots strides by, aware, as we are, of Brando. She enters a block of flats, has a demented exchange with a dippy old concierge (Darling Legitimus, say the credits), goes up to investigate a vacant apartment. There, by design or more likely by accident, is Brando again, still in a trancelike state, or hiding like a hurt animal. The apartment, ratty, dusty, peeling, empty except for some draped and junky furniture, is to be the center of the movie, the place Brando establishes as an oasis for himself and the girl (round-faced Maria Schneider), in which they have no names, no identities, no links with anything beyond the apartment walls.

There is a good deal of surrounding action. The girl seems to be starring in a television documentary about her own life (she is the daughter of a French army officer) which is being made by her young lover (Jean-Pierre Leaud, from the Antoine Doinel films of Francois Truffaut). Brando, as we are to discover, is in flight from the messy suicide of the French wife he loved. Paul, the Brando character, had led a life of vagabondage which took him from a Midwest farm to Cuba to Tahiti and then—happily—into the small, shabby residential hotel owned by his wife's mother (Maria Michi).

The relationship he establishes with the girl in the deserted apartment is brutally, coarsely, impersonally sexual. The language is probably unprecedented in its abrasive candor, and we are left in no doubt that some intricate and unconventional things are going on. But even to identify them is to give them an explicitness which they do not really have. Ultimately, what is happening is left mostly to our imagination. The graphics are less specific than those in "I Am Curious (Yellow)," although that is probably not the most helpful comparison in the world.

But what is crucial is the emotional coloring of these goings-on. And the coloring is pale, chilly, off-putting rather than erotic. The images are designed to convey not the physical specifics but the complicated, contradictory and highly charged emotional states of the protagonists. If I may repeat myself, "Last Tango" more than any film I have yet seen deals with sexuality coolly and objectively as it dominates the relationship (as initially it *is* the relationship) of two complex, fully realized and entirely credible contemporary characters. They may be extraordinarily unusual figures, and yet they are believable; and whether or not we accept them as making a comment on their society, it is hard not to accept that they have some things to say about the relationships between men and women.

Brando and the girl have tried to create an entirely physical relationship, and it does not work. It begins for Brando in a kind of terrible anguish which he hopes to mask with a brutally impersonal sexual association, and the scenes in which he tries to assert the nature of this association are cruel and discomforting. But if there is a brief release, there is no relief and no escape, no alternative to the need for a deeper sharing. Both of them recognize this; but it is the girl who cannot cope with the truth of it. Bertolucci, as I suggested earlier, has set up a reversal of roles, in which for once it is the woman rather than the man who flees from deeper needs which impose a dependency on her. Brando as a free and equal love object might have been acceptable; Brando as a creature of pathos is not.

The ending, which I do not intend to give away, is the least satisfactory part of "Last Tango," I think, because it simply avoids the long-term implications of everything the movie has seemed to be about. It is unpersuasive as story and evasive as a conclusion.

If "Last Tango" is chilly in its detached examination of the characters, it is also finally very affecting indeed, thanks overwhelmingly to the strength of Brando's portrayal. His performance as the Godfather was a particular triumph for the actor as craftsman and technician, creating a character with guile and the tools of voice and visage. But it is impossible not to believe that much of Paul grew out of Brando's own innards. There are two or three extended scenes—Brando suggesting that he ought never to have had a name, another recalling his boyhood and his mother—that feel like improvisations which have gotten out of hand, gone beyond the needs of the exercise and beyond make-believe. No one, you think, could possibly have written or even outlined them. Whether they are truly autobiographical becomes a matter of gossip; what is important is that they have a clenching sincerity and intensity which seems to leave mere craft far behind. Brando is always impressive on the screen; it is hard for me to remember when he has been so moving.

Miss Schneider is a triumph of casting—petulant, self-indulgent, and convincingly terrified as someone who has gotten in beyond her depth. Massimo Girotti has some very effective moments as Brando's wife's sad lover. Luce Marquand is colorful as an old-crone friend of the girl's. Gitt Magrini is the girl's mother and Miss Michi is convincingly emotional as the wife's mother. Vittorio Storaro did the exquisite cinematography and Gato Barbieri, who did the music and its urging, noodling alto sax solo, has made a crucial contribution to the mood of the film.

"Last Tango" does not betoken a revolution but it is a long evolutionary step forward in the screen's ability to deal not exploitively but coolly with human sexuality in the context of complicated human relationships. Indeed, what Bertolucci's story says is that sexuality can be neither a refuge from nor an alternative to more thoroughgoing relationships and responsibilities.

The sadness and the danger is that even though "Last Tango," seen as coolly as it regards its events, looks to be shocking but not exploitational, it certainly has been treated exploitationally. Movies are a marketplace commodity and profit is their iron law of survival. And United Artists, which is distributing "Last Tango," is also stuck with $11 million or more worth of "Man of La Mancha" and cannot be blamed for wanting to extract every dime the dance will yield. Yet allowing the impression to stand that "Last Tango" is somehow more prurient than it really is invites a double backlash—from the disgruntled young studs who are already tossing beer cans at the screen in New York (according to a published report from Rex Reed) and from those forces in the society who are already unhappy with the freedom of the screen and who imagine, sight unseen, that "Tango" is glorifying a kind of behavior which it, in fact, is not.

"Last Tango" is a strong, disconcerting, sobering motion picture, an examination of some of the most guarded but universal fears, desires and pains in human nature. It acknowledges the pleasures of the flesh, but acknowledges also that they are never without consequences, and that nothing we do is without consequence.

For the mature audience for which the film was made, it ought to be possible to see it that way.

Paper Moon

The film, delightful as it was, became a sort of high water mark for both director and stars, and a third straight hit for Bogdanovich, after which a law of averages seemed to catch up and the later films, well made as always, seldom captured critics or audiences. Miss O'Neal was in several more films, including a remake of "International Velvet," but nothing equaled her engaging vivacity as a ten-year-old in "Paper Moon."

IN HIS LIFELONG HOMAGE TO THE MOVIES, Peter Bogdanovich has mastered the making of them so that "The Last Picture Show" and "What's Up, Doc?" both had a terrific professional sheen. But he also paid careful heed to kinds of tales the movies told, and his own work is becoming a notably entertaining anthology of the movie form.

From the suspenseful violence of "Targets," his first independent feature, to the social drama of "Picture Show" and the zany comedy of

"What's Up, Doc?" Bogdanovich in "Paper Moon" moves on to remind us that there is no one quite so irresistible as a beguiling child star. It is some reminder, too. Tatum O'Neal, puffing cigars, using language that would curl your naturally straight hair, outconning her con man pal with the wiles of an elderly gypsy, is the most robustly entertaining young lady to hit the screen in a very long time.

What sets her apart from television's juveniles and from the few young movie folk who have come along is a kind of innocent wickedness which leans as much toward the wickedness as toward the innocence. There is nothing inadvertent about the mischief she gets into; she is right with Mark Twain's young men in her premature awareness that not everything is okay with the world and in fact that there is evil, greed, lust and other grown-up diversions.

The period is the 1930s. The film is correctly and luminously black and white (the superb photography is by Laszlo Kovacs). The score is a skein of radio sounds from Paul Whiteman to early Jack Benny.

Miss O'Neal is Addie Loggins, lately orphaned and being reluctantly delivered to a distant aunt by Moses Pray, played by her father, Ryan O'Neal, with I should think mixed emotions. His daughter could steal scenes from a train wreck or a forest fire and she certainly commandeers every moment of "Paper Moon."

O'Neal is a mobile grifter working penny-ante swindles, mostly delivering unordered Bibles to new widows with a heart-tugging story that the late lamented had intended it as a surprise. Miss O'Neal proves brilliantly effective at this and other dodges. The team acquires a world-used carnival girl (Madeline Kahn) and her maid (P.J. Johnson). They run afoul of a bootlegger and his nasty cop brother (both nicely done by John Hillerman), setting up a long and inventive chase sequence.

Alvin Sargent did the screenplay, from the novel *Addie Pray* by Joe David Brown and it is lovely make-believe fun, with none of the sugary sweetness that usually goes with moppet fare, and indeed with only a rough-cut sliver of sentiment here and there. Addie's ingenuity in setting up the downfall of the carnie girl goes beyond anything even a malevolent ten-year-old could concoct, but it hardly matters. Similarly, some of the language goes beyond what common sense says even a plain-spoke girl of the limberlost would use—and you wish the script hadn't. Yet at its best the dialogue has a wonderful natural ring and bite.

The performances are all effectively in support of Miss O'Neal, and they are all excellent. Miss Kahn, the hysterical fiancée in "What's Up, Doc?" is obviously a very versatile comedienne, and Hillerman, who was also in "What's Up, Doc?" is a fine character actor. In a large company of small parts, Burton Gilliam is an amorous desk clerk and Liz Ross, Yvonne Harrrison, Eleanor Bogart and Dorothy Forster are defrauded widow ladies.

The film was shot in parts of Kansas and Missouri which progress has left largely untouched, so that Polly Pratt's design generates a total sense of period.

O'Neal has said that his daughter would do no more acting until she is older. But on the strength of this performance, the world is going to be as hard to resist as she is. She is just plain marvelous and "Paper Moon" is a tough, funny, beautifully calculated diversion.

American Graffiti

This film reportedly returned more money in relation to its scant million-dollar cost than any film in the studio's history. Yet Universal, with no confidence in Lucas, whose one previous feature failed, almost torpedoed "American Graffiti" before he had finished it. But the film's quality and its resounding success led on to "Star Wars" and all of Lucas's unparalleled career.

GOING IN, "American Graffiti" as a title tells you almost nothing about what to expect from George Lucas's masterfully executed and profoundly affecting movie. Coming out, you realize that the title has tipped us off to almost everything.

On the surfaces of one sultry September night in 1962 Lucas finds all the markings which gave that moment in young American life its characteristic, fleeting flavor. Some of the notations are in the garish neon signeries of the Modesto-like city (actually, part Petaluma, part San Rafael) where Lucas himself grew up. Some of the notations are musical: the bass-loaded early rock of the Heartbeats, the Regents, Buddy Holly, Bill Haley and the Comets and, on camera, Flash Cadillac and the Continental Kids. (In all, there are forty-two songs and thirty-five groups on the nonstop collage of period sounds, and I'm not sure who would have guessed a dozen years ago that they could set up such a powerful and complicated nostalgia.)

It was Lucas' place and his time—he is now twenty-eight—and the great and satisfying significance of "American Graffiti" is that it marks one of the first attempts, and by a long shot the most impressive, by a new generation of film-makers to look at their own experience. I am not much given to superlatives, but I think "American Graffiti" is one of the most important American films of the year, as well as the one most likely to move you to tears. It is a kind of collective spiritual autobiography, because most of Lucas's collaborators, including his co-authors Gloria Katz and Willard Huyck, are also his contemporaries, who, like him, were coming to majority just as the Age of Kennedy was at once beginning and ending. What is so striking and so admirable about his and their reexamination of the last hours of settled youth is the affectionate but unfalsified tone of the reminiscence, which recalls the passing moment with amazing exactitude but also with detachment. The past has been put in perspective; it has not been revarnished to fit the fancies of a later time.

A lot of events have been crowded and condensed into this one final night, when high school has resumed with a sock hop and last year's seniors have not yet left for college. There is a very large cast of characters, all carefully drawn and enacted with such credible naturalness that you are tempted to think Lucas found and recruited them on the spot (not so). There are latent violence, danger, sadness, true romance and not a little mousing around. But running through it all is a lovely and persuasive innocence. The main drag mating dances of the hot rods, glistening T-birds and chromed-up fan-tail Chevies look like "Carnal Knowledge" on wheels, but the end results are closer to "Marty" with manual shift.

The retrospective mirror in which Lucas and his friends studied themselves and their summer of '62 revealed that there had been plenty of bragging and hoping, and naiveté along with the savvy, but more loneliness and uncertainty than lust or wrath beneath the ducktails and the beehives.

The night's nerve-center is Mel's Drive-in with its roller-skating waitresses and its young, waiting crowd. Paul Le Mat is the burly, moody, T-shirted owner of the town's hottest undefeated hot rod. Ronny Howard is the nice square kid torn between flying off to college in the morning and staying behind to be with his girl, Cindy Williams. Richard Dreyfuss is the shy loner, the intellectual so unsure of himself he is still hesitant to take his scholarship and tackle an Eastern school. Charlie Martin Smith is head of the awkward squad, the thick-lensed, bucktoothed Vespa-rider who suddenly gets custody of a real car and with it new pretensions and (wow!) access to a sporty older (eighteen) blonde (Candy Clark). Bo Hopkins, Manuel Padilla, Jr. and Beau Gentry are the movie's nearest equivalent to villains, gang members who commandeer Dreyfuss for a small crime and a large, dazzling prank. Wolfman Jack has been imported (somewhat improbably) to be the local deejay in residence who supplies the town's and the film's thumping Greek choral effects. He is terrific.

The form is episodic, a night-long and into-the-morning interweaving of several storylines, almost all of them touched often or continuously with some of the warmest and most human comedy that has happened by in a long time.

Young Smith's newfound braggadocio at the wheel of the car, his nervous attempts to buy some liquor for the blonde and the painful consequences to his car and his stomach are all sensationally funny because, like so many of the doings in this California town, they have happened in just about this way in other towns and other times, to different tunes and with different blondes and love-struck boys.

There is a nice moment when Ronny Howard and his date, now squabbling, are forced to dance the first dance, as last year's king and queen, in the ice-blue spotlight at the sock hop. How could any squabble survive the music and the memory? It doesn't.

The invention never falters. The reluctant relationship between the hot-rodder and the strong-willed twelve-year-old chick (Mackenzie Phillips) he finds himself chauffeuring would sustain most movies all by itself. In common with much of the action in "Graffiti," it starts as fun and ends as a revelation of unexpected depths and truths.

Beyond the qualities of its observations, "American Graffiti" is also a considerable technical achievement. The problems posed by shooting almost entirely at night, and frequently from cruising car to cruising car, were obviously monumental. But Haskell Wexler, who was the supervising cameraman, and his crews brought it off so unpretentiously that we accept it as given, and pay attention to the characters and the relationships rather than to the ingenuity that was required to let us watch.

The level of the performances from a largely unknown cast is another of Lucas's uncommon achievements. Dreyfuss, also now visible as Babyface Nelson in John Milius's "Dillinger," is probably the closest to being Lucas's alter ego in the movie, and so moves closest to our attention. Dreyfuss is a fine young actor, certain to be better known soon, and he gives the character a roundness which is partly expressed, partly implied by remarkable powers of implication. His loner is wry, quick-witted, nobody's fool, reserved but no stranger to romance, better at perceiving others than himself. You get the feeling the character will be heard from creatively, whatever his momentary doubts.

The women are also first-rate and Miss Phillips (the daughter of John Phillips of The Mamas and the Papas) makes a film debut hardly less startling in its youthful professionalism than Tatum O'Neal's was in hers.

Candy Clark makes the dumb blonde more than a stereotype. A dozen or more lesser parts are well worth citing. Among them: Harrison Ford as a rival hot-rodder, Terry McGovern as a sympathetic teacher, Jim Bohan as a town cop, Jana Bellan as a waitress with eyes for Ronny Howard, Scott Beach as a loyal Elk.

As the movie ends, Lucas in the closing crawl lets us know what lies in the future for some of his characters, and the impact is devastating. We see with brutal swiftness that that late summer's night was indeed only a fleeting moment, a prelude. Only the memories and the wisps of exuberant melody are frozen in time; the lives went variously on. The nostalgia may be real enough, but it has been stripped of any easy sentimentality and it is placed in the whole setting of those lives and the country's life. That night is a comment, not a refuge and the movie is more than a trip back home.

Francis Ford Coppola produced the picture for Universal under the banner of his American Zoetrope collaborative in San Francisco. Gary Kurtz, who, like Lucas and co-author Willard Huyck, came out of the USC cinema department, served as co-producer. Verna Fields and Marcia Lucas did the very adroit editing with Walter Murch in charge of the sound montage and rerecording.

It is not news that the film schools are producing notably gifted young moviemakers. Coppola himself, Lucas with his first feature "THX-1138" and John Millius, also from USC, have established that. The excitement of "American Graffiti" is that Lucas has deployed his creative vigor and skill to provide entertainment and insight from the materials of his own past. But the particulars of that past have been so artfully documented that their echoes carry far beyond Modesto.

The accuracy, the affection, the understanding and the humor which color the film all the way through make it one of the most rewarding attractions of the year. To miss it is to miss something quite special.

The Exorcist

"The Exorcist" was the first of a small number of films that led me to think audiences may respond, perhaps subconsciously, to stories raising the possibility of Otherness—powers outside ourselves. Did the decline of traditional religious practice leave a vacuum to be filled or re-filled by the forceful idea of God and Satan, or of nondenominational good and evil? Or was it just the thrill of those pea-soup eructations? I conclude it was something more, not necessarily intended by the filmmakers.

WHAT THE INDUSTRY CALLS the want-to-see, the anticipation for a film which precedes the reviews or the word of mouth, has probably been higher for "The Exorcist" than for any other film of 1973.

William Peter Blatty's scarifying best-seller about a movie star's daughter possessed by the devil was not the first about demonic possession, but deriving its details from a contemporary case history as it did, his book had a rare credibility. And Jesuit-educated Blatty saw it all not only as an incomparable horror story but as a true contest of good vs. evil, God vs. Satan.

The movie, which Blatty produced and wrote and which William Friedkin ("The French Connection") directed, is now here. It is a genuinely shocking movie, which in its ferocious strength and bloodcurdling events denies any possibility that what we are witnessing is anything but a titanic struggle between God and the Devil localized in the deranged and cruelly abused form of an innocent twelve-year-old girl. In its uncompromised treatment of its theme, "The Exorcist" becomes quite as much a movie landmark as, say, "Who's Afraid of Virginia Woolf?" did in its year for its own reasons. It is strong and frequently revolting stuff. Readers of the book are advised that it has been delivered with only the most minor trims. Those who never read the book are seriously forewarned that it is a long shriek from the parlor game devilishness of "Rosemary's Baby."

Ellen Burstyn, from "The Last Picture Show," is the movie star, finishing a film on location in Washington and living divorced in Georgetown with her daughter (played with endearing innocence and then with frightening unrecognizability by Linda Blair, a Connecticut schoolgirl). There are inexplicable rustlings in the attic, laughed-off complaints that the girl's bed is shaking, then a crude prank during a dinner party. A spinal tap (shown in needlessly clinical detail) reveals nothing physiologically wrong.

The possession tightens—strange voices and vile language from a terrified and then withdrawn and surly child. Psychiatrists have nothing to offer but many-syllabled evasions. The mother's campy director (Jack MacGowran in his last role) dies mysteriously and ghoulishly during a visit to the girl. The mother, understandably hysterical, at last seeks out Father Karras (Jason Miller), a priest-psychiatrist at nearby Georgetown University.

In the movie, as in Blatty's expertly paced book, the race to exorcise whatever demons are in possession of daughter Regan runs a nerve-tearing, accelerating parallel with Regan's maniacal and destroying furies. The exorcist himself is an old, frail archaeologist-priest (Max von Sydow), obviously modeled on the Catholic philosopher-theologian Teilhard de Chardin, who was himself said to have performed an exorcism in Africa. Von Sydow is just back from a dig at Nineveh, where we see him in the film's prologue, Blatty's effective device to suggest the timelessness of the struggle about to begin.

At the technical level, Friedkin's movie is startlingly clever. (The special effects are credited to Marcel Vercoutere.) The girl's bed shakes jarringly and rises; the girl levitates; her skin erupts in open wounds; "Help me" appears in welts across her abdomen; her room is suddenly wind-whipped and icy cold, breaths steaming. Her face is the most ghastly and distorted since Dorian Gray's, thanks to makeup man Dick Smith.

The swift and unexpected resolution is, of course, the book's and the movie's secret, and its meaning, even more in the movie than it was in the book, is for the viewer to speculate on.

The most disappointing change from book to movie is, in fact, the loss of Blatty's always-brief considerations of what it all means: Why an innocent girl? Was what we have seen murder or martyrdom? Who won, and what kind of read-out is there, if any, for all of us, skeptics and believers alike? The movie plays, spectacularly, as a jolting drama which can be enjoyed (in the most flexible sense of the word) as an adult suspense shocker with overtones. But the reading of the overtones is left to the audience, even though the existence of those overtones is by no means confined to those who can believe that the battle has been indeed between the forces of God and those of the Devil. By strong inference, the events also can be taken as good vs. evil, and as aimed at a kind of self-loathing in which modern man frequently finds himself.

Jason Miller gives a darkly forceful performance as the priest who has deep doubts about his own faith and heavy guilts about his abandonment of his Greek immigrant mother (Vasiliki Maliaros). As the girl's distraught mother, Ellen Burstyn is clearly the up-to-date star actress rather than a movie queen, and her portrayal of a woman driven to the edge by events beyond reckoning is stark and strong. Her own language is strong even before things go wrong, which is probably in character but which seems a dramatic miscalculation because it makes the daughter's sudden obscenities slightly less jolting (though they still jolt). The surprise of the cast is William O'Malley, a Jesuit priest from Rochester, New York, a high school teacher and drama coach, here playing a Jesuit priest, Karras's confidant. No promotional cameo, his is an important supporting role and O'Malley brings it off with an easy and likable professionalism. Lee J. Cobb's part as the homicide detective who is more perceiving than he lets himself appear is brief but effective. Von Sydow is also effective as the dying priest trying with his last strength to save a life. In less dignified hands than his and Miller's, the crucial moments of the exorcism would come off less successfully than they do. Kitty Winn (from "Panic in Needle Park") plays Miss Burstyn's secretary, and very well.

Dissonant, eerie excerpts from the work of Penderecki, Webern and other modern composers make up the striking and enhancing musical background.

1974

Blazing Saddles

What might be called the new horse-laugh latitudes of the movies were ideally suited to Mel Brooks, the veteran comedy writer who found a second home in Hollywood and who does not so much walk as ignore the line between good and outrageous bad (but funny) taste. "Blazing Saddles" was the most requested repeat at the Z Channel in Los Angeles and there were those who just wanted the channel to make a loop of the infamous campfire scene and play it continuously.

"NEVER GIVE A SAGA AN EVEN BREAK," says the gloating slogan for Mel Brooks's new comedy, "Blazing Saddles," and they don't write ad-lines that come any closer to catching the full, rich flavor of the product.

His mock-down, knock-down, bawdy, gaudy, hyper-hip burlesque western is irreverent, outrageous, improbable, often as blithely tasteless as a stag night at the Friar's Club and almost continuously funny. It is a two-hour revue sketch with overtones of *Mad* magazine, Lenny Bruce, the *National Lampoon* and the Old Howard. It is to Zane Grey as Little Annie Fanny is to Daddy Warbuck's wide-eyed ward.

It embraces such antic visions as Brooks himself playing both an oblique-eyed lechering governor (named as a very in-joke after a real French vaudeville star whose act was the most bizarre of them all) and a Yiddish-speaking Indian chief.

There is also Madeline Kahn (from "What's Up, Doc?" and "Paper Moon") doing a maliciously exact counterfeit of Marlene Dietrich in a burnt-out torch song written by Brooks and called "I'm Tired."

Among the additional treasures are Harvey Korman as the suave, irascible and incompetent chief villain, hysterical at the loss of his rubber frog in the bathtub, and Gene Wilder as the fastest gun in the world, drinking himself shaky after being outshot by a six-year-old. Footballer

Alex Karras is a weak-brained giant who puts his whole head in the campfire to light a cigar.

It is all blazing nonsense, which conjures up most of its humor by relocating present foolishnesses in its false-front parody of the past. A few too many of the laughs arise in the shock effect of strong language from unlikely sources, but in a joky enterprise like "Blazing Saddles," it is the batting average which matters and Brooks has a grand season.

The story, dreamed up by Andrew Bergman and scripted by Bergman, Brooks, Norman Steinberg and Richard Pryor, establishes Cleavon Little as a cool black dude with Gucci saddlebags who swaps the hangman's noose for a suicide mission as sheriff of a snarling and ungrateful town jeopardized by Korman and his cutthroats under the vacuumheaded leadership of Slim Pickens. As the late Bobby Clark classically remarked of his revival of "Sweethearts," never was a thin plot so complicated.

Looking for messages in "Blazing Saddles" is like going to a weighing machine for advice. What Brooks wants us to do is laugh our untroubled heads off, and he will try anything to achieve this welcome result. There are elaborate sight gags, a pie fight, some rousing and ridiculous street brawls, a takeoff on a Busby Berkeley dance routine (apoplectically choreographed by Dom DeLuise as someone suspiciously called Bubby Bizarre).

"Blazing Saddles" may at that have an instructive tone, if not a message, in the sense that when you take everything as crazy, overturning tradition, form, logic, dignity and ceremonious duty, you do sort out what is foolish and isn't, what was and what wasn't. The derision is amiable and if the hero is black, the comedy really isn't, although it is an interesting tattle-tale gray. Virtue triumphs, even, although it dismounts and climbs into a studio limousine for the ride into the sunset.

For the adult and not easily offended audience for whom Brooks had done this mad frontier frolic, "Blazing Saddles" offers an extraordinary quantity of unrestrained laughter. As with "Where's Poppa?" you are not invariably sure that you ought to be laughing, but you do.

John Morris did the score, with unexpected help from Count Basie and his prairie swingers. The performances without exception are farceplaying at its polished best.

The Conversation

Coppola's very scary film about the electronic invasion of privacy gave him an unprecedented second Academy Award nomination for best picture in the same year, along with "The Godfather II." The Oscar went to the latter, along with four others. Seldom has a filmmaker so well bracketed the range of his skills, from intimacy to sweeping scale.

FRANCIS FORD COPPOLA HAS A WAY with the very large film and a taste for the very small film. He followed "Finian's Rainbow" with a quiet and sensitive drama of a housewife at the breaking point, "The Rain People." Now he follows the big-scale bloodlettings of "The Godfather" with a stunning, personal, low-budget, compact (in fact claustrophobic) social document called "The Conversation."

The conversation at the core of "The Conversation" takes place in a busy San Francisco square at noontime: a pair of young lovers, you'd have said, taking a lunch-hour stroll together through the pigeons and the sunning winos. But they are grim-faced and preoccupied, as if they probably ought not to be meeting at all. And indeed they are being shadowed electronically—by a directional microphone atop a nearby building, from a van, from a tape recorder in a battered shopping bag carried by an anonymous man in the anonymous crowd.

Managing the triangular eavesdrop is Gene Hackman as Harry Caul, an overhearing genius able to invade even public privacy with all the unthinkable, unblockable resources of modern science. Written, Coppola says, in the late 1960s, "The Conversation" and its frightening demonstration of just how unprivate we have become—anywhere—is as up-to-date as Watergate. (Caul uses the same Uher model 5000 tape recorder which gave the President's secretary such trouble.)

The focus of Coppola's dramatic interest is of course Harry Caul himself, who until this caper has been able to imagine that he is as impersonal, professional and free of responsibility as his sophisticated gear. I just deliver the tapes, just do my job, he says, in the way that men have sought to absolve themselves for centuries. Hackman, who has so often played lower-class, low-IQ, high-voltage characters so effectively, creates in Caul a kind of engineer Everyman, a tidy, colorless, intelligent bachelor so thoroughly nondescript you would overlook him on a desert island. He has a sometime mistress, but his marriage is to his work and his only real animation comes when he is either solving a technical problem or noodling on the tenor sax to his jazz records.

Around Harry and his taping of the curious exchanges between strollers Frederick Forrest and Cindy Williams (from "American Graffiti" and "The Migrants"), Coppola spins an intricate and fast-breaking mystery. Who is the chief to whom Harry's assignment is worth a cool $15,000? Who is the aide all too eager to get the tapes? What makes the tapes worth stealing, once Harry has been seduced to sleep by a call girl (Elizabeth MacRae)?

At a convention of tappers and anti-tappers, Harry meets an East Coast competitor (Allen Garfield) whose praises for Harry's ingenuity become indictments of Harry as an unwitting accessory to murders prompted by the evidence on his tapes. It seems to be a lesson of our time that spies never make it in from the cold because they have the cold always with them—the dank paranoia they have spent a whole career generating and finally succumb to. And the conversation, the caper, his reluctant conscience plus his own galloping paranoia begin to get to Harry.

Coppola's movie takes on overtones of "Blow Up"—what is real, what do I dream, suspect, fear? The plot at last has a phantasmagoric quality and neither we nor Harry can be entirely sure what has happened, where into a pattern of betrayal Harry's handiwork fits, who may now spy upon the spy. "The Conversation" is a movie which seems to me to work at every level: as a message picture dramatizing the nightmare possibilities of privacy breached; as an intricate and suspenseful plot; as an engrossing character study of a man become the captive of his own dark skills; as a social document fascinatingly detailed in its look at the techniques of electronic eavesdropping. From Harry's loft laboratory to his girl's basement apartment, the San Francisco milieu is exactly caught.

Hackman's portrait of a man's confidence collapsing, of a plumber forced to examine the consequences of his work, ranks in its understated and internalized way with the very best he has yet done. The picture is virtually all his and he takes us with him from astonishment to contempt to pity. Robert Duvall has an unbilled cameo as the chief whose world the tapes destroy. John Cazale is Hackman's aide. Michael Higgins is the chief's suave and sinister aide. Teri Garr is Hackman's briefly seen girl. All the performances are coolly right.

Coppola inverts the usual Hollywood pattern, using the blockbusters as leverage to be able to make such personal work as "Rain People" and "The Conversation," which he sandwiched in between "The Godfather," writing the final script for "The Great Gatsby" and shooting "Godfather II," now nearing completion. But if the budget and the scale changes dramatically, Coppola's ability to generate excitement and tension does not.

Produced at his American Zoetrope facility in San Francisco, "The Conversation" can have cost no more than a slight fraction of "The Godfather," but it is a powerful and important picture, ominously fascinating in the wiretap age. It arrives almost totally unheralded and obscured by the pageantry attendant on the same studio's "Gatsby," but you have to hope Coppola's dynamite demonstration that the air has ears finds its astonished audiences.

Chinatown

"Rosemary's Baby" may have been Roman Polanski's biggest commercial success in the U.S., but "Chinatown" was his masterpiece. The sardonic views of filmmaker and author were perfectly matched. It is a sizzling film noir drama that soared above the genre to illuminate a significant chapter in Los Angeles history.

THE NAME OF RAYMOND CHANDLER does not appear in the credits of the Robert Evans-Robert Towne-Roman Polanski "Chinatown," but if ever a film were an homage to one man's vision of a time, a place and a lifestyle, "Chinatown" is it.

"Chinatown" is also the finest American film of the year, which is not saying nearly enough because it has been an emaciated year for American films so far. But in its total recapturing of a past, in its plot, its vivid characterizations, its carefully calculated and accelerating pace, its whole demonstration of a medium mastered, "Chinatown" reminds you again—and thrillingly—that motion pictures are larger, not smaller than life; they are not processed at drugstores and they are not television. They are, at their best, events calculated to transport us out of ourselves, as "Chinatown" does.

If Chandler does not appear in the credits he is in the production notes, acknowledged by author Robert Towne as a principal inspiration for the story, along with Carey McWilliams's *Southern California Country* and Morrow Mayo's 1933 book, *Los Angeles*.

Jack Nicholson, Gatsby-dapper and hair parted in the middle 30s style, is a former DA's man, turned private eye specializing in divorce work, and so exchanging one kind of disillusion for a lesser one. He's doing better at it than Philip Marlowe ever did, with a swell suite of offices complete with concealed bar, and a secretary at the other end of the intercom. Like Marlowe, Nicholson is a cynical wisecracker as snappy as his belt-in-the-back jackets and fedoras. But underneath he is a battered idealist, proud of his integrity to the point of naiveté.

Towne's plot weds the essential Chandler format to Dashiell Hammett's strong social consciousness, and it is the wedding which makes "Chinatown" more than a Sunday excursion to a colorful past.

The redhead (Diane Ladd) who wants Nicholson to get the goods on her errant husband (Darryl Zwerling), the chief engineer of the Water Department, turns out not to have been his wife after all. The Mrs. is Faye Dunaway in plucked eyebrows and a look of anguish. In the great tradition, Nicholson has been suckered into a plot more ornate than it seemed by several million bucks' worth. The engineer is found stone cold dead in Stone Canyon Reservoir; the redhead vanishes and so does the girl who may and may not have been the dead man's playmate. Nicholson is hassled by a pair of bad guys, including Polanski himself in a short, savage cameo as a knife-happy killer who leaves his signature on Nicholson's nose.

The trails always lead somewhere; this one leads to a confrontation with John Huston (in one of his best, strongest and least mannered roles) as a super-rich villain out to get richer by fetching water at public expense to thousands of acres he has bought dust-cheap in the San Fernando Valley.

The detours lead to John Hillerman as a corrupt Water Department official, to a shoot-out and chase in an orange grove, to an evil nursing home, to Echo Park and, ultimately, to Chinatown—yesterday's enclave rather than today's tourist attraction. But the movie's Chinatown is not so much a place as a condition—a state in which idealism is probably as dangerous as it is useless, and cynicism is good sense. Nicholson has been there before with a badge on. The hard wisdom, which he defied and has now defied again, was to do as little as possible.

As in Ross Macdonald, to fill out the *hommage à trois*, the present villainies have blood ties to the buried past. It all comes together in a swift and shocking finale which is, with everything else it is, a stunning film sequence.

The break with the fictional past is chillingly unsentimental and unrelieving, more modern Europe than old Los Angeles, and daring in a time when the marketplace seems to demand good cheer. But "Chinatown" is also unforgettably strong, and for the sake of the art-form you have to hope there are still audiences who want to be gripped and held rather than merely cuddled.

For his first solo venture as a producer, Robert Evans assembled an unusually gifted team. The original script by Robert Towne (a contributor to "Bonnie and Clyde" and "The Godfather," Oscar-nominated for "The Last Detail") provides the unshakable foundation. It is literate, intricate, respectful of a great form, ambitious and successful in its attempt to convey the whole spirit of a small city verging on its explosive tomorrow, propelled in part by rough giants who had large thirsts and large visions.

John Alonzo's photography and the deep-textured production design by Richard Sylbert really do bring alive the Los Angeles of the 1930s, from the bungalows of Echo Park to the mansions of Pasadena and the paneled elegance of the Windsor restaurant. The five dozen vintage cars are an autophile's dream. Anthea Sylbert did the right, non-camp costumes. The music by Jerry Goldsmith is marvelously well considered, declining to be yet another assemblage of period recordings, instead accenting an unmuted solo trumpet to catch the bluesy spirit of the period.

Nicholson this time lets a major strain of both naiveté and concern shine through the wise-guy bluff. The result is yet another masterful, individual and engrossing characterization. Faye Dunaway begins as the fairly standard *femme* perhaps *fatale*, but finally lets us see convincingly the torment behind the cool, and she is touching indeed.

Polanski's control is sure throughout and the gradual increase in tempo he and editor Sam O'Steen create is enormously impressive. The point of view, touched with cynicism, seems to be both Polanski's and Towne's, but there is a compassion which is more pronounced here than in Polanski's earlier work. No one will accuse him of sentimentality, but "Chinatown" is, with everything else it is, a work of feeling.

The Chandler faithful should be in the vanguard of those who run, not walk to see that they still make movies in our day.

Earthquake

"Earthquake" was prophetic, not of the Northridge horror, but of Hollywood's steady trend toward ever-larger "event films." The $8 million budget, worth noting then, is ironic in a day when $80 million budgets no longer raise a gasp and many exceed it. Irwin Allen's thriller had starry casting in depth and some well-defined sympathetic characters, sometimes scarce in the latter-day swollen epics.

THERE IS A SAFETY NET strung across the rococo ceiling of Mann's (formerly Grauman's) Chinese Theater these days, and whether it is a psychological gimmick like the nurses patroling the aisles during horror films or whether the plaster gingerbread has really been shaking down, I don't know.

I only know I am glad the netting is there, because when the sound effects for Universal's "Earthquake" cut loose like the world's largest jukebox running amok, you fear for the walls as well as for the ceiling's rattled cherubs.

The high-volume, low-frequency vibrations which constitute what the studio showmen call Sensurround (invented, as near as I can tell, by Pat. Pending) succeed very nicely in making themselves felt as well as heard and they set up an anxiety which makes watching "Earthquake" a very ambivalent experience for anyone who, so to speak, has been there before.

At that, the stirring sonics are only part of the exhilarations of "Earthquake," a thriller which would be effective enough without the augmented gadgetry. Like "The Poseidon Adventure" (which it outdoes), "Earthquake" is a display of motion picture special-effects wizardries which is heroic, astounding, fantastic and at least a little sobering.

Houses disintegrate like matchboxes—but they look like houses, not matchboxes. Skyscrapers crumble in rains of plate-glass shrapnel. The Hollywood Reservoir Dam yields to the aftershocks of a quake measured at an unimaginable 10-plus on the Richter scale and three billion gallons of water roar down Cahuenga Pass. (The quake may for the moment be make-believe but it hits an all-too-believable Los Angeles, and we watch the cylindrical Capitol Records building, among other landmarks, lose its facings.)

Charlton Heston as an engineer surveys the carnage and says, "For the first time in my life, I'm ashamed for my profession. Why do we build these forty-story monstrosities?" The preview audience cheered and applauded. Between "Earthquake" and the forthcoming "Towering Inferno," it is going to be a hard year for architects, engineers and high-rise rental agents.

The astonishing ingenuity with which the miniaturists, matte artists and fearless stunt designers and performers have simulated the thundering, spitting, burning, crashing, roaring horror of a catastrophic quake is the haunting heart of the film. But the human dramas played out within it are more than incidental puppetries, and if not exactly Bergmanesque, at least recognizable dilemmas. George Fox and Mario Puzo (of "The Godfather") did the script.

Heston is a self-made man who married the boss's daughter and now watches the last civility drain out of the relationship. Ava Gardner is the spoiled but also scared wife, and it is a strong performance. Genevieve Bujold is a young widow with whom Heston could imagine a new life, and Miss Bujold is uncommonly vivacious and sympathetic. George Kennedy plays an uncompromising policeman in a compromising world. Lorne Greene is Heston's tough, wise, father-in-law. Walter Matuschanskayasky is a barfly dolefully resembling the Walter Matthau he became. Ex-evangelist Marjoe Gortner is vivid as a grocery clerk who goes nutty in his National Guard uniform, with Victoria Principal as an intended victim. Richard Roundtree is a trick motorcyclist hoping, with manager Gabriel Dell, to give Evel Knievel a run for our money. Barry Sullivan is a seismologist who tries to tell mayor John Randolph what's coming. Lloyd Nolan is a hardworking doctor. They and the rest of a very large cast move swiftly and expertly under the guidance of Mark Robson, who both produced and directed. John Williams' superior score is *molto agitato* and immense. Chamber music would never have done.

It is, of course, the disaster picture to end all disaster pictures, although it won't. It is a spectacular piece of picture-making which looks to have cost even more than the $8 million it is said to have cost.

Yet, for an earthquake-zone audience, it is not really escapist fare which you can leave behind in the foyer. You sense now and again that the picture-makers realized they were succeeding even better than they wanted to and tried, mostly through the Matthau characterization, to remind everybody that this was a movie entertainment. Still, never did an entertainment leave so many uncomfortable intimations of the stinking, starving, demoralizing chaos that would or will follow the big jolt the seismologists have been promising us for years.

"Earthquake" may play more comfortably in places where the earth stands still and the plaster needs no nets.

Lenny

One historian called it "rampant with the new permissiveness," and true enough it was another film unthinkable only a few years earlier. Yet for all its difficulties in seeing Lenny Bruce whole, so I thought, its sincerity was palpable, its shock value not large, and it received six Academy nominations, including best picture. Hoffman and Valerie Perrine were also recognized. "Lenny" remains a significant marker on the evolution of film.

THE IRONY WHICH IS THE WHOLE POINT of "Lenny" is that these days you can make a movie saying all the things Lenny Bruce kept getting busted for saying. Today the movie won't raise an eyebrow or a lawsuit in Boston, and possibly not even in Memphis or Charleston, West Virginia. The only shock left is remembering that we were so recently so uptight a society as to send a man to jail for using words familiar to (if not endorsed by) every American of puberty and past.

The movie has been shot in perfect black and white (color would have been hopelessly inappropriate to a man whose career alternated between underlit nightclubs and black and white headlines). It was directed by Bob Fosse, who finds in another time and place the same kind of link between what entertains a society and what bedevils it that he found in "Cabaret."

The decadent charms of Joel Grey & Co. mirrored the deeper sickness of a newly Nazi Germany. Lenny Bruce, working to the edgy strains of the late bop–early cool sounds (Miles Davis dominates the score), was a kind of reluctant avant-garde for a society moving into furious battle with its puritan traditions. He was only a short step ahead of everybody else, but it was an exceedingly painful step. What may well have begun as an accidental lark became an obsession which at last left him unable to work, reinforced his addiction to drugs and pushed him toward the fatal overdose (in August 1966) which may or may not have been accidental.

The movie, scripted by Julian Barry from his successful play, is severe, earnest, uncompromising, very strong and ultimately very depressing stuff. It centers on not one but two of the year's most conscientious and impressive performances: Dustin Hoffman's as Lenny, Valerie Perrine's as his sweet, spontaneous, screwed-up wife, Honey. Ms. Perrine, eye-catching as Montana Wildhack in "Slaughterhouse-Five" and coolly accurate as a stock-car groupie in "The Last American Hero," didn't really do anything to prepare us for the power and depth of her portrayal of

Honey, the easygoing stripper spiraling down into the addled despairs of addiction. The year has not yet produced a more assured and affecting piece of acting, over a range from girlish humor to pitiable blank-eyed freakiness and it is a performance, not an accident, as the nominating Academy will almost surely acknowledge.

"Lenny" is an unreservedly admirable film, artful and imaginative, and I am not quite sure why it misses being the overwhelming experience it intended to be and ought to be.

Partly, I think, the trouble is that the film works too hard at making a martyr of Lenny, a war casualty in the fight for freedom of speech. The script and Hoffman's performance—however immaculately he reproduces tapes of Bruce in action—somehow make him less complicated than it seems certain he was. He had come along a hard, embittering, knock-about road, and he had to have been an odds-on favorite for trouble even if he had not had a cause thrust upon him. The movie does not deny the unattractive aspects of his life or the long captivity to drugs, but they are made secondary to his troubles with the law over those dirty words.

Hoffman's Bruce is finally a romanticized figure, warm and likeable, not so much salacious as mischievous, an advocate of sanity, not shock. What I think the portrait misses is the bitterness, hostility and rage which had been fermenting throughout a hard life and then spilled over in performances which were assaults on the audiences and the society.

In the film's most effective scene, essentially one very extended long shot, Hoffman in a bathrobe and unmatched socks tries to put a monologue together in a Chicago nightclub when he is drugged out of his mind and hardly able to stitch one word to another. He is then almost, but not quite, a tragic figure, a man dimly perceiving he is out of his depths, not only at that moment but in his tilting with the world. What he becomes instead of tragic is a figure of pity. It is not quite the same thing and it makes all the difference to the impact of the movie, because Bruce is then seen to be what he was, a relatively minor entertainer who did not so much change history as anticipate it. You are left with that central irony of a man who ran out of time.

Fosse and cinematographer Bruce Surtees beautifully catch the flat neon world of all-night cafeterias, the smoky squalor of strip joints and coffeehouses, the gray anonymity of hotel rooms and cheap apartments. As in "Cabaret," atmosphere becomes the shaping force on character that it is.

The film belongs virtually entirely to Hoffman and Perrine, although Jan Miner has some very effective moments as Bruce's showbiz mother,

Sally Marr. Gary Morton does a brief satiric cameo as a Catskill comic tightly tailored to the image of Milton Berle. Rashel Novikoff is delightful as Lenny's shocked aunt.

But in general the film's point of advocacy shows up most heavily (and damagingly) in the subsidiary characterizations—an agent (Stanley Beck) dripping with hypocrisy, a *Time* reporter (John DiSanti) like never was on heaven or earth, and thick-sketched and stereotyped policemen, lawyers and judges.

Fosse and music supervisor Ralph Burns have conspired wonderfully well to compile a "found" score out of the small group wails of several nightclub combos accenting the strippers or bringing on the comics, together with those Miles sides which were apt to be the background sounds of all the better grass parties in Lenny's 60s.

The exposition moves expertly back and forth in time, from Honey and Mama and the agent chattering memories into tape recorders, back to love at first sight in a Baltimore strip joint where Honey was a headliner and Lenny a very bad clean-beginning comedian. The span is maybe a dozen years, but he and she both age a lifetime within that period, and they look it. A more straightforward chronology might have heightened the impact of Bruce's rise and decline, but it might well also have made the film an even steeper downer, and I think the intercutting of early and late was the better choice.

If "Lenny" leaves us with mixed feelings about Lenny, it offers a strong suggestion that as a society we have made some progress. The furor he caused seems unimaginable only a decade later, and the threat to the common weal he represented (working as he did to audiences of paying, consenting adults) was imaginary then, as now. He may have been tasteless, but the only danger he presented was to the dignity and the credibility of law.

The last irony of his delayed victory is that a latter-day Lenny would be unable to shock us with dirty words. The expletives have been depleted of shock by common usage, as he said they would be.

"Lenny" may miss being a masterpiece, but it is one of the season's notable achievements. Marvin Worth, a longtime friend of Lenny, was the producer, with David V. Picker the executive producer.

The Towering Inferno

The late Irwin Allen personally defined the "shake and bake" genre, as it was called at the time, first with "Earthquake" and then with "The Towering Inferno." The question became, What could filmmakers do for an encore? The unfortunate answer has been volcanos, tornadoes, wicked extraterrestrials and unstoppable viral plagues, all testing the limits of what constitutes entertainment, since not all of Allen's successors have so expertly set interesting characters within the effects.

THERE ARE THEORIES IN ART that form follows function, that art is the elimination of excess and less is more. The movies have confirmed those theories from time to time, but they are even better at disproving the living hell out of them, demonstrating spectacularly that more is more and nothing succeeds like excess.

"The Towering Inferno" is $14 million worth of Holy Cow! Spend more—efficiently—and you get more. More stars, more effects, more scale, more suspense, more crises, more impact, more of that feeling in the foyer that you have got your ticket's worth and then some. Irwin Allen's tale of a catastrophic fire in the highest (138 stories) of the high-rises is the most successful of the raucous run of multiple-jeopardy movies—so seemingly untoppable, to coin a phrase, that it becomes hard to imagine what would serve as an encore except bubonic plague or some other natural calamity in which the horror would overbalance any conceivable entertainment value.

Like the original "Airport" and the recent "Earthquake," "The Towering Inferno" generates a powerful empathetic fright because almost all of us have been there, have known the close-at-hand scare of a stove-top or wastebasket blaze or the shuddering threat of a fire siren in the night, the clanging engines roaring to a stop just up the street. There is, compoundingly, a little or a lot of claustrophobia in each of us, entrapment being a kind of ultimate fear. The difference in impact may be that you think about earthquakes and feel about fire. Both of the season's spectaculars leave you shook up—pleasurably, for the most part, but not without aftershocks. In the case of "The Towering Inferno," I dare say there will be an epidemic of very nervous jokes in the elevator en route to the thirty-fourth or fifty-first or eighty-second floor after the coffee break.

Allen's "Poseidon Adventure" featured wondrous special effects and sets, populated by characters which made kindergarten stick figures look like Rembrandts. This time, with a very starry cast which cost a bundle but is eminently worth it and with a slick Stirling Silliphant script drawn from not one but two novels, the firemen don't have all the lines. The cast matches the technical wizardries.

We are talking about traditional, superlative-seeking, romantic melodrama strewn with villainous villains, heroic heroes and heroines, vivid snapshots of lesser characters, the delivered promise of eyewitnessing great events and glimpsing the machineries of our times, otherwise hidden. Just as a firefighting documentary, "Inferno" is engrossing. For what it is and intends to achieve, it can all be done well or less well. "The Towering Inferno" does it damned well, with style and flair and continuously growing suspense and drama. It is almost impossible to withhold belief and concern.

Paul Newman is the rough-hewn architect (right out of "The Fountainhead," I couldn't help thinking) whose tallest triumph, a soaring glass obelisk on the San Francisco skyline, is about to have its gala dedication. His arrival by helicopter is a fine Bay tour behind the main titles and his reception in the office amid a cacophony of queries is lovely traditional exposition. The heliport, the office, the first worrying question from an aide (Norman Burton) will all figure largely in the plot. Indeed, the plot begins to smolder before we are five minutes into the film, even as Newman has a satiny reunion with Faye Dunaway, while the big builder—William Holden—awaits. Fred Astaire mysteriously cons a cabbie out of his tip and O. J. Simpson as the chief of security wonders what's goofing up his control panels.

The subplots—Robert Wagner as the resident PR man dallying with his adoring secretary (Susan Flannery), Jennifer Jones as a rich widow who is con man Astaire's quarry, Robert Vaughn as an arriving senator making his mark in urban renewal—are crisply laid in while a burned-out circuit breaker catches some waste in a storeroom. The tuxedos and the furs arrive only a little ahead of the firemen, led by an apprehensive Steve McQueen who is all but told to use the service entrance so not to alarm the partygoers.

But the fire won't wait or be contained, and there are some gruesome sequences (born of very daring stunt work coordinated by Paul Stader) of the first victims becoming human torches. "The Towering Inferno" is strong stuff, not for children or the overimpressionable. The party guests are trapped in the nightclub on the 135th floor, while the fire climbs inexorably toward them and the high winds keep the helicopters from landing on the heliport (although one tries, disastrously).

The sequences within the narrative escalate in scale and complexity—children and their mute mother rescued from their burning room; a long, scary passage down a stairway interrupted by an explosion, with Newman and Miss Jones helping two children; McQueen and some of his men roping their way down an elevator shaft; a breeches' buoy rigged from the nearest (much shorter) building; an exterior scenic elevator caught halfway down; the final last gamble involving the top story water tanks.

As always there are things which hindsight says might have been done differently. The whole elevator rescue sequence is almost the more which becomes too much, a piling on of spectacle which is also the most difficult of the make-beliefs in terms of ordinary logic and the hardest to make believable.

The story's principal villain is Richard Chamberlain, never so nasty since "Petulia," here a sneering, sniggering coward. He is Holden's son-in-law and also the subcontractor who cut costs on all the electrical gear. He gets his comedownance, does he ever. It is a fine piece of acting.

"The Towering Inferno" is a message movie and, in the calm beyond the holocaust, architect and fireman agree they have got to consult together before more deadly high-rise chimneys are designed and built. It has been a terrible year for high-rise rental agents, and producer Allen says he is already a marked man. Allen also insists that firemen tell him there is only one truly fire-safe skyscraper in the whole country, a government building just completed in the Northwest. The movie itself stresses the point that even the building codes are inadequate, that what might be all right for four stories is calamitous for forty.

McQueen, calm, deadpan, efficient, is the center of the picture; and both he and Newman, rugged and resourceful, remind you what movie stars are and why they can be worth the kingly sums they are paid. Allen directed the action sequences himself, as he evidently did on "Poseidon," and they are marvelously done. John Guillermin is presumably responsible for the sure-handed dramatic sequences, which establish personalities and relationships with economy and clarity if not great depth.

Astaire is outstanding as the con man finding love and conscience late. Miss Jones handles a knockabout role with enthusiasm and grace. Susan Blakely is sympathetic as the wife who loves Chamberlain despite himself. Vaughn, perhaps out of his private affinity for politics, makes a notably believable senator. Wagner and Susan Flannery are gone almost before we know it but move persuasively from love to last agony. Wasted in "The Klansman," O.J. Simpson gives an assured and solid performance. Don Gordon, often a villain, is here first-rate as a good guy and McQueen's chief aide. Holden, a man aghast at what he has helped bring about, is effective, although you sense that the part could have been better written.

John Williams's music is very potent stuff, ominous and urgent, fully underlining everything we watch, in a return to an earlier-day Hollywood regard for music's role in heightening drama.

The Godfather, Part II

"The Godfather, Part II" confirmed Francis Coppola's enormous skills as a filmmaker, a master of scale as well as intimate characterization. The film also supplies the missing pieces of a large historical mosaic, which was to receive a final panel, a mournful coda, in "Godfather III," a trilogy without equal in American film.

WHAT YOU COULD SAY is that "The Godfather" was such a hard act to follow that the filmmaker preceded it instead. Actually, what now exists is one six-and-a-half-hour film, of which "The Godfather, Part I" was the middle half and of which "The Godfather, Part II" now provides the opening and concluding quarters. (I hope one day we'll be able to see it re-parted chronologically.)

The scale on which Francis Ford Coppola and Mario Puzo have told their tale is epic, spanning six decades and three generations, with a glimpse of the fourth. Their commercial success is already established as heroic, and there is no reason to doubt that "Godfather II" will join the top moneymakers of all time. But the creative, aesthetic success of this long enterprise is also, I think, on the heroic scale. "Godfather II" is quieter, less propulsive, less furiously violent than "Godfather I" and it demonstrably lacks the hypnotic patriarchal figure of Brando as Don Corleone. Still it is compellingly watchable. The new film settles for its own strengths, and they are considerable, to say the least.

It gives us, superbly, the Mafia-dominated Sicily of 1901, from which the don-to-be flees as a small boy after his father, elder brother and mother have been murdered by the village chieftain. I don't remember the first glimpse of the Statue of Liberty and the cattle-pen chaos of Ellis Island (with impatient clerks improvising names which families would carry for generations) ever caught more authentically.

As in "Godfather I," Coppola and his cinematographer, Gordon

Willis, have engineered their color palette with superb and subtle ingenuity. The first Sicilian sequences are sun-bleached and flinty. The New York of the 1900s is redless, like faded lithographs, and has the sepia tone and the composition of the documentary stills of Jacob Riis and the other slum decriers of the period. Much of the latter-day action, particularly in the family fortress-encampment on Lake Tahoe, is heavily shadowed, closed off, both isolated and besieged. Few movies have used visual tone so varyingly to heighten, almost subconsciously, the operative mood of a story.

The young Vito Corleone (clerk-named for his home village) makes his way in the Italian ghetto of lower Manhattan that was to be updated 70 years later in Martin Scorsese's "Mean Streets." Indeed, the young Vito is played by Robert De Niro from "Mean Streets" and "Bang the Drum Slowly." It is a sensational performance, advancing Corleone from the thin, pale youth working for pennies in a grocery store to the solid leader of his family, returning in triumph to settle the old score in Sicily, parlaying thievery and murder into power and respect. De Niro, hoarse-voiced and imperiously handsome as he grows in assurance, does an amazing job of preparing us for the Brando we remember.

The makings of an American overlord are half the story. The rise and fall of Michael constitute the other. To a great extent, "Godfather II" can, I think, be seen as a corrective, erasing any lingering romanticizing of the characters and the lifestyle that might possibly remain from Brando's foxy grandfather, romping among the tomatoes, or from Michael's reluctant turning from his own straight pursuits to honor his father's business.

Al Pacino, in yet another outstanding portrayal, moves Michael still further, from the cool and unemotional mastery of all he surveys to the prisoner of his own paranoia—fearful, vengeful, isolated from everything he genuinely loves, but too repellent to be pitiable. He has survived a Senate hearing (beautifully familiar) but lost his cover and his respectability.

The narrative flow so irresistible in "Godfather I" is intermittent here—and, in a couple of instances, surprisingly muddy and hard to follow. What "Godfather II" offers are environments and characterizations. Its texturing of the Sicilian background and the tough, testing immigrant life in New York is meticulous and enlightening.

The characterizations include Lee Strasberg, practicing what he has preached to generations of actors, creating a vivid portrait of an aging, ailing, rival Jewish rackets boss, complete with small nervous cough and deceptively folksy charm. Robert Duvall is on hand again as the family's legal counsel, ruthlessly loyal. John Cazale is Pacino's weak older brother,

craven but dangerously resentful, and Cazale makes it a fine piece of acting. Talia Shire is Pacino's self-indulgent sister who hates his guidance but
comes home as one of the last loyalists. Michael V. Gazzo is vivid as a sec-
ond-level mobster caught in power plays between Pacino and Strasberg.
G.D. Spradlin is a smoothly corrupt Nevada senator trapped in the family
coils. Diane Keaton is again Pacino's proper New England wife, an out-
sider who finally can take no more of what she finds inside. She is touching as a victim, even if her scenes as written play less convincingly than
those involving the family itself.

James Caan and Morgana King make brief appearances in the roles
they established in "Godfather I." (Brando enters an off-camera room,
and it is curious how potently we imagine his presence.) Mariana Hill has
some fine, flaring moments as weak brother Cazale's trampy wife.
Francesca deSapio is sweetly innocent as De Niro's wife and Amerigo Tot
is a faithful bodyguard.

The scenery ranges from Sicily to Cuba and the film is reported to
have cost upward from $15 million. The Cuban episode, in which
Strasberg and Pacino conclude a deal with Batista just as the Castro
forces topple him into exile, almost becomes a movie within a movie, although the elaborateness of it outruns its usefulness by a large margin.

Peter Zinner was chief editor with Barry Malkin and Richard Marks.
Although the film runs three and a third hours, it seldom lags, despite its
far-spaced flashes of violence. Dean Tavoularis did the production design,
crucial to the film's intentions, and Nino Rota the lush score, which occasionally reprises his original "Godfather" theme and which was conducted
by Coppola's father, Carmine.

In its way, "Godfather II" is more daring than the original, taking the
risks inherent in establishing the context for a movie we have already
seen and adding what becomes a kind of sullen epilogue to a movie which
left us breathless. The risks were worth taking, and the reward is that a
single monumental segment of the American experience is neither
glorified nor patronized, but made comprehensible and real, transmuted
into drama of both scope and depth.

1975

Shampoo

*In the candor of its dissection of sexual mores After Hays and Be-
fore AIDS, "Shampoo" is yet another of those films that could not
have been dreamt of before the late 60s. It does not so much portray as dissect a slice of society and a slice of time. It can be dis-
liked but not found inaccurate.*

"SHAMPOO" IS "ALFIE" WITH AVOCADOS, or "Advanced Carnal
Knowledge," or "Lather Ye Rosebuds While Ye May," or "The Decline
and Fall of Beverly Hills," or all of them.

Its language wipes out whatever reticences were left in the screen's
playback of life as spoken. Its images manage, fairly ingeniously, to keep a
few letters shy of X; and yet the combination of word and half-seen deed
makes "Shampoo" seem more explicit than "Last Tango in Paris," and Warren Beatty outrevels Marlon Brando by a few square inches of sacroiliac.

The talk and the tarryings-on will enliven a lot of cocktail conversation for the next little while, and "Shampoo" is one of those movies likely
to attract business because it is notorious rather than because it is admirable—because it will be culturally necessary to say you have seen and
heard Julie Christie in the Bistro scene.

But, as in the cases variously of "Who's Afraid of Virginia Woolf?," "I
Am Curious (Yellow)," "Carnal Knowledge," "Midnight Cowboy" and
"Last Tango," the notoriety is a notoriously unreliable preparation for the
actual experience of seeing "Shampoo."

It is not a titillation but a downer (or at least a soberer-up), a chilling,
hard, unsentimental (though far from insensitive), accurate and unattractive piece of social reporting which will be worth studying a century from
now to know what a part of our times was like. And while "Shampoo" is
unquestionably about sexual relationships and sexual attitudes, they are
understood to be symbolic and symptomatic of a larger national malaise.

"Shampoo" is indeed almost too heavy-handedly a political picture. Its very brief action centers on Election Night 1968; the party at the Bistro is a Republican victory celebration and Nixon and Agnew make their by now grossly ironic promises from television sets in the background.

What links the sex and the politics is opportunism, a kind of operational chaos resulting from the lack of any long-range values still regarded as important and commanding. Lacking any confidence in love and singularity in relationships (or any really deep-seated social idealism in politics), the consequences are compromise, cynicism and a despairing accommodation.

Warren Beatty, whose idea the story was and who wrote the script in collaboration with Robert Towne, the author of "Chinatown," plays a very fashionable Beverly Hills hairstylist, functioning for a clamoring gaggle of overrich and underattended women as a combination of guru and gigolo.

He has an enraptured steady (Goldie Hawn) and a still-haunting previous steady (Julie Christie). But he is also tending to the wife (Lee Grant) of a fat-cat investment counselor (Jack Warden). And anybody else he can get astride his Triumph.

Beatty, who works for somebody else (Jay Robinson, flighty like a fox), wants to open his own shop. The banks can't imagine what the collateral is (funny scene). Maybe Warden will; the visitation sets the climactic central evening in motion. Warden is presently keeping Ms. Christie. Perhaps Beatty will escort her to the party, playing the beard as a favor. Goldie Hawn gets to attend with the commercial-maker (Tony Bill) she's just auditioned for. Ms. Grant will be there to complete the sextet.

It is for a while a Georges Feydeau farce, played out not in the rooms and corridors of a trysting Parisian hotel but upstairs at the poshest restaurant around and then at a pot-fogged party at a Hefnerian mansion.

Of all the stud heroes or antiheroes the recent movies have given us, Beatty seems the most complicated and the most believable. He is not an unfeeling exploiter like Michael Caine in "Alfie," not a near-psychopath like the Nicholson character in "Carnal Knowledge." He does not seem incapable of love; it is just that loving as opposed to making love has never struck him as all that necessary. Making it with those ladies was partly a reward for having to listen to all the chatter but mostly pure pleasure which somehow kept reassuring him, as he says, that he would live forever.

The Beatty character strikes me as being as carefully accurate a portrayal of a particular male psyche as can be found, comparable in its candor to the projection of the female psyche in Erica Jong's novel, *Fear of Flying.*

The women in "Shampoo," if they are not a mother's dream of comportment, are also not caricatures, not unsympathetic; they are individuals, not objects. Ms. Grant comes closest to being a stereotype in her jealousy, her scheming and her sexual frenzy. Yet the actress's skill carries the part beyond the jokey distortions and reveals the harder, sadder truths about fear of emptiness, fear of rejection, fear of aging.

It is, obviously and harshly, a quick tour of a world of no fixed values and with no heroes or heroines in the traditional molds. Goldie Hawn is, I guess, the closest approximation of a traditional heroine, loving Beatty and wanting only a steady and loving relationship with him, and sickened and disgusted to find quite what a free-swinger he is. Their final meeting is a razor-sharply written and performed scene, Beatty stammering through a defense of a lifestyle he has acted out rather than thought about, Ms. Hawn listening with horror and fury. It is a mature and touching achievement for her.

The director was Hal Ashby, demonstrating again his skill at evoking sensitive and rounded performances. Julie Christie, as she did in her first major triumph in "Billy Liar," plays a free spirit who knows that freedom is relative and that the negotiations with the real world are continuous and delicate. She knows that love is a luxury not everyone can afford all the time, although sometimes the knowledge is so bitter it cannot be borne, and her drunken fury at the election party is a stunning revelation.

Like Ms. Grant, Warden takes a caricature of a figure, posturing and nearly ridiculous, and finds in it the truer dimensions—the confusions of a man working to understand a world whose ground rules have changed or vanished, a man too smart not to know finally that he looks ridiculous masking his loneliness as simple lust, and trying to hold on to youth and love in a world that overvalues one and undervalues the other. Warden, allowed to overact in "Duddy Kravitz," plays here with a sort of increasing restraint that gives the character at last an odd and affecting dignity.

Tony Bill, the actor turned producer ("The Sting"), gives interesting depth to a brief part, making the film man who comes into Goldie Hawn's life more than a casting-couch conqueror, suggesting that he cares about the girl, even if it is not clear that they live happily ever after. Carrie Fisher has a short, strong scene as Warden's daughter. Brad Dexter does a fine cameo as a dumb senator.

Laszlo Kovacs did the photography, which records Beverly Hills down to the last palm frond. Paul Simon did the music.

Beatty is not a tragic figure, and we cannot weep for him any more than he can really weep for himself. Like Alfie, he is temporarily out but not down. But what he and we have had is a terrifying glimpse of the sterility and isolation of his life, in which the penalty of openness is the closing off of the possibility of love. He has seen the beginnings of wisdom, and the bitter truth that he probably cannot act on his wisdom.

"Shampoo" seems already to be dividing its audiences—between those made uncomfortable and annoyed by some shock of recognition, and those who find insight and perhaps even negative guidance if not consolation in exactly the same shock of recognition. It is an unsparing picture, but not unsympathetic. "Carnal Knowledge" was more coldly clinical in its dissections. "Shampoo" lets us in on the pain, and the numbness, of its protagonists.

The Day of the Locust

My embarrassed confession is that this review demanded, so I thought, some minor fixes—not to change what I said originally but to say it more precisely. It was a painful review to write because I have admired John Schlesinger from "A Kind of Loving" and "Billy Liar" forward and because the effort was so earnest and admirable. But films work or they don't and, alas, this one didn't work for me.

THE MIDDLE- TO LATE-1930s must have been a glorious time to be the kind of pessimist that novelist Nathanael West evidently was. Capitalism had taken sick in 1929 and there were widespread fears for its recovery. Fascism was on the march and only a foolish dreamer could pretend that another world war was not near at hand. There was a kind of pre-apocalyptic tension in the air and it must have given a grim satisfaction to a man who seems to have seen life as a primarily absurd spectacle.

There are apocalyptic intimations in the air again, an erosion of confidence all along the line, and it would be a more than reasonable guess that West's masterpiece, *The Day of the Locust*, might play as a parable for our later day, setting up sympathetic vibrations and stroking familiar and edgy dissonances. But given the material and the tender, lavish and ravishing care with which it has been treated, it is astonishing that John Schlesinger's "The Day of the Locust" should play so remote, bloodless and untouching, so merely artful.

Even though the end-of-civilization riot to which the novel and movie build has been lifted (so far as you can decipher) from the protagonist's deranged and nightmare vision, it is treated like an actuality rather than a surrealist fantasy. The spectacle seemed to me to be impressive at last, only as logistics, as film production. The movie contains some prodigious feats of design, of period re-creation, of size and motion, of performance. It fails of that start-to-finish control and continuity of its tone, fails in its own approximation of reality. At its most effective, it achieves something of the absurdist sense that West got in the novel, and so that you under-stand Hollywood is not the subject but is (for West) a grotesquely appro-priate symbol of all the absurd, shallow, lost, denied dreams of the society and the system.

But there are then mismatches, shifts in the handling and the tonality that thrust us back to a more straight-line plotting and a more traditional development of character and relationships. The idea may have been to make us care both at an abstract intellectual level (think about the system and what it does to people) and at gut-level (look at him, look at her, ca-sualties of the system). But if you can sometimes have it both ways, you can't here. The film is too considered, too calculated, too *made* to gener-ate emotional responses to its own material. (Responses to films are hard to calculate. The apocalyptically inclined may bring their own recogni-tions to the film, but they do the film's work for it, I think. "The Day of the Locust" is a curiously closed entity, positioned in a kind of aesthetic limbo, for all the period décor.)

The story is of a young Yale man (William Atherton) come west to in-vade the movies as an art director. He sets up in a decaying U-shaped stucco apartment complex whose décor is Failed Moorish. The other ten-ants include Burgess Meredith as an old vaudevillian reduced to door-to-door selling, his movie-struck daughter (Karen Black) and a horse-playing dwarf (Billy Barty) with a shrewish wife. A partial row of movie seats rests in the courtyard and there Madge Kennedy takes the sun.

Atherton's (or West's) Hollywood also comes to include Donald Sutherland as a rich midwesterner who seems to have elected to retire to Hollywood, Richard A. Dysart as a cynical studio executive, John Hillerman as his aide, Natalie Schafer as the madam of a very toney brothel, Geraldine Page as Aimee Semple McPherson by any other name, Bo Hopkins and Pepe Serna as pals who train and bet fighting cocks.

It is a colorful congregation, placed in a colorful world by production designer Richard MacDonald. Conrad Hall has bathed much of the ac-tion in the golden sunlight of yesterday and "Locust" is extravagantly sumptuous and seedy all in the same images. The craftsmanship is fault-less, and a long sequence of some sets collapsing on a sound stage is almost as remarkable as the climactic riot that is said to have cost $1 million and to have employed one thousand extras.

The problems are several. One is that Waldo Salt's script never quite brings Atherton's character into focus. He is neither the innocent corrupted nor the cynic confirmed, neither the narrator-witness (like Nick in "The Great Gatsby") nor a hero so despairing that his frenzy before Grauman's is credible and moving. Karen Black is just right as Fay Greener, tough enough to keep hoping, too dumb to see she'll never make it. But the relationship with Atherton never rings true; he is too smart not to see through his own infatuation, and unlike Maugham's Mildred, human bondage is the least of her desires. Sutherland, though he gives an earnest and crafty performance, simply seems too young, intelligent and vigorous to be the hapless, impotent Homer, goaded to his own last agony amid the premiere at Grauman's. He is an actor in a funny period haircut, acting, and the camera works him over all too consciously.

Meredith, grimacing through heart attacks, sweating in the summer sun as he peddles patent cleansers, tippling the blues away, has a tour de force part (as John Mills did in "Ryan's Daughter," a comparison that springs to mind) and it is to be watched with enjoyment and admiration, not with belief. It's a film of sensational set-pieces. Geraldine Page (unrecognizable until you've seen the credits) makes a formidable white-robed healer, crying simultaneously for a green collection and healed limbs. The pieces make the film intermittently brilliant, like an incomplete mosaic, but they don't confirm the grand design.

Extras aside, it is a huge cast of able performers. Lelia Goldoni is Karen Black's friend who has found it easier being a call girl. Jackie Haley is a nasty brat being pushed into the movies by his mother (Gloria Le Roy). Barty, Hopkins and Serna provide first-rate characterizations. Hillerman establishes the sycophantic, protective personality of the studio aide in a handful of words. William Castle, the director, plays a director and convincingly, although I think the typecasting a mistake because it further confuses the intent of the film, like using Dick Powell, Jr. (looking incredibly like his father) as a celebrity arrival at the premiere.

Few movies are ever such obvious and sustained labors of love. The logistics were mind-boggling, and no expense was spared. It is almost embarrassing to be unable to react more enthusiastically to a film for which such hopes seemed possible. With its flaws, it is a better and more admirable film than most. In the end, its patient, painstaking, accurate literality is the film's undoing. *The Day of the Locust* was an assertion of style; the movie is all too substantive.

Jerome Hellman was the producer and John Barry oversaw the music, mostly period recordings, with Louis Armstrong's "Jeepers Creepers" as the theme song.

Jaws

Some films are absolutely review-proof, and "Jaws" was overwhelmingly one of them. With papers running timely stories about real shark attacks, there was a stampede to see the fake thing. Shooting the film was a nightmare but when things calmed down, Steven Spielberg emerged as a major director, well and truly launched. Even now, I continue to think that the PG rating was a real goof.

THE FIRST AND CRUCIAL THING to say about the movie Universal has made from Peter Benchley's best-seller, *Jaws,* is that the PG rating is grievously wrong and misleading. The studio has rightly added its own cautionary notices in the ads, and the fact is that "Jaws" is too gruesome for children, and likely to turn the stomachs of the impressionable at any age.

A severed leg drifts toward the sea bottom, a severed arm and other shark-chewed remains are studied ashore, a man dies horribly in the jaws, spewing a last gout of his own blood; a child dies and the sea foams red. Careful studies by the Children's Film Foundation in England have confirmed what common sense suggests: Children identify most strongly with what happens to children on screen, are most impressed and terrified by the violence done to or endangering other children. "Jaws" is nightmare time for the young.

Even the mature are apt to be jolted harder by "Jaws" than by the earlier jeopardy films. Violence done to the helpless, always the hardest to watch, is here compounded because the victims are in the water, an alien environment, demanding and potentially dangerous at best. The inability to flee or fight back, as in a nightmare of paralysis, is real and only too easy to identify with. It sounds, all of it, like a backhanded compliment for a potent and well-made movie. But while I have no doubt that "Jaws" will make a bloody fortune for Universal and producers Richard Zanuck and David Brown, it is a coarse-grained and exploitive work which depends on excess for its impact. Ashore it is a bore, awkwardly staged and lumpily written.

The opening sequence, an underwater camera giving a swift shark's-eye view of the depths, over the ominous murmuring basses of John Williams's good score, is excellent, carrying the promise of suggestive power. Then an abrupt and jolting cut takes us to a beach beer party to establish the great shark's first victim. The tension rises again as we are allowed to imagine the evil lurking beneath the water's placid, moonlit surface.

Land and sea quarrel thereafter. Peter Benchley's story, which he adapted with Carl Gottlieb, has Roy Scheider as the sea-fearing resort town chief of police, trying in vain to close the beaches over the opposition of the merchants led by Murray Hamilton. A reward offered for the shark evokes a comical flotilla of amateurs. Most of this, despite an intense performance by Scheider, is flat-brush melodrama, broad and obvious. Richard Dreyfuss arrives as the rich boy who, after a childhood experience, has become a dedicated shark expert. Robert Shaw is the local shark hunter, more than half-mad, a poor man's Captain Ahab who, having survived the shark-infested seas after a wartime torpedoing, is out to exterminate the species. If the whole project from manuscript forward has been a commercially calculated confection, the tipoff in the movie is the stubborn refusal of the key characters to come into sharp focus.

Hamilton is a caricature of greedy shortsightedness. Shaw, raking fingernails across a blackboard to gain attention, stewing shark bones and humming chanteys, is undeniably colorful but his actions, ranging from the shrewd to the suicidal, serve the needs of a pot to be kept boiling. They don't reveal even the logic of madness. Dreyfuss, in a lively, individual and sympathetic performance, comes off best, even if the demands of the plot make him alternately very wise and surprisingly inexperienced.

But, at what seems long last, the three men set to sea in quest of their Nantucket Moby Dick and the adventure which is the heart of the movie begins. It is well and suspensefully done, the footage of real sharks joining indistinguishably with the chompings of the fearsome model. John M. Dwyer is credited with the special effects and Ron and Valerie Taylor the filming of actual sharks. Bill Butler was the cinematographer, and he must have had his hands full. Rexford Metz did the underwater work, including a sequence of the Dreyfuss character in a shark cage under heavy attack.

Young Steven Spielberg, who was the director, shows as he has before an uncommon flair for handling big action. He, and the script, are much less successful in the man-to-man confrontations than in the man-to-shark meetings. Intimacy is not yet his strength.

The ending is pulp story hokum, calculated, I suspect, to affirm that it has all been in gory good fun; the nightmare was only a dream. Still, it would not be surprising if DON'T GO NEAR THE WATER turned out to be the motto along the ocean beaches this summer. The frights, like those in "Earthquake" and "Towering Inferno," are not put away by happy endings. The argument has always been that tragedy, violence and terror, witnessed, purge us of them. The Grand Guignol theater of Paris, with its bloodlettings and eye-gougings ingeniously faked, was thought to have denatured shock by making it amusing. After "Jaws," you do wonder what it was that was purged, and what it takes to entertain these days.

Nashville

Altman has always seemed to me an action painter among filmmakers, getting the gesture onto celluloid instead of canvas, but with the same speed and seeming spontaneity. Sometimes the gesture appears to interest him more than the whole picture, and occasionally he even appears to have lost interest before the last reel. But in "Nashville" he gets it all right, in a wonderful, unique bafflement of sounds, images and moments.

ROBERT ALTMAN'S "NASHVILLE" must fulfill a dream every filmmaker has had at some time: to escape the bonds and boundaries of the straight-line story with its restraints and exclusions and to use the wide screen as a tapestry to catch at least a moment's worth of the immense diversity of life in a time and at a place. The easy analogies are to the dense and teeming canvases of Brueghel, to Hogarth's serial vision of London, to the picaresque early English novels, to Joyce's *Ulysses* as it immortalized a day in Dublin, to John Dos Passos's ranging view of America in *U.S.A.*

The comparisons imply a forbidding and formidable ambition, but while Altman and Joan Tewkesbury, who wrote the script, clearly intend "Nashville" to be larger than Nashville, the film—whatever its powers of suggestion—is a rollicking and vivid entertainment, done in the primary emotional colors of the country and western music which it uses, examines and celebrates. The humor ranges from slapstick to satire; the heavier emotions are similarly widely ranged from poignant to painful.

The invention is amazingly varied, which is also to say uneven, though not troublingly so.

"Nashville" is undoubtedly the best and most assured film Altman has yet made, certain to be his most commercially successful since "M*A*S*H" and the most consistently revealing of his unique and remarkable gifts as a filmmaker. It is also the most original and provocative American film in some time.

His moment's worth of life is five days of Nashville as the capital of country and western music, and his collective star is a superb cast of two dozen principals who weave in and out of each other's lives, sometimes touching, sometimes not. The plot, insofar as there is a mechanism to link the beginning and the end except by the passage of time, is the effort by Michael Murphy as a suave campaign manager to put together a musical rally for his man, an unseen figure who seems to be a well-modulated demagogue running as an independent on the Replacement Party ticket.

Altman began as a documentary-maker, learning to make the most of tight budgets and to put a lot of energy and impact on the screen, learning as well to catch and convey the reality of men, events and things. "The James Dean Story" was his first conspicuous success and it is still a model of its kind. His strengths from his feature beginnings with "Countdown," a low-budget moon-landing adventure at Warners, and notable ever since, have been the vitality of his images and the naturalness of his performances. Like directors as different as Jean-Luc Godard and Ken Russell, Altman abhors a vacuous screen, and he can make almost anything interesting on it. He has an uncommon affinity for losers and survivors, rogues and drifters, eccentrics and outcasts, the hopeless hopefuls and the shaky successful. He has sometimes been better at the parts than the wholes (as in "The Long Goodbye" and "California Split") but his instincts for that existential half world between security and failure are sure, accurate and special, and he is never dull.

No wonder that Nashville is as perfect a site for his particular sight as "Tommy" was a vehicle for Russell. The pressures to get there, to make it, keep it and extend it are dynamics which Altman explores as well as anyone now working.

His Nashville is Mecca with a mouth organ, Paradise with pearl-button shirts and handmade boots, and it is the symbol of escape and success for every three-chord guitarist, cheap-rhyme songwriter and cornbread vocalist not only in Grand Ole Opry country but a world away.

Altman and his scenarist see it all and populate it with some surprising performances. Henry Gibson, the sniffy poet of "Laugh-In," is sensational as an established Nashville star, mean and anxious beneath the oozy and unctuous drawling charm, and entirely susceptible to the idea of running for governor. Ronee Blakley is another of the successes, a Gibson protégé who has been pushed beyond her ability to cope by her ambitious husband-manager, Allen Garfield. Miss Blakley, making false starts, chattering aimlessly and collapsing emotionally before a large audience, is a creature of pity but she is also a sharp comment on the folksiness which is orchestrated as carefully as a minuet, and on the high pressure behind the low-key entertainments.

Karen Black has a briefer turn as another Grand Ole Opry star, trying harder because she is not No. 1, and singing three songs she wrote herself. Very good, too, in the sophisticated country idiom (and dress) into which the Nashville style has evolved. Keith Carradine is one-third of a third Nashville success, a trio (with Allen Nicholls and beautiful Cristina Raines) reminiscent of Peter, Paul & Mary, which is running aground on romantic shoals. Carradine also complicates the life of Lily Tomlin, who is very affecting in a straight part as a gospel singer and the mother of two deaf children.

Timothy Brown is a successful black country singer. (The production notes blandly remark that his latest hit makes him the pride of Nashville, a nudge at Charley Pride which the faithful will get easily enough and which you could dreadfully say helps make "Nashville" a *roman à clef*.)

If Altman has fun with the anxieties of the haves, he is terrific with the aspirations of the have-nots: Gwen Welles as a tone-deaf waitress whose big break is a cruel disappointment at a stag smoker, Barbara Harris whose first break is suffocated by revving hot rods and whose second is for an audience too stunned to hear her. In her laddered tights, she just about makes off with the film, adding another to her list of unforgettable presences.

Elsewhere in the tapestry are Ned Beatty as a show business attorney (and Tomlin's indifferent husband) trying to help Murphy line up stars for the rally; Shelley Duvall as a C&W groupie, collecting beds like albums; Robert Doqui as an embittered dishwasher; David Arkin as a showbiz chauffeur; Scott Glenn as a star-worshiping GI; Bert Remsen as Barbara Harris' furious farmer husband; Jeff Goldblum as a later-model easy rider; David Peel as Gibson's son who knows he'll do better as a lawyer; Barbara Baxley as a nightclub owner remembering the good days of working for the Kennedys; David Hayworth as an intense songwriter-fiddler.

The inventions work variously well. Keenan Wynn is touching as an old man trying to make his groupie niece care that his wife is dying. Geraldine Chaplin is an expert and amusing parody of a BBC radio journalist trying to get the sense of Nashville for an overseas audience sure to be confused by poetic descriptions of rusting buses. There is also a barbecue which Altman uses mostly to give cameos to his publicist, Sue Barton, and to visitors Julie Christie and Elliott Gould. The Wynn and Chaplin sequences in particular, although they are ably done, wear an air of premeditation and insertion which the other elements, as broadly drawn as they sometimes are, don't have.

I think it does not reveal too much to say that "Nashville" ends with a death, unexpected, unprepared for and unsatisfactory, even if it is agreed that a crazy unpredictability, and latent violence, are part of life and inherent in society. The argument here seems to be that the movie is putting together a tableau and revealing no more than the characters choose to reveal. It is a defensible position, yet it leaves the event looking rather much like a convenience, and not the most telling way to make the point Altman had in mind both about the milieu and the larger society. Still, it does not much diminish an extraordinary achievement—not the least of which is that the film came in for less than two million dollars, despite its scope and population. There are twenty-seven new songs, several of them all or partly by the principals themselves, including Gibson ("Two Hundred Years" and the rousing "Keep A'Goin'"), Lily Tomlin ("Yes, I Do"), Ronee Blakley ("Down to the River," "Bluebird," "Tapedeck in His Tractor," "Dues" and "My Idaho Home"), Dave Peel ("The Heart of a Gentle Woman"), Carradine ("Honey," "I'm Easy," and "It Don't Worry Me"), Allan Nicholls ("Rose's Café"), Karen Black ("Memphis," "Rolling Stone," and "I Don't Know If I Found It in You") and Altman himself ("The Day I Looked Jesus in the Eye"). In many instances, Richard Baskin, the picture's musical supervisor, was the collaborator.

Unless you are congenitally unable to hear country music except as buzzsaws hitting hickory knots, you are likely to find the songs lively and enjoyable, and several of them are certain to make the charts. The sound was endemic where I grew up, at Future Farmers dances and in the spaces between commercials for Peruna tonic and Colorbak shampoo, and for me, as I suspect for many others, it manages to be at once contemporary and nostalgic.

The feeling of the film itself is entirely contemporary, of course, and Altman invites us to read as much out of it as we will, or can. Like "Shampoo," but more successfully, it hangs a political backdrop for its foreground events, although I'm not sure that the link-up between the imaginary Hal Phillip Walker and the real George Wallace, despite the alliteration, is to be taken any more concretely than the identification between Sen. Tunney and the Redford character in "The Candidate."

"The Candidate" was about campaigning in the television age; "Nashville" more than anything else is about manipulation—the manipulating of stars, careers, events, politicians, consumers of records and concerts, the manipulating of emotions which somewhere down the line were or are honest.

The movie can also be said to be about the frustrations of failure and the resentments of fame which can fester into hatred, and about the shrewd and cynical calculations behind the public charm, about racial hypocrisy and about dopey aspirations toward a kind of success which is made to look especially shallow. There is in fact an unusual and sustained double tone in "Nashville"—between the generally light, robust and melodic course of events and the dark, sardonic subtext of implied comment on those events. Altman appears to find Nashville as potent as a symbol of a system whose values have got out of whack as Nathanael West found Hollywood. In both places, real feelings are the casualties—the singer babbles dazedly of a different childhood, the nightclub owner weeps for a lost idealism, the wife hungry for love finds only a savagely demeaning one-night stand, Wynn can find no one to grieve his dead wife with him. (That sequence pays off philosophically, at least.)

Seldom is the same footage so warm and so chilling, and where "Day of the Locust" fails by the heavy hand, "Nashville" succeeds by its deceptively light hand. It is a dazzling effort, and at mid-year there is no better film in sight, or close.

Dog Day Afternoon

No director with a profile deliberately kept as low as Sidney Lumet's has done such consistently original (and high profile) work year after year. The motivation and the language of "Dog Day Afternoon" would have been un-doable a decade earlier. Yet perhaps no one then would have conceived a crime film with so much to say, or imply, about sexual confusions and the cruelties of frustrated love.

THE EXECUTIVE BLESSINGS and the go-ahead dollars may have come from the Golden West, even as they have for movies to be shot in Burbank or Bulawayo, but the finished product which returns west from

New York looks different, acts different, feels different. There is a New York style within American filmmaking. It has not lately been seen as often as it was in the 1960s, but it exists and is unmistakable.

It is compounded of differences in location (and a particular emphasis on location), of differences in casting (drawing on a whole repertory company of highly disciplined actors not often seen in movies) and of less obvious differences in tone and intent. Like the city itself, the movies out of New York have been harder-edged, intense, often bleak in their life-view.

You think of Martin Ritt's first feature, "Edge of the City" twenty years ago, and of Elia Kazan's "On the Waterfront" and of Sidney Lumet's "The Pawnbroker." Delbert Mann's "Marty" recorded the triumph of two people finding gentleness and each other against the odds in a lean, lonely city. The more characteristic visions and movies of the city have been harsh, even in the comedies ("The Out-of-Towners," "Taking Off") as well as the dramas (Jerry Schatzberg's "Panic in Needle Park," Lumet's "Serpico," with its portrait of pervasive corruption).

"Dog Day Aftenoon" is the quintessential, undisguisable New York movie, as unrelocatable as Rikers Island or the IRT subway.

It is by the man whose work as much as any other man's helps define the New York style: the Lumet of "The Pawnbroker" and "Serpico," with Al Pacino now once again his all-stops-out star. Based on a bizarre news event, it retains the raucous urgency, the look and the feel, of neighborhood life. It is crowded with singular charcters who in a crisis situation behave for the most part as real people rather than fictional creatures.

"Dog Day" is so eccentric and original a work that it does not categorize easily: frequently very funny, it is not quite a comedy; increasingly suspenseful, it is far from being a caper movie; frequently affecting, it is still pretty cool-eyed and ironic. But from start to end it is engrossing and unpredictable, and although hindsight raises a few questions, "Dog Day Afternoon" works as it plays.

Based on a *Life* magazine account by P.F. Kluge and Thomas Moore, the movie details the inept stickup of a small Brooklyn branch of the Chase National Bank in August 1972, an event which before it was done had escalated to a large-scale siege and an attempted escape on a jet with hostages. Pacino and a morose, slow-brained associate (John Cazale, who played his weak older brother in "Godfather") invade the bank just at closing time. As in real life, a third plotter (Gary Springer) chickens out and splits even as the heist begins; it is a sign. The plan was simple: to grab the loot and scoot—and no one wants the plan to work more than the branch manager, Sully Boyar, and his staff, headed by Penny Allen.

Everything goes wrong. Most of the cash has already left by armored car. Pacino's attempt to burn some evidence sets off alarms and the police are outside, in force, before Pacino and Cazale can take off. The siege, and the revelations, begin. Pacino has a shrill, domineering mother (Judith Malina) and a fat, whining wife. He also has an unhappy transsexual lover (Chris Sarandon) and has said marriage vows with him. What made the real robbery a magazine story and a movie was that the idea behind the robbery was to finance a sex-change operation for the lover.

It is not the stuff of your run-of-the-till bank job, and a certain percentage of the audience is certain to be repelled by the premise within the premise. The movie carries a double suspense—the suspense inherent in the material and a suspense over its handling of the material, which could have lent itself to sniggering bad taste and cruel exploitation. But Lumet and screenwriter Frank Pierson have moved carefully and calmly, finding the situation as their audience must in general find it—ludicrous but also sad and touching.

Sarandon (in one of the year's most difficult acting chores) makes the lover extravagantly hysterical but he preserves the viewer's sympathy. He is funny, but he is nature's victim, not a joke.

Pacino's performance dominates the film and he gives another measure of his remarkable range, moving maybe 50 points down the IQ scale from the ice-cold intelligence of Michael in the "Godfather" films and the warm intelligence of Frank Serpico to this preposterous figure named Sonny, a lifelong loser growing more bombastic as he gets more scared and uncertain—defying what looks like every law officer east of the Alleghenies and worrying about food for the hostages, planning an escape with a near-moronic partner who imagines Wyoming is a country someplace overseas.

It's a very theatrical role and there are moments when you wish for a little less. Then again, there are quiet moments when the bravado has subsided, and Pacino gives us insights into a man for whom nothing has ever gone quite right and who is not too dumb to know how defeated he is. Part of the defeat—and central to the movie—is being around at a time when the society is liberating itself sexually, but into a kind of chaos in which everything is obtainable except love. Sonny is in fact an unlikely recruit to the gay community and seems, as Pacino plays him, like a man who has lost himself more than found himself and who is trying desperately to find any love, rather than new sex.

His robbing partner, Cazale, is even more crippled, mumbling of purity and sickened by the sight of a woman smoking a cigarette. The suspense of the movie arises from Cazale's murderous loathing of a world he fears because he knows so little about it. Cazale's performance, like Pacino's, is the art at its best.

Pierson's dialogue sounds accurate down to the last semiliterate snarl.

The reservations come later. "Dog Day" plays extremely well, its shifting moods orchestrated with sure skill, its large and generally little-known cast performing with easy authenticity. Some of the problems are with the back story. You do wonder how the characters played by Pacino and Cazale ever hit it off. You don't have the feeling they could have planned a cup of coffee together. Judith Malina as Pacino's mother is a vile caricature of Momism such as might have sprung fully grown from the brow of Philip Wylie. Susan Peretz as Pacino's wife is presented as a weighty grotesque who would drive any man into other arms. You learn enough about where Pacino is coming from to wish you knew a lot more.

Charles Durning as the detective in charge of the siege and the man negotiating with Pacino gives a performance as vigorous as Pacino's own, and it works because he is dealing with an armed man who is not the brightest guy on the block. James Broderick is the chilly FBI man, some-how more menacing than Pacino.

"Dog Day Afternoon" is essentially an intimate, even a claustrophobic movie, but it calls for big moments—the jeering crowds (who are on Pacino's side), the battalions of encircling lawmen, the edgy procession to the airport. Lumet, cinematographer Victor Kemper and editor Dede Allen cope very nicely indeed.

The conflicting emotions the movie stirs up throughout continue to the swift finale, which is satisfying (no giveaways there) but leaves echoes. One of the echoing messages is that a movie as unorthodox in its choice of materials as "Dog Day Afternoon" must be in good hands, and be far more entertaining, invigorating and instructive than formularized stuff. It is indeed.

One Flew Over the Cuckoo's Nest

Milos Forman said years later he got "Cuckoo's Nest" because he was "cheap and available." He had indeed been in limbo because the studio had dumped his fine first American film. His Oscar-winning work here confirmed his ability and predicted the quality and originality of the films to follow, like "Amadeus." McMurphy remains Nicholson's best performance.

WORKING THE NIGHT SHIFT as an aide at the Palo Alto Veterans Hospital fifteen years ago, Ken Kesey used the quiet hours on the wards to write the novel which probably more than any other spoke to the angers and anxieties of a generation that was shortly to start ripping the campuses apart in frustration.

One Flew Over the Cuckoo's Nest used an unquiet ward of a mental hospital as a symbolic battleground for the life-celebrating loner versus the suffocating system. The novel, a continuing bestseller, became a frequently produced play and has now become one of the year's strongest, best-made and most engrossing movies, offering still another demonstration of Jack Nicholson's phenomenal powers as an actor. The acting honors are shared by Nicholson with a large and almost totally unfamiliar but meticulously well-chosen supporting cast. He and they constitute an ensemble whose quality is such that they always seem characters colliding and never actors acting.

Nicholson is R. P. McMurphy, the jailbird transferred from the penitentiary to the state mental hospital to be checked over to see whether he's really crazy or only faking it to stay off the work details. He may or may not be crazy, but he is an original from his first whooping dance after the handcuffs come off. He runs like an affable typhoon through a ward whose rule of survival is Don't Make Waves. If he is the perfect symbol, with rumpled hair and a stubble of beard, of the nonconformist who doesn't so much want to change things as to be let alone, the perfect counter-symbol is the cold-eyed, calm-voiced boss of the ward, Nurse Ratched, to whom conformity and sanity are the same thing. Their clash of personalities and philosophies can be felt from their first size-up encounter, and the escalating tension, the swirling, smoking hatred, the inevitable drive toward an explosive end generate a dramatic excitement that is very rare indeed.

Louise Fletcher, who after a long absence from the movies appeared in Robert Altman's "Thieves Like Us" in 1974, is the nurse, ruling her charges with the seeming sweet reason and patronizing primer-simple style of a teacher disciplining slow children. She is a monster whose domineering contempt masquerades as understanding patience and whose sadistic aim is clearly custodial, not curative. As a performance it is frighteningly fine; the nurse is monstrous without ever being a monstrosity; the hatreds are veiled with a motherliness as starched and pure as the uniform.

Nicholson does his own unveiling. McMurphy may not be the brightest guy in the world but he is not the dumbest and he is sly enough to clown over his deepest feelings about the nurse and about the men she has cowed so thoroughly. (Most of them, unlike Nicholson, are voluntary and could leave if they dared to.) It is the muted quality of their warfare which makes the relationship between Nicholson and the nurse so particular, suspenseful and deadly.

Noisy, back-slapping, confident and alive, Nicholson is from the start the leader of the ward. He energizes a platoon of losers: a stammering, love-starved boy (Brad Dourif), a giant Indian (Will Simpson), a quavery complainer (Sidney Lassick), a bearded drop-out (Delos V. Smith, Jr.), a jealousy-crippled husband (William Redfield), a jovial dimwit (Danny DeVito), a Mutt and Jeff pair (William Duell and the tall, morose Vincent Schiavelli).

Nicholson organizes a crazy basketball game, a loud protest over a World Series telecast, even an afternoon outing on a fishing boat. He then attempts a break-out which embroils two chicks from town (Louisa Moritz and Marya Small) who invade the cuckoo's nest with a party's worth of booze, some of it to beguile the night man, Scatman Crothers. The bizarre and orgiastic romp reveals, as only dramatic moments can, just how close comedy and tragedy are linked.

"Cuckoo's Nest" is one of the most involving films in a long time and most viewers will, I think, feel during the party scene a kind of exasperated anxiety which is wrenchingly strong—the emotional pull movies can develop but rarely do. And if the whole drama is a message and a metaphor, there is a message in the orgy as well, which is that we can nicely seduce ourselves into forgetfulness about the perils and the dilemmas that face us.

Milos Forman, whose smashing social comedies with edgy overtones from Czechoslovakia, "Loves of a Blonde" and "The Fireman's Ball," introduced him to this country and whose "Taking Off" revealed that he had an accurate eye for the American scene too, directed "Cuckoo's Nest" from an adaptation of the novel by Lawrence Hauben and Bo Goldman. It seems important to say the novel because there is absolutely no feeling of a play having been opened up. It is easy to imagine how effectively the drama could have been centered on the ward.

But from its mood-establishing opening footage behind the titles of a barren winter plain backed by snowy mountains, a motionless chill landscape broken by the lights of a lone car speeding through the bleak dawn, "Cuckoo's Nest" is a movie, ranging naturally throughout the hospital, out in the yards, into the town, out on the water. Forman's sensitive handling of the cast is by itself stunningly productive.

The movie was shot, remarkably, at the Oregon State Hospital at Salem, whose own director, Dr. Dean R. Brooks, plays the director of the fictional asylum—and very naturally and subtly at that. Haskell Wexler was the principal photographer, with credited assists from two other top talents, Bill Butler and William Fraker. The feeling throughout is of naturalism, which is to say neither of overaccentuated gray and gloomy shadows nor of stage-lit sets. The exposition and the editing, like all the performances, are of the consummate art which refuses to draw attention to itself. The one convention is the musical score by Jack Nitzsche (who did "Performance" a few years ago), but it is quite effective—intermittent and suggestive, reinforcing the emotional intensity of the drama.

The energy inherent in the McMurphy character made it almost inevitable that the Nicholson performance should be a tour de force. But oddly enough it is the restraint and the ambiguity of the characterization, not the splash of it, which make it unforgettable. This figure is still another fresh and individual creation—not intentionally heroic, not deliberately a destructive antihero, earthwise but nothing like as neurotically intelligent as the men played in, say, "Easy Rider" or "The Passenger." He is crafty, clever and compassionate and he is in the end a hero because his instincts leave him no choice. He is more than a show-off or a pop-off, and in what is possibly the subtlest performance of his amazing career, Nicholson makes his eyes let us see how much more he knows and feels than he lets on. He is here closest to the sailor of "The Last Detail," whose cynicism could not quite override the caring.

Kirk Douglas had played in "Cuckoo's Nest" on Broadway and tried for years to get a movie going. It was finally his actor son Michael who found a backer in Saul Zaentz of Berkeley's Fantasy Records (from Dave Brubeck to Creedence Clearwater). Zaentz had also financed the fine and equally tough-minded "Payday." "Cuckoo's Next" seems likely to be a far more substantial commercial success than "Payday."

"One Flew Over the Cuckoo's Nest" is calculated to restore your faith in the discipline and the emotional effectiveness of inspired fine moviemaking.

1976

Taxi Driver

Robert De Niro's "You talkin' to me?" monologue to a mirror, his trick, forearm-mounted pistol snapping into position, is one of those unforgettable movie moments. As a study of urban paranoia at its most lethal, "Taxi Driver" created a foreboding of violence to come as few films ever have—and the violence came. In the calm beyond the violence, the film suggests that we all live uneasily ever after. It was one of the decade's most potently disturbing films.

THE STREETS GET MEANER, A LOT MEANER, in "Taxi Driver," Martin Scorsese's nerve-scraping new film about the making, or more accurately the triggering, of a psychotic killer. Robert De Niro, who was Harvey Keitel's disastrously easygoing pal in "Mean Streets" three years ago, is an ex-Marine living in a roach-ridden room in Manhattan and getting ready to reenter civilian life. He keeps a journal, painfully written in a childish script and revealing a mentality that is at best early adolescent and a personality already blotched with paranoid alarms and resentments.

Paul Schrader's script is not explicit on the point but you have a feeling from the beginning that Travis Bickle, the De Niro character, has just now come out of an institution—and probably not the Marine Corps, but something subsequent to it. Sitting in that room, sifting reality through his peculiar dark maze of a mind, Travis is at the very first sight a ticking bomb. And whatever else anybody comes to think about "Taxi Driver," it has a muscle-tensing, skin-prickling, apprehensive suspense that builds from those first unsettling moments like an air-raid siren.

He becomes a cabdriver, volunteering for the night shift, happy to take the unpopular trips to the high-danger ghettos of Harlem and Spanish Harlem and the crime-thick warrens of the city everywhere. It is a life that would test the optimism of a saint, cruising past the pimps, the pushers, the jeering, fighting streetwalkers, the dead winos and the lost children. It's like being a ferryman to Dante's inferno. It sickens Travis further, compounding his paranoia with a crusading, avenging contempt toward the dregs of society he carries in his taxi or sees from it.

Scorsese demonstrated in "Mean Streets" (and in his first film, begun as a graduate student at NYU, "Who's That Knocking on My Door?") that he knows and can put on film the seedy despair and the stony oppressive cruelty of the Manhattan underside. The first images of "Taxi Driver" are abstract forms finally taking recognizable shape as car lights moving through the steam that curves from manhole covers like the smokes of hell. It is a surreal metropolitan nightmare, and it establishes the tone of jangling anxiety and incipient violence that rises at last to the film's bloody climax.

(The R rating reportedly came out of negotiations and re-editings to avoid an X. It remains, as they say, a very hard and violent R.)

Travis/De Niro is not alone in this world. Peter Boyle is a cabdriver pal who talks incessantly and knowingly without saying anything at all. Cybill Shepherd is a campaign worker for a presidential candidate (Leonard Harris) and Albert Brooks works with her. Harvey Keitel is a pimp and one of his charges is a thirteen-year-old runaway, played with a stunning blend of innocence and world-weary wisdom by Jodie Foster, who came to fame in the bizarrely different world of Walt Disney. Murray Moston is her kindly protector.

In what is possibly her most effective casting since "The Heartbreak Kid" and "The Last Picture Show," Cybill Shepherd plays a cool, ambitious WASP princess, amused for a while by the attentions of a dopey cabdriver who has spotted her through an office window and who tries to take her to a porno flick, seemingly unaware there are any other kind. Scared off, she sets the bomb to ticking faster.

In the end, Travis is a walking arsenal, bent on assassination as the suicidal first step in a purge of society's evils. Along the way he tries to pry Jodie Foster loose from the life she leads, and amidst the rising tension there is a scene between them of unusual tenderness, the child treating the man, rightly, as a child.

The astonishing thing about "Taxi Driver," and I don't see how to avoid talking about it, is a kind of coda which follows the bloodbath and in which Travis himself seems to have been purged and is back on night duty, an ironic hero. Is he a renewed time bomb, ticking again? There is no effort to say he is, and some suggestion that he is newly calm.

It is in fact the coda which makes it difficult to come to an easy assessment of "Taxi Driver." De Niro's performance and all the others,

Jodie Foster's in particular, are all strong and convincing. The raindrops falling on his hood, the wipers blurring the abstract expressionist clumpings of neon signs and traffic lights, hubs and bumpers giving back the city's image, grow overfamiliar and self-conscious before the film is done, but before the familiarity sets in, Scorsese and cinematographer Michael Chapman have caught the grimly garish look of the city by night, the gray sterility by day.

The lesson, I presume, is that there are invisible men among us, ignored equally as threats or as wounded individuals crying unheard for help and sympathy, and that the taxi driver is a potent symbol of metropolitan anonymity. Fair enough, except that you might have to drive far to find more assertive personalities than most of the New York cabbies I've ridden with.

The problem with "Taxi Driver" as a study on the making of a potential mass murderer is that it seems to start too late in the process. If there are clues to Travis they are further back in his past. What got him to that demoralizing room in which we meet him matters a lot, and if it was only the Marine Corps and its training to obey, kill and feel righteous, you'd have said the script should have made it clearer, instead of leaving it doubtful.

The larger problem is the ambiguous coda, with what seems to be a currently fashionable and idiot thesis that violence is good for what ails you, a right rite of passage to maturity and mental health. Whether the film is saying this, or suggesting that society in its willful blindness is doomed to reinfect itself endlessly, is also unclear. And the ending as it stands seems curiously tacked on and unconvincing. Granted, it goes against the tidy resolution and melodrama, the stage highpiled in corpses; but it's not certain what at that point the message is—only that there was evidently intended to be one.

The film is already famous as having the last score by the great composer of film music, Bernard Herrmann, who finished recording it only hours before his sudden death. His music is unquestionably a prime source of the abrasive and unnerving power of "Taxi Driver." There has not been so full, insistent, eerie and ominous, doom-pushed, throbbing and needling a film score in years. Herrmann leaves us a definitive example of supportive film music in the grand tradition.

All the President's Men

The achievement, the smashing achievement of "All the President's Men" is that it was a paper chase made thrillingly dramatic. The break-in itself and a shadowy meet with Deep Throat in a parking garage were as traditionally suspenseful as it got. The rest was paper and, above all, newspaper, and at last a newsprinter clacking out the story of Nixon's resignation. But Pakula had made real history—and a civics lesson—superbly watchable.

MORE WATERGATE? After three years and more of revelations, denials, the puncturing of denials, the hearings with both their drama and their dronings, the piling up of names, dates and details until the memory sagged and blurred under the accumulated weight, all before the historic resignation which was like the breaking of a national fever?

Yes, more—in the form of a classic motion picture. "All the President's Men" is, quite beyond anything else, an engrossing mystery movie, with atmosphere, suspense, surprise, conflict, danger, secret messages, clandestine meetings, heroes, villains and a cast of leading and supporting characters that might have emerged from an unlikely collaboration of, let us say, Gore Vidal and Raymond Chandler. Except, of course, that they and the events and the drama are real, and the reality of their time and deeds has been recreated with unenhanced honesty and unsparing detail that must thrill anyone who looks for excellence in movies.

What "All the President's Men," dramatized by William Goldman from the book by Bob Woodward and Carl Bernstein of the *Washington Post*, brings to these familiar events is a clarity born of historical perspective but also a newly quickened feeling of national concern. The central drama and suspense of "All the President's Men" is in its reminder of the narrow margin of our safety, the fresh realization of how close the cover-up came to working.

At one level, the movie has a historically happy ending. The good guys won and the *Washington Post* teletypes clack out a final litany of the events that electrified all our lives—the hearings, the indictments, the convictions, the resignations. At another level, the film invites no comfort. It was a narrow and almost accidental escape and the weight of a corrupted government had been tilted against the truth as never before. But never again? The movie makes no preachment but you are bound to think anew that forgiveness and forgetfulness ought to be two starkly different commodities.

"All the President's Men" is not least a newspaper drama and in my experience the best of those ever made: the least sentimental, the most accurate (even unflatteringly accurate) in its depicting of editorial processes. Robert Redford, who bought the movie rights to the book and is the producer as well as the costar, and Dustin Hoffman are stars indeed and here cast in heroic molds. But one of the satisfactions of the film is that they do not do star turns. They are working actors acting the parts of working journalists with a rumpled tie-askew believability.

The first happy accident of Watergate was night watchman Frank Wills's discovery of a taped door latch, which led to the busting up of the burglary back in June 1972. (Wills plays himself in the movie.) The next happy inadvertence was the teaming on the story of Bernstein (Hoffman), an inexperienced cityside hand, and Woodward (Redford), a relative newcomer on the staff who had evidently not yet found his feet or got a secure hold on his desk. They become collaborators, although the movie does not indicate that they became close buddies. (Despite the starry teaming, "President's Men" does not join the roster of palship pictures.)

Hoffman's Bernstein is the principal author, who invaded the action in the first place by doing an unsolicited rewrite of Redford's initial story. (The first pleasure of the movie's reportage of newsroom dynamics is its study of Woodward's bristling burn at Bernstein's meddling, and his grudging admission that Bernstein's draft read better.) Hoffman is the traditional investigative reporter, cajoling, flattering, applying pressure where it will work, not above a little dirty-trickery to get at a reluctant and evasive source.

Redford's Woodward is a man learning about himself as he explores the story, taking a toughening stance, feeling the moral outrage of the situation he and his partner are uncovering.

The curious happy accident of Watergate was Woodward's source, whom one of the editors dubbed Deep Throat, an informant never yet identified but apparently someone in the Justice Department who first fed Woodward cryptic hints in the manner of the Delphic oracle and later gave some more practical confirmations. Deep Throat is played, in deep shadow in a parking garage where he and Woodward meet, by Hal Holbrook. He is a fine study in nervous limited helpfulness, finally provoking Redford to a snarling outburst against all the timidity.

For their newspaper and its top editors and its publisher, the Woodward-Bernstein stories were at the beginning sensitive, explosive, potentially libelous. The cover-up (as came clear later) made it nearly impossible to get on-the-record proof of anything. The crucial effort to trace funds from the Committee to Re-Elect the President to the Watergate burglars and the Justice Department-White House controllers was a job that might well have thwarted "Mission: Impossible," even in a two-part episode.

The publish-and-maybe-perish decisions rose ultimately to the office of the *Post*'s executive editor, Ben Bradlee, portrayed to laconic perfection by Jason Robards. The drama within the drama is the convincing of Bradlee that the Watergate pieces will hold water. Robards as Bradlee, in from a black-tie dinner to read copy, puts feet on desk and then, decision made, does a kind of light-foot walk along an aisle of desks, lightly touching each as he passes. He is going away from camera, but somehow the departing view is of a man who has bit the bullet and found that he likes the taste. It is one of the most pleasing movie scenes I can remember, understated but hugely expressive.

The editors on the line are Jack Warden as Harry Rosenfeld, the *Post*'s Metro editor, and Martin Balsam as Howard Simons, the *Post*'s managing editor. Both are a very long way from Walter Burns (as most modern editors are, so far as I know), the same long way that "President's Men" is from the boozy child's play of "The Front Page" generally. In their own anxieties, doubts, testings, guidance, encouragement and support, they become, like everyone else in sight, absolutely credible figures. Nobody yells, as they'd have to yell now, "Stop the computers, I got a great story," and nobody fakes a watch theft.

The movie is a story of process—a press procedural in the way that Ed McBain's 87th Precinct books are called police procedurals. The procedures are watched for the emotional tonings as well, and the play-off of personalities (the doubters and believers) at the daily budget meetings to determine the play of stories on page one is seen to be the OK Corral with invisible sidearms. For working newsmen there is the wry shock of discovery.

The movie is not short (two hours and fifteen minutes) but it ends with startling suddenness. The script follows the book, which is to say it does not carry forward into the hearings and the agonies in the Rose Garden preceding the resignation. But as the movie ends, the cover has been lifted; the revelations are by now self-generating, the links to the unprincipled operatives in the White House (unprincipled in the sense that even now there looks to have been no motivation beyond power and political survival) have been firmly made. The triumphant ending is not a surprise not to be given away. The surprise and the riveting interest are in the beginnings, the stumbling and then increasingly surefooted advance into the murky wastelands of democracy abused.

It is a movie doubly thrilling, as a superlative piece of movie making and as a revealing and important perspective on an unparalleled piece of American history.

The director was Alan J. Pakula, whose hallmark here as before is a meticulous naturalism. The performances he has evoked are in some paradoxical way both low-keyed and high-energy, reflecting the tension of all the characters whether it finds expression or is revealed in strained silences.

In a very large assembly of fine and accurate work, Jane Alexander as a distraught CREEP bookkeeper is outstanding, as is Stephen Collins as Hugh Sloan, the campaign executive who opted out rather than be an implicit accessory to the tricks being turned around him. Robert Walden has a brief but charged cameo as Donald Segretti, displaying the moral numbness that seems to have been invaluable in campus politics at USC, and still finding that losing is the only regret. John McMartin is economically effective as the doubting foreign editor of the *Post*.

George Jenkins's production design is a source of immense strength to the film, and his re-creation of the *Post* newsroom at the Burbank Studio, accurate to the contents of the wastebaskets, is not less than astonishing. But at that, it is (like all the other settings) only a place where things take place. It is a background, interesting and informative, but the foreground figures matter.

David Shire did the music, which echoes rather than insists upon the drama.

The star charisma of Redford and Hoffman will, I hope, help assure the film of a wide audience, but the measure of the integrity of the undertaking is that they use their craft to meld into the men they play. No stars lurking about in raked fedoras with a fifth of Old Inspiration in the bottom drawer. "All the President's Men" has the fidelity of a documentary, but let no one doubt that it is history recreated as high drama. Knowing how it all came out does nothing to untie the knots in your innards or turn down the mind's alarms.

Family Plot

"Family Plot" was Alfred Hitchcock's final film—a melancholy milestone for anyone who loved the master's touch. It was not at the top of the canon, but far from an embarrassment for an ailing man in his mid-seventies. The long plummeting sequence of an out-of-control car (meticulously storyboarded) is pure Hitchcock and the intricate story is lightly, tastily amusing.

THE MOVIES, YOU ARE REMINDED with a jolt, are even now only four-score years old, a mere flicker on the long, expressive face of history. More to the point, we are still in the presence of men who helped to invent the language of the movies and to define what the movies could hope to do.

One of the pioneers, bless us all, is still working. Not only that, Alfred Hitchcock is working with a young man's wit, style and tireless craftsmanship. It is astonishing to realize that he entered the industry in 1920, worked at the famous UFA Studio in Berlin along with the men who made "The Cabinet of Dr. Caligari," directed his first feature there in 1925 and his first English feature, "The Lodger," in London exactly a half-century ago.

"Family Plot" is Hitchcock's fifty-third movie. It is atmospheric, characterful, precisely paced, intricately plotted, exciting and suspenseful, beautifully acted and, perhaps more than anything else, amusing. It is not as traumatically scary as "Psycho" nor as gruesomely violent as "Frenzy." It is a suspense comedy that is probably closest in spirit to "The Trouble with Harry."

The particular rewards of "Family Plot" include the most extensive and appropriate movie role that the richly talented Barbara Harris has yet had. After her tantalizing moments in "Harry Kellerman," "Nashville" and points between, it is nice to see her at full length. She is teamed with Bruce Dern, an able actor who often seems a whole lot better than his parts, but who here has a large opportunity of which he makes the most.

The match play is against William Devane as a suavely pyschopathic jewel thief and murderer, and Karen Black as the helpmate who hadn't realized quite what a wierdo she has on her hands.

The script, by Hitchcock's collaborator on "North by Northwest," Ernest Lehman, is from a book by Victor Canning, and it is in effect Ross Macdonald-told-funny—past and present crimes related to a tangle of family relationships.

Barbara Harris is a cool medium, helping Cathleen Nesbitt commune with her late sister. Miss Nesbitt wants to atone for past cruelties by leaving the family wealth to the sister's boy, given away for adoption these many years ago. Can Harris and her voices locate him? For the fee, she and her larcenous but slow-brained boyfriend Dern, a part-time cab driver, could find Judge Crater.

The trail leads to a weedy small-town cemetery and a surly filling station proprietor (Ed Lauter). What connection could all this have to a super-slick kidnapping in which the ransom is a million-dollar diamond? There is a connection, we can all rest assured, and Hitchcock and Lehman make the story lines join sharply. There is a careening, out-of-control car ride down a mountain road that is pure Hitchcock in that fright and laughter cling together.

Also in the Hitchcock vein is a kind of startling shift of sympathy. His central figure is usually an innocent accidentally beset by perils he can neither identify, nor, apparently, successfully fight. This time his innocents are only relatively innocent. They are small-time con persons quite prepared to put their own tax on Miss Nesbitt's inheritance. But they find themselves in a game far more deadly than their own, and we find ourselves rooting for them—not so much to win as to survive.

If in "Frenzy," Hitchcock seemed to be keeping up with his younger contemporaries in the graphics of violence, he here edges into the graphics of language, no less unnecessarily. A little with-itness goes a far way. The wordage is not profoundly off-putting but only a minor disappointment in a work whose satisfaction is in our reintroduction to the special and timeless world Hitchcock creates and sustains so well.

Indeed, the lesson of "Family Plot" for young filmmakers (and possibly for the customers who know what they are liking but are not sure how to define it) is the importance of setting and keep a tone. Tone is an elusive word, and the quality is easier to spot when it is inconsistent and a movie lurches from light comedy to heavy farce by way of messy violence. The delight of Hitchcock's company is that an impeccable entertainment like "Family Plot" declares its intentions from the start and then plays out its make-believe at the same level of reality (or non-reality) straight through to the winking end. He scares, baffles, surprises and startles you, but he doesn't confuse you, and it makes a good deal of difference.

The performances are all splendidly assured, although Devane may be a shade too urbane for the rotten fellow he conceals. Particularly good in support are Marge Redmond as a saleswoman linking past and present and Katherine Helmond as a bitter widow. Ed Lauter is a fine menace and William Prince a swiped bishop. It is a shiny production. Hitchcock will be seventy-seven in August, but you would hardly guess it.

Network

Articulate anger, bordering on satiric rage, is rare in film. Appealing to a safe consensus is the norm and the idea is, if you're going to get mad, pick a safe target or better yet just don't make any waves. Paddy Chayefsky's "Network" was a soul-invigorating change of pace and it was cheered by multitudes who know they are addicted to television and are mad as hell but who, unlike Howard Beale, are going to take it forevermore. Chayefsky's furious prose is sadly missed.

HE HAS THE ELDER-STATESMAN BEARING of an Eric Sevareid, the reassuring warmth of a Walter Cronkite, the back-from-the-wars dash of a Chet Huntley. Smiling serenely, he faces the evening news audience out there in televisionland. The ratings have been awful, he says; he has been fired and, after all these years in the trade, he doesn't know how to do anything else so he is going to blow his brains out on camera a week hence.

He is Peter Finch as Howard Beale, the gray news eminence of a fictional fourth network and the symbolic center of Paddy Chayefsky's coruscating and corrosive assault on commercial television, "Network."

Chayefsky does not bite the hand that fed him when he was one of the then-young medium's best dramatists, he rips it off at the shoulder. It has been a long while since a movie attacked anything as savagely (and knowingly) as Chayefsky attacks television. He writes like a hellfire preacher, raging against television for its craven commercialism, its enslavement to the demon ratings, its amoral willingness to try, seduce, corrupt, exploit and compromise anyone or anything in its desperate struggles to get and hold the attention of the audience.

But his jeremiad is not only about the misuses and degradations of the medium and its powers, it is also about the all-pervading, life-changing, soul-crippling, reality-distorting influence of television even when (presumably) it is noble and swell.

"The tube is gospel," cries Finch, "the ultimate revelation. It's the most awesome goddamn force in the whole goddamn world. Television is a goddamn amusement park, it's not the truth. We're in the boredom-killing business!"

Chayefsky's own script for "Hospital" a few years ago made the same kind of outrageous indictment of its subject matter and was outrageously funny much of the way. Then he seemed to blunt the edge of his wrath by providing a plot and a burlesque denouement that let everybody off.

"Network" is a far angrier and far more persistent and intent piece of work, although once again Chayefsky, pushing the material beyond satire into the merely ludicrous, comes dangerously near to suggesting it's all been in fun, all a joke. This time the passion and the eloquence of the denunciations, together with the electric energy of Sidney Lumet's direction, make the message indelible. But "Network" for all its vitality and impact is still a rough-hewn movie whose fire is intellectual and whose attitude toward all its characters is so cold that the viewer, denied the chance to root for anyone, acknowledges the anger but takes the lessons to mind and not to heart as well.

Finch as Beale is, of course, going crazy, but even his old buddy Bill Holden, as a Murrow-like figure now the head of the network news operation, doesn't realize how fast. Finch asks for another airing, to bow out with dignity. He gives instead a ranting put-down of the nonsense television news is.

Since all the world loves the sore loser and the indiscreetly nutty, Finch is a hit, propped in place by Faye Dunaway as the unslakably ambitious, conscienceless, rating-mad head of new programming and by Robert Duvall as the coldly efficient chief executive of the network, overseeing it for its shadowy new conglomerate owners.

Dunaway, a vile-tongued cartoon of the female executive, has no end of vile ideas—a new anthology series, the Mao Tse-tung Hour, built around actual terrorist acts filmed by the terrorists themselves, and a new news show which resembles "Let's Make a Deal" and features a soothsayer as well as the bonkers and collapsing Finch, and which apparently delivers no news whatsoever.

Chayefsky engineers some acidly wonderful moments large and small. The director and his staff in the control room are so focused on camera moves they don't hear a word when Finch announces he's going to shoot himself. Later, as Finch goes into full prophetic tirade, he urges the householders to throw open their windows and cry, "I'm mad as hell and I'm not going to take it anymore." Amidst thunder and blue lightning, the windows of apartment towers in Manhattan do indeed open and there is a caterwauling chorus in the night. It is a remarkable bit of scene-stealing, a kind of Capra populism gone mad.

Introduced as an individual, Finch has become a remote, lost symbol only, beyond reach as well as beyond normal belief. In a slightly realer mode, Holden (now fired) and Dunaway, representing everything he despises, begin one of the most psychologically unlikely affairs since Harold made it with Maude. There is an extraordinary scene—out of some other script—in which Holden leaves his tremulous wife (Beatrice Straight). The structural reason for the romance is clear enough; Holden can take over from Finch as Chayefsky's denunciatory voice, cutting Dunaway down to size as a hollow and loveless end-product of television, incapable of caring or concern, no longer sure what is image, what real. "She learned about life from Bugs Bunny," he says, both in sorrow and in anger.

The author has a lot on his mind, also including alarm over how much the Arabs are buying of America (Chayefsky names real places and institutions) and further alarm about the multinational corporations that are taking over as the structure of the world. (Ned Beatty is the soothing voice of the corporation cosmology and he creates a dynamite cameo quite removed from his usual redneck sheriffs.)

Duvall, a fine actor, makes his hard-line professional executive believable if not sympathetic and lets us watch the very human deflating of a corporation man suddenly bereft of his corporation. There are vivid snapshots by Marlene Warfield as a Communist turned grasping television producer, Arthur Burghardt as a terrorist turned equally grasping producer and Kathy Cronkite as a willing captive of the terrorists (an unpleasant borrowing from real life).

The performance, given those whip-sharp Chayefsky lines, are cracklingly good: Finch going spectacularly, frothingly mad; Holden as the burnt-out case who has watched his own pride erode along with the erosion of the quality of the news; Dunaway in a recklessly busy, uptempo and unlanguid characterization quite unlike what she's done before. The Dunaway role will offend feminists who do not like successful women portrayed as emasculating competitors, and it is indeed a cruel cartoon, well-played.

Whatever its shifts of gaze from Finch to Holden to Dunaway to Duvall to Beatty to the audience, and despite its shift from satire to burlesque by way of romantic melodrama, "Network" has vitality and a provocative excitement that is forever rare. It is marvelously literate, a quality also forever rare.

Owen Roizman's photography catches the sights as Chayefsky catches the sounds and intimations of the network world. Elliot Lawrence's music is precisely and, I imagine, deliberately like the swelling anthems that announced "Ed Sullivan" and "Your Show of Shows."

Rocky

Predicting that "Stallone is now and forevermore a name and talent to conjure with" was as easy as prophecy gets. What prophecy does not show is the troubling effect great fame and vast money can have on both art and life. But a twentieth anniversary screening of "Rocky" at the Motion Picture Academy revealed how well the film still plays and how thrillingly conceived it was. Stallone, on hand at the screening, was again for the night the young hopeful on the verge of everything.

GRAPEVINES CAN BE SKILLFULLY NOURISHED, if there is something genuinely worth talking about. As long ago as midyear the escalating word of mouth out of carefully cast private screenings was that a little movie called "Rocky" was very, very special.

And so, by all that makes movies movies, it absolutely is. In one warming stroke it revives and restores the vital tradition of the low-cost and unpretentious movie which creates stars instead of hiring them and which commandeers the rousing affection of its audiences by proclaiming the possibility of love, hope and triumph in the lives of ordinary men and women (who are anything but ordinary in their sympathetic individuality).

"Rocky" was written by and stars Sylvester (Sly) Stallone, a sturdy young actor previously remembered as a costar with Henry (The Fonz) Winkler in "The Lords of Flatbush," another low-budget and less-heralded film, shot in 16mm, which became a large critical and commercial hit. Stallone is now and forevermore a name and talent to conjure with.

His Rocky is part Marty, part the Brando of "On the Waterfront," a lumbering nice-guy loner who lives in a really crummy apartment with a goldfish, a pair of turtles named Cuff and Link and a poster of Rocky Marciano. He makes small change as a strong but awkward club fighter ($42 net for a win) and earns his keep as a collector for a flashy waterfront loan shark (Joe Spinell). He is a strong but lousy collector, too good-hearted to deliver overdue notices in the form of broken fingers and arms.

He has eyes for the chronically shy and repressed clerk (Talia Shire) who works in a pet shop and is the sister of his beefy and beefing pal (Burt Young) going lame and alcoholic among the cold carcasses in a packing plant.

The simple plot of Stallone's working-class fairy tale is that Rocky, as the patsy in a promotion stunt, gets a shot at the heavyweight title held by a tycoon in trunks here called Apollo Creed but satirically modeled, in all his extravagant and lucrative showmanship, on Mohammed Ali. In its straight-line development, in parallel, of the love story and the big fight, "Rocky" seems wonderfully guileless, but it is the innocence won of an artful sophistication crafty enough to conceal itself. The director was John G. Avildsen who, off of "Cry Uncle," "Joe" and "Save the Tiger," has learned how to do much with little and how to catch the sights, sounds and feelings, almost the aromas, of life as it is ordinarily lived in real places.

"Rocky" seems as brilliantly orchestrated as a fine if raucous symphony, alternating tumults and solitudes, humor (Rocky is a joke-maker, usually intentionally, as Marty and the Brando character weren't), anger, small rejections and small victories, building to an ending which is surprising, ingenious, logical and blissfully pleasing. (At the two screenings I've attended, "Rocky" got roaring, standing ovations the likes of which I can't ever remember at a movie before.)

The establishing of Rocky's lifestyle and his world, Philadelphia at its scruffiest, is daringly careful, deliberate and meticulous: a slugfest in the local church arena, the squalor of the dressing room, the bruised walk home down streets that are not mean but terminal, the monologue in his rooms, being deprived of his gym locker in favor of a more promising fighter, a chewing out by the shark and his taunting bodyguard-driver (Joe Sorbello).

But the birth of love, in its comedic way, is lyrically affecting. The first date on an ice rink, deserted on Thanksgiving night, is one of those indelible movie sequences. (It is also a product in part of a fortunate necessity. The budget did not allow for the extras the script called for but the scene works much better with the rink empty. The girl takes off her glasses and—it was ever so—is seen to be most tenderly beautiful. Talia Shire, twice nominated for Oscars before, is one of the film's several contenders this time, for her intelligent, sensitive and touching performance.

Rocky's training, revealing Stallone's own grueling five-month preparation for the part, is fascinating to watch. Thanks to a newly developed body-held camera, cinematographer James Crabe was able (without impossibly extensive tracking platforms) to follow Stallone jogging before dawn through all of Philadelphia, a literal opening-up which appropriately symbolizes the opening up of Rocky's world, and his chances. The exultant climax of the training is another unforgettable moment which gets well-deserved applause.

One of the strengths of "Rocky" is the relative freshness and unfamiliarity of most of its cast. All are talented professionals with considerable lists of credits, but you sense you are seeing them for the first time, as the characters they are intended to be, not as actors acting. The one very familiar face is Burgess Meredith's, as the sour old manager of the gym, a former fighter for whom all of the breaks have been bad, unless he can hitchhike on Rocky's luck. It is a vivid characterization, recalling his failing salesman in "Day of the Locust." But for all its skill, it is still identifiable as a performance and the one element you might have wished changed for the purposes of the ensemble.

For the rest, highest honors for the art that does not show itself as art: Carl Weathers as the champ, realizing from round one that he has taken on more than he can kid to the canvas, Burt Young as the brother who is dying inside and knows it, Thayer David as the promoter with a heart like the carbon steel vault of a bank, Spinell and Sorbello as the hoods.

Stallone's own performance is a once-in-a-lifetime coming together of man and material. He makes Rocky colorful, not too bright (although he and Ms. Shire brighten and blossom as events move forward—it is part of the pleasure of the fantasy) and altogether engrossing and heroic.

The film involves boxing, but it is not truly about boxing. ("Rocky" does not attack the sport but it is not an endorsement, either. It remains possible to hate the sport and love the picture.) It is much more about the redeeming and ennobling powers of real love and about the possibility of overcoming whatever is defeating in our fates or within ourselves. And how long, we may well ask, has it been since any movie—particularly any movie as credibly rooted in a grittily identifiable real world—was saying anything like that?

The movie is hardly less a miracle than the story it tells. Stallone, not overwhelmed with work, drafted his rough treatment and took it to a pal, Gene Kirkwood, who handily enough is a material-finder for the producing team of Robert Chartoff and Irwin Winkler. They elected to go ahead on a very tight budget (about $1.3 milllion) and even guaranteed the completion money themselves, which is unheard of among producers. If the film had gone over budget, they would have been stuck personally.

But all the endings seem certain to be happy for everyone involved. The street-flavored music (and the instantly memorable main theme) by

Bill Conti are just right. Richard Halsey was the editor, and the art direction by James H. Spencer may not make him Philadelphia's Man of the Year but is first-rate. Kirkwood is credited as executive producer for Chartoff and Winkler.

Bound for Glory

The range within which a filmmaker can create sensitive and insightful work has never ceased astonishing me. Having done "Shampoo," his look at a rather fragrant slice of contemporary life, Hal Ashby was back a year later with "Bound for Glory," a look at two crucial years in the life of Woody Guthrie, an angry troubadour in a diametrically different time, an America of hard times and thin hopes. As an act of portraiture of a man and his world, it remains a milestone film.

EVEN DURING THEIR PERIODS OF DARK and timid banality, the movies keep us hooked by their capacity for surprise, as an art form and as a commercial form.

"Rocky," in its unstarred and unpretentious way, is a surprise. And so, in terms of its cost, subject matter, structure, pace, length and serene defiance of what you would have said is ordinary commercial wisdom, is "Bound for Glory," which is one of this year's most admirable and triumphant surprises.

It may well be that just as "Save the Tiger" owed its existence in part to the money Paramount made on "The Godfather," "Bound for Glory" owes its uncompromised existence to the emboldening profits spun for United Artists by movies as different as "The Return of the Pink Panther" and "One Flew Over the Cuckoo's Nest," last year's largest, happiest surprise.

Woody Guthrie, a wandering, unionized minstrel out of Texas, radicalized by the Dust Bowl poverty and cruel unemployment of the late 1930s and 1940s, particularly among the migrant tides of farm workers he knew best, told it all in his episodic, anecdotal and candid autobiography, from which the movie takes its title.

Guthrie died in 1967 after a long bedridden battle with a wasting hereditary affliction called Huntington's Chorea (from which two of his daughters now suffer). But dozens of his songs went into the language and into the repertoires of a whole later generation of popular folk singers and groups. The name lived on, and "Bound for Glory" now provides the complicated personality (not nearly as simple as his catchy tunes) that goes with it.

Director Hal Ashby ("The Last Detail," "Shampoo") and screenwriter Robert Getchell ("Alice Doesn't Live Here Anymore") use two years' worth of the autobiography to reveal the making of Woody Guthrie and to paint, with an angry fidelity not seen since "The Grapes of Wrath," a portrait of Depression America in which he moved and in which he found his calling. He is at the start an unprosperous sign painter in the dying Dust Bowl town of Pampa, Texas, where most of the signs say FOR SALE and the residents, their flivvers piled high with household goods, are starting the slow pilgrimage toward dreams of bounty in California.

From the beginning it's an unposed and unconcealing portrait that we get of Woody and from Woody (who knew himself well and was too honest not to tell it), Ashby, Getchell and David Carradine, whose controlled and considered performance is an impressive achievement within the total achievement of the film.

Guthrie is married, has two small daughters, lives in crowded domesticity with a father, brother and sister. He fiddles at square dances, hangs around the filling station, whiles away the afternoons playing guitar at the local cafe and jumps at the chance for a little action with one of the local girls ("Things ain't dead here yet, after all"). He's a footloose loner in a foot-tied situation and it can't last. He leaves a note, grabs his hat and a clutch of paintbrushes and hitches a first ride toward Los Angeles and away from the despairs of home. (We've just watched a dust storm, an awesomely convincing special effect engineered by Albert Whitlock, who did much of the work on "Earthquake.")

The introduction to Guthrie is a measured series of tableaux, atmospheric and revealing, a mosaic more than a narration, and it asks a kind of readjustment from audiences conditioned by now to the jump-cut pace of television and many movies. But patience yields its pleasures—encounters with a traveler at the filling station, with a sick woman and a crazy man.

The slow journey to California is an introduction to the glories of the land and the tribulations of its workless wanderers. All of it has been interpreted in images of extraordinary power by Haskell Wexler, who catches in color—dust-hazed, sun-bleached, smoke-shadowed—the austere beauty and the feeling of humanity in extremis to be found in the black-and-white still photographs of Dorothea Lange, Walker Evans and the others who did their historic documentation for the Farm Security Administration in the 30s.

There are the long roadside waits for rides, the roadblocks over the California border turning back those who cannot show $50 in cash as proof they can support themselves for a while, the crowded freight cars and the waiting railroad detectives. And, in California, there are the soup kitchens and the sprawling shanty camps where hundreds of able-bodied men queue for a handful of jobs as low-paid pickers.

Hard times, against which Guthrie's weapons are his guitar and his indifference to (or his fear of) worldly possessions. Amidst a melee at a worker camp started by club-wielding goons, he meets a radio country-western singer (played by Ronny Cox) who is a fearless organizer but who can also handle the possessing world on its own terms. Through the organizer, Guthrie begins to find wider fame, singing on the radio, and also singing the gospel of a union for farm workers in the fields and at fund-raising cocktail parties (radical chic commenced early).

He strikes up with a rich widow (played with classy charm by Gail Strickland) but cuts out when it, too, begins to feel like possession. He imports his patiently uncomprehending wife (Melinda Dillon) and the children, but domesticity wears no better for him than it did before, not when the price of it is toning down his militant songs to satisfy the sponsors. He splits to go rambling again on what somebody else's lyric called side-door Pullman cars, and gets the whey kicked out of him for singing union in a fruit-packing plant.

The movie leaves him at a turning point—turning away from a nightclub gig that would have enriched him but made him a fake cowboy, turning east for Manhattan and the international fame (though not the riches) he would find as a crusading troubadour who sang both the glories ("This Land Is Your Land") and the ills of it. There would later be another wife and other children (including Arlo of "Alice's Restaurant"), recordings and concert tours, sing-alongs and hootenannies, but the movie's two years are the crucial ones.

The aura of dedication and loving care that emanates from "Bound for Glory" is not often found anywhere in film. Guthrie's longtime manager and close friend, Harold Leventhal, was an involved co-producer with Robert Blumofe. Yet the movie seeks constantly to reveal Guthrie neither as a mythic figure nor an unblemished hero but as an exceptional and contradictory man, capable of compassion for the masses and of callous disregard of family obligations, a lover of earthly pleasures who could also courageously put them at risk and forswear them. Guthrie was probably more politicized than the film makes him out to be, yet he can be seen to be part of the distinctively native grass-roots radical tradition. And, although there is no doubt where the film's own sympathies lie, it remains a portrait rather than a polemic.

To the end, "Bound for Glory" remains a succession of strong scenes, linked by and disclosing the evolving character of Carradine as Guthrie, wry, quizzical, quiet-spoken, strong-minded beneath the easygoing and at times Gary Cooperish charm. It is an earnest and hardworking performance by Carradine, who comes a long way from Kung Fu.

The other performances are hardly less remarkable, and "Bound for Glory," like "Rocky," reopens again the question of the necessity of star casting and raises welcome doubts. Melinda Dillon is sensationally real as the devoted wife stuck with the bills and the kids while her man goes strumming off to his crusades. (The versatile Ms. Dillon is unrecognizable in a wildly different second role in the film, as a black-wigged Memphis Sue, a twangy country-western singer with whom Guthrie does a radio show.) Gail Strickland is equally affecting as the gracious woman Guthrie uses and discards. Randy Quaid, the luckless sailor from "The Last Detail," is good again as a luckless migrant worker, and Elizabeth Macey is a wisp of iron as his wife.

Throughout all the supporting cast, notably including all the extras, Ashby has found a gallery of just-right faces: Mary Kay Place and Sondra Blake as one-night fancies; Ji-Tu Cumbuka as a freight-riding friend, John Lehne as a radio station executive, Lee McLaughlin as a crazy man, and Miriam Byrd Nethery as a sick woman.

Most of the music is Guthrie's, performed in Guthrie's own idiom by Carradine himself. But composer Leonard Rosenman has also woven Guthrie's themes into a full orchestra score, often at slowed and poignant tempos. The score, too, is a courageous choice (another among them all) and it works—lifting the film beyond the events of the moment and into the longer considerations of history, matching the timeless sweep of the landscapes Guthrie celebrated, reminding us that Guthrie was more than another itinerant minstrel.

The deliberate pace, like the mosaic structure, is demanding but rewarding. (Amazingly, the executives at UA encouraged Ashby to restore several minutes to what he had presented as his final cut.) The final running time is just over two and a half hours, yet a second viewing proved to be even more satisfying than the first.

Elegant may not have been the word for Guthrie, but he is now the subject of an elegantly crafted, hugely beautiful and interesting film, which reveals a loving integrity in every frame.

1977

Annie Hall

This was Woody Allen's twelfth film, including two early ones to which he was a contributor. His one-a-year pace has made him the country's most prolific and continually surprising director. It's hard to think of another major filmmaker whose career has shown such an ever-growing command of the medium, not only its technical aspects but its power to convey the subtle stresses of contemporary relationships and metropolitan living. The stand-up comic has become one of our most thoughtful observers.

MARRIAGES AND OTHER RELATIONSHIPS often end not with a bang but a withering away of whatever it was that made the relationship work. And in the time beyond the end there is neither hatred nor despair but a shared affection that is strong enough to do almost anything except make the relationship work again.

"Annie Hall," Woody Allen's newest and most personal film, is more than anything else a love poem in the form of a heartfelt comic Valentine to a romance that was, and, being over, can now be seen with a calm, considered admiration and gratitude. Not without pangs and a taste of bittersweet and now and again a twinge of what if. But the past tense of *que será, será* is "what used to be, used to be," and growing up is getting to know it, accepting that lives move on.

"Annie Hall" is not only Allen's newest film, it is also his best. It seems the most directly and obviously autobiographical. His character is called Alvy Singer but he would not be startled to see Woody Allen in the mirror. He is a stand-up comedian working the college circuit most profitably and making the jokes mostly on himself as a postgraduate neurotic signaling to all the girls around in the coffeehouse code words of psychiatry, comp. lit and Erica Jong.

But the jokes, which are several and marvelous, are more transparent than ever as a cover for the character's real angers and concerns—his needs to escape and succeed, to be secure, to tell the sharp-toothed truth about everything he finds preposterous and pretentious around him. There are jokes about Singer's paranoia over the anti-Semitism that he detects in the society, but it is impossible not to feel the rage and the fear beneath the jokes. You sense, not as a message but as a reflection of deep feelings, that Singer may become less insecure, but never entirely secure.

It is a movie in the form of a personal statement. And after swift silent titles, austere white letters on black, Allen in a waist shot addresses the camera for a monologue that tries to find the truths of a life in old jokes. (Groucho wouldn't join a club, he said, that would accept him as a member. Singer/Allen wonders if he is incapable of relationships with girls who would have him.)

The autobiographical impact of "Annie Hall" is doubled (approximately) because Annie Hall is the vibrant and splendid actress Diane Keaton, who is, of course, not only Allen's most frequent costar but also formerly a romance and presently the object of the affection revealed herein. Whether, as could well be, not one of the delicious detailings of the script (which Allen wrote with Marshall Brickman) has a basis in historical fact, you have to believe that the fever chart of the friendship cannot have read greatly different, and that in the making of the movie there must have been odd echoings for them both.

The coordinates are imagined, that is, but the sweep of the graph is true. It is also quite universal in this day, which is why "Annie Hall" becomes more than a succession of sharp scenes and fine lines; it becomes a love story of high emotional power—a comedy with tears, or close to them—that many among us can identify with.

Allen uses all the devices of the movie form—the direct address to the camera; having children speak as the adults they would become (the children being his least favorite grade-school contemporaries); standing in the scenes as he and Keaton act out memories or dramatize fantasies. With all the trickeries, "Annie Hall" takes only a fleeting hour and a half, but carries us from a childhood home (a quaking shambles built beneath the roller coaster at Coney Island) to a 1972 now, two marriages and several relationships later.

The movie belongs primarily to Allen and the wonderfully adept comedienne that Diane Keaton is. But there are also microscopically accurate portrayals in support, one of them by Tony Roberts as an actor pal who goes Hollywood and is last seen wearing an asbestos bee bonnet to keep off alpha rays that age a person. The other women include Janet Margolin as an early wife—an ambitious literateuse who finds joy in the

New York Review of Books and only there. Carol Kane is another wife, discovered at an Adlai rally and reduced to a cultural stereotype, Barnard, dissertation and all, by Allen in a funny expressing of love at first sight. Shelley Duvall is a contributor to *Rolling Stone* who is into everything except reality. Singer-composer Paul Simon plays a record producer who catalyzes the end of a relationship but who also lets Allen unload his acid asides on the Southern California lifestyle, on which he is perhaps the most devastating commentator since an earlier Allen, Fred, famously remarked that it was a swell place to live if you were an orange. Allen, Woody, asks what we are to make of a culture whose prime achievement is letting you turn right on red.

Another of the supporting players is Marshall McLuhan, who helps Allen enact one of his fantasies, stepping out of a theater queue (they're all waiting to see "The Sorrow and the Pity") to berate another customer whose opinions (about McLuhan) have been driving Allen batty. McLuhan as McLuhan is perfect, an unbeatable twinning of medium and message.

In the movie's most biting sequence, Allen visits Keaton's prototypically WASPish family in the midwest, an exercise in culture shock unmatched since "The Heartbreak Kid." Colleen Dewhurst and Donald Symington are the parents, Helen Ludlam a bigoted old grandmother whom Allen sees seeing him as a Hassidic Jew, flat hat, beard and ringlets, long black coat and all. Christopher Walken plays Keaton's uptight brother.

Jonathan Munk plays the young Allen, sharp-tongued from an early age, and Johnny Haymer helps Allen have his delayed say about the Borscht circuit comics, loud and awful, for whom Allen wrote jokes before he realized he could do it better himself. Haymer is them all, wrapped in one.

There are lovely lines to remember. Allen watches Keaton park after their first ride and says, "It's okay, we can walk to the curb from here." But more than in any previous Allen film, it is the feeling that stays in mind.

Allen has enlarged his command of the movie form every time out, from the gags of the early work to the elaborated exercises in style of "Everything You Always Wanted to Know About Sex" to the ambitious undertakings in time fore and aft of "Sleeper" and "Love and Death." "Play It Again, Sam" got closer to the soul, in its guarded way, of any of the films until "Annie Hall." It shows a control, confidence and maturity, an ability to let the guard down and reveal the man beneath the clown mask, and it is a great pleasure to watch.

Charles H. Joffe produced. The excellent photography is by Gordon Willis, the tight editing by Ralph Rosenblum, and Mel Bourne was the wide-ranging art director.

Star Wars

Even my enthusiastic review could not predict that the "Star Wars" trilogy and its re-release in 1997 would propel George Lucas past Steven Spielberg as the largest-grossing filmmaker in history (for a month or two, anyway). Nor that his film would launch a new wave of special effects films, nor that his investment of hundreds of millions in computer images and digital technology generally would turn the industry inside out again. Harrison Ford said on the "Today" show, "Who knew that this simple country priest would grow up to be pope?"

GEORGE LUCAS HAS BEEN CONDUCTING a lifelong double love affair, embracing the comic strips on the one hand (or with one arm) and the movies on and with the other. Now he has united his loves in "Star Wars," the year's most razzle-dazzling family movie, an exuberant and technically astonishing space adventure in which the galactic tomorrows of Flash Gordon are the setting for conflicts and events that carry the suspiciously but splendidly familiar ring of yesterday's Gene Autry serials.

The sidekicks are salty, squatty robots instead of leathery old cowpokes who scratch their whiskers and say "Aw, shucks" a lot, and the gunfighters square off with laser swords instead of Colt revolvers. But it is all and gloriously one, the mythic and simple world of the good guys vs. the bad guys (identifiable without a scorecard or footnotes), the rustlers and the land grabbers, the old generation saving the young with a last heroic gesture which drives home the messages of courage and conviction.

There are inspirations (rather than borrowings) from the other movie forms, including the swashbuckler with its captive and endangered princess, the monster film with its creatures both good and evil, and almost any form with its second male lead wavering between cynicism and idealism but making the right choice in the very nick of time.

Tributes to the movie past have often been campy spoofs which suggest that it was all rather quaint. "Star Wars" is a celebration which, in the ultimate tribute to the past, has a robust and free-wheeling life of its own, needing no powers of recollection to be fully appreciated. It employs some of the dramatic devices out of the past for the good and simple reason that they worked well (and probably because they evoked strong and positive responses in the souls of those of us watching).

The magical mechanics of the movies seem to have been invented for simulating space travel, as Georges Melies saw before 1900 and as Stanley Kubrick demonstrated so spectacularly in "2001: A Space Odyssey" in 1968.

Lucas's film cost significantly less than Kubrick's even after inflation. But the small army of inspired technical-effects creators he assembled has worked wizardries in some ways more lavish and varied than Kubrick's own. (There are seventy individuals and five firms cited in the credits for the miniature and optical effects unit alone, in addition to the nearly four dozen creators listed in the main technical credits. The cast list, conversely, has to include bit parts to reach a scant two dozen.)

"Star Wars" is Buck Rogers with a doctoral degree but not a trace of neuroticism or cynicism, a slam-bang, rip-roaring gallop through a distantly future world full of exotic vocabularies, creatures and customs, existing cheek by cowl with the boy and girl next door and a couple of friendly leftovers from the planet of the apes and possibly one from Oz (a Tin Woodman robot who may have got a gold-plating as a graduation present).

After a once-upon-a-future time crawl establishing the story line—the brave rebels encamped on a secret star and darting out to do battle with the vastly larger imperial forces—Lucas plunges into the thick of things. His script takes it for granted we know the lingo (we don't but that's the fun of it) and who's who. We catch on quickly.

Mark Hamill is our likable young hero, a sort of interstellar Jack Armstrong, rocketing around in the space-time equivalent of a Ford roadster and eager to try bigger stuff. He's the orphan of a warrior who died bravely at the treasonable hand of a friend (David Prowse). Events thrust Hamill into cahoots with his father's old comrade in arms (Alec Guinness) and with the princess (Carrie Fisher) trying to get a desperately important secret message back to the rebels. It could undo the Imperials and their cruel leader (Peter Cushing). Harrison Ford operates a sort of nonscheduled space ship; no questions asked about cargo or passengers. Just the cocky sort to take our friends through hostile Indian country to the next settlement. (Through hostile space to the next star, that is; the old ways creep in.)

What happens and how it all ends hardly matters. The narrative pace is jet-propelled or rocket-thrust and the invention is continuous, the crafts and sets and space complexes genuinely amazing in their minute detailing and believability.

During production, Lucas said he was after a used future—a tomorrow that looked lived in and dented and tarnished. And, fittingly, one of the charms of the movie is that much of the gear does look as if it should be run through the nearest capsule wash or be had at with the chrome polish.

Some of the exteriors were shot amidst the lunar landscapes of Tunisia and Death Valley, so that the visual reminders of the dry gulch and box canyon West are inescapable. And there really are those rustlers, dealing in stolen robots and other hot goods. If it is the larger-than-life fun which the movies have been and still are, Lucas provides majesty as well. John Williams has a score of unstinting dimension, soaring string sections and thundering basses and brilliant horns, which, performed by the London Symphony Orchestra for the superlative sound system, lifts you out of your seat.

The finale borrows from the battle films at their most bravely hokey—the shrinking band of good guys fighting against ever-longer odds until there is only one chance left at saving the day. The uses of the movie past extend to the calm after battle when heroes take their just salutes and we leave with the cheering thought that there may well be further adventures awaiting us all.

Lucas's script and his film are a warm mixture of remarkable professionalism and an ingratiating innocence that is almost childlike (the squat robot is called Artoo-Detoo, for R2D2). Then again, many of us in our young days read Flash Gordon (envying Alec Raymond's way with a drawing pen) and Buck Rogers, and believed with childlike faith (now seen to have been justified) that this was not yet the way things were, but would be. Lucas has taken us all back to the future and he has done it in a style both wonderfully ambitious and blessedly unpretentious. His characters speak neither in biblical cadences or an ornate Slav-Oriental accent but in a wisecracking colloquial vein that derives equally from Cockney and Kansas City.

The awesome list of technical credits almost defies individual applause. But clearly production designer John Barry was a central shaping influence (he also did "A Clockwork Orange"). Cinematographer Gil Taylor, with a past as various as "Dr. Strangelove," "A Hard Day's Night" and "Frenzy," mastered a whole new range of challenges. The special effects crucially involved John Stears ("Thunderball" and other Bond films) and John Dykstra, who worked on "Silent Running." The makeup men included Stuart Freeborn, who turned Albert Finney into Hercule Poirot, and Rick Baker, who created the later King Kong. A western barroom scene is populated with mutants and monsters that are a fantasist's dream of heaven.

It is, all in all, hard to think of a place or an age group that would not respond to the enthusiastic inventiveness with which Lucas has enshrined his early loves. "Star Wars" proves again that there is no corporate substitute for the creative passion of the individual filmmaker.

New York, New York

Daring, defined as going riskily against the audience's conventional expections, was a characteristic of some of the best films of the 70s. Occasionally it made the films admirable rather than instantly likable. Scorsese's film had lots of music and was set in the world of music, but it was not a musical. It re-tailored some of the film musical stereotypes to become an essay on male chauvinism vs. female resistance and resilience in a telling that was cool to the point of chilliness.

THE PRELIMINARY CREDITS are in a slim and elegant typeface that might have been designed for Fred Astaire and Ginger Rogers and intended to convey a particular kind of sophisticated innocence. The name of the movie then rises like an additional big city skyline behind a night aerial shot of blinking Manhattan, thereby hinting of a slightly gaudier but still innocent screen vision of life. But Martin Scorsese's "New York, New York" is nothing so simple as a tappy-toe trip through a tuneful past. It is (among other things) a revisionist view of innocence, and in particular it is a scathing portrayal of the male innocence now called chauvinism and here revealed in all its cruel and damaging stupidity.

"New York, New York" is in all ways a surprising work, both brilliant and grueling, a nostalgically accurate account of the music scene in the immediate postwar years when the big bands were fading in favor of vocalists and bop. But it is also a stormy and bitingly well-observed story of a relationship which becomes "Who's Afraid of Virginia Woolf?" orchestrated for thirteen pieces and a girl singer.

Now and again the movie seems like two forms or two periods joined somewhat uneasily together: the sing-me-a-dream Hollywood musical about show business lashed to the tell-it-like-it-is social and psychological realism of a later day (indeed, of Scorsese's day, as depicted in "Mean Streets," rather more than in "Taxi Driver"). It is a genuine musical drama—the music executed with uncommon verve and fidelity to its era, the drama watched with uncompromised honesty.

There are two soloists, and Robert De Niro and Liza Minnelli give performances that convey intensity, consistency, depth, charm and pathos. For De Niro, his wisecracking but ruthlessly egocentric tenor sax player is another confirmation of his versatility and dedication, most notably his self-effacing willingness to be actively unlovable. Minnelli (whose rise from band singer to movie and nightclub star gives the story resonances of "A Star Is Born") does the best dramatic performance of her film career to date. And in the role's bittersweet blending of private unhappiness with roaring public acclaim, there are the most obvious echoes yet of her mother, enhanced by the most evident vocal resemblance (the full-volume vibrato especially) she has recorded so far. (Minnelli is reported to have said that it is the role more than any other she wishes her mother had lived to see, and there is no doubt that Judy Garland would have been very proud indeed.)

The script, written by Earl Mac Rauch and Mardik Martin from a story by Rauch, commences on VJ-Day in Times Square with De Niro just out of uniform and into the most civilian civvies he could find—white pants, two-tone shoes and an incandescent souvenir-of-New York sports shirt. He makes toward the hotel ballroom where Tommy Dorsey (William Tole, who looks and plays amazingly like Dorsey) is doing those fine charts on "Song of India" and "Opus One." There won't be a dry eye over fifty in the house.

Looking on in a USO uniform is Minnelli, sitting it out while her pal (Kathi McGinnis) decorates the dance floor. De Niro, seeking whom he may devour, comes on strong, and it is an amusing line of chatter. It is almost meeting cute in the Hollywood tradition, except that already there is an edge of discomfort or uneasiness. The come-on is a little too strong and persistent, and impersonal. The tension, it grows clear, is what Scorsese and his writers are going on about. The story marches on in a kind of split-level or multi-level way, observing the rubrics of the movie musical but with a new dissonance you do not so much hear as feel: two funny scenes in hotel lobbies, an audition that she saves (establishing a pattern of wisdom vs. male arrogance), necking in the rain. Romance, all on his terms. They join a dance band, fictional, whose leader is played with wonderful sardonic credibility by Georgie Auld, the big-band veteran of the Artie Shaw wars and much more, who also blows the sensational tenor-sax solos fingered by De Niro. One of the not-so-small miracles of "New York, New York" is that De Niro took pains to learn the saxophone, so that he looks like he's playing and not just wiggling his fingers (which is what usually happened in Hollywood musicals).

The nostalgic amusements of the dying big-band era—the tedium of the bus rides between one-night stands, the awfulness of the ballrooms and the cigar-chewing cupidity of the proprietors, the soap opera antics of the sidemen—play off against the sharpening portrait of De Niro and of a relationship that is heading for the shoals, as probably becomes evident too soon for the picture's good. All of De Niro's presumptions of male superiority, of the greater importance of his work, his career, his needs— emotional and other—are so deep-bred and inherent he can't even think to question them. A later generation sees this quickly enough. The matter for speculation is whether even a character so accurately perceived for his time would have remained so steadfastly and blindly chauvinist, despite all the evidence of its cost to himself as well as to others. You wonder, and regret, that the writers didn't let him wise up just a little.

Along the way there are scenes of brutal power, confrontations between De Niro and Minnelli in which their mutual needs ricochet futilely off his arrogance, and the suspense is how long a traditional female submissiveness will stand for it. One of their scenes, a pummeling fight in a '41 Buick late at night on the eve of a childbirth, has a lacerating ferocity that nothing in the hothouse terrors of "Virginia Woolf" can match. Friends, we have come several choruses beyond "Orchestra Wives."

The rise of the Minnelli figure parallels the shifts in the popular music scene, and her career gives Scorsese a chance to do a fine send-up of the Hollywood production number, an item called "Happy Endings"— one of several originals, including the excellent title song, by John Kander and Fred Ebb—fitting with appropriate irony into the backstage story. The documenting of her career leads him as well to a vast nightclub scene with a belting finale in the various traditions of the movies and of Judy Garland's final appearances. The ending has its own suspense and it is not for a reviewer to give it away; and saying that it is an affirmative ending does not give anything away. (What in the circumstances constitutes affirmative may divide the women in the audience, as well as the women and the men.)

"New York, New York" is a very long movie, about two and a half hours by present measure, and it once was four hours long. It is here and there possible to guess but not to miss what must have been shot and discarded. Even now there are scenes, particularly those that provide further evidence of De Niro's self-destructive mix of superiority and jealousy, that could be quickened to spare the audience the additional pain of a point already well made.

The technical sheen of the film is stunning. The design by Boris Leven gives the feel of a period now gone, and Laszlo Kovacs's cinematography seems to have been toned gold for memory, notably in the early sequences. Many of the scenes are on a grand scale, and the film moves easily from intimacy to spectacle and back again.

The other performances are all shadowed by De Niro and Minnelli, but very honorable mentions are due to Lionel Stander as an agent, Barry Primus as the piano player who remains a close pal throughout and Mary Kay Place as a parody of the bad band singer, who follows Minnelli into the band. Diahnne Abbott has an attractive cameo as a Harlem singer in the image of Billy Holiday. Don Calfa does an excellent bit as a record producer not about to be out-glibbed by De Niro. Auld, as noted, is authenticity itself as the band leader, and some of the movie's most amusing moments recall the Pal Joey stories by John O'Hara, an earlier unsentimental look at the band and nightclub business.

Although De Niro's cast name is Jimmy Doyle, it is not hard to see "New York, New York" as a direct continuation of Scorsese's very personal work. It is in a real sense a movie about New York, in all its vitality, allure and cruelty as well, and also a story from a male-dominated ethnic heritage more specifically Latin than Irish, of which the De Niro figure is product and victim. Doyle is a thin disguise.

"New York, New York" further establishes Scorsese as one of that handful of young American directors of great and increasing command of the craft, with a strong and independent vision, and something to say. What he is dealing with in "New York, New York," despite the period charm and the irresistible music, is stern stuff, an unconventional musical, an unyielding romantic melodrama, a dazzling but finally chilly work that must engross and sober its audiences. Those sax solos are noodling and warm and lovely, but they mirror someone else's soul.

Irwin Winkler and Robert Chartoff were the enterprising producers.

Close Encounters of the Third Kind

What I should have commented on more forcefully was the fact that Spielberg's extraterrestrials were friendly critters so far as anyone could tell—a distinct change from the sci-fi/fantasy tradition of hostile aliens eager to steal our water, blood or souls or just destroy us. Benignity was so well-received that Spielberg used it five years later to make "E.T." one of the biggest box office successes in history.

STEVEN SPIELBERG'S "Close Encounters of the Third Kind" is assured the annual Godot Award as the most awaited movie of the year. The subject matter and the security blanket Spielberg wrapped around it have made millions eager for a peek and now, by damn, the full look is at hand.

And "Close Encounters" proves to be a magic act with dramatic interludes. The interludes range downward from so-so (the movie is oddly like "Jaws" in that way) but the magic is so thrilling that nothing else matters much. The special effects conceived by Spielberg and executed by Douglas Trumbull and a staff that seems to number in the hundreds are dazzling and wondrous. That's not surprising; the surprise is that "Close Encounters" is so well-leavened with humor. Despite its cost (said to have been $19 million ultimately, with additional millions for advertising and promotion) and despite its scope, "Close Encounters" stays light on its legs, mystical and reverential but not solemn. It is a warm celebration, positive and pleasurable. The humor is folksy and slapstick rather than cerebral, as if to confirm that our encounter is with a populist vehicle.

The effects resemble those in "2001: A Space Odyssey" and "Star Wars." You can't, after all, make westerns without horses, or science fantasy without sky and stars and brilliant ships sketched in an approaching tomorrow. But "Close Encounters" is not Stanley Kubrick's film, with its ecstatic and incomprehensible mysteries of infinite time and space, and not George Lucas's, with its primal wars of good and evil fought in some futuristic past. Spielberg's movie says that once upon the present time the visitors from an unidentified elsewhere arrived upon earth and manifested themselves, raising hell with the electrical gadgetry and assorted souls in and about Muncie, Indiana. The earth-shaking reverberations caused by the spacecraft's energy system (which makes model trains and vacuum cleaners roar alive unbidden but amusingly) are made to seem more startling than terrifying. It seems significant that the aliens are presumed to be friendly rather than hostile—as if to say that intelligent life elsewhere is surely too intelligent to go in for the kind of bloodletting that has characterized planet Earth from the start.

Spielberg symbolizes this trust in the slight and wide-eyed person of a child (Cary Guffey), who could not be more pleased, amidst the incandescence and the roaring, than if a circus parade had passed in front of his house. It is also as if the communication between Them (whoever they may be) and us is innocent and loving.

Despite the best efforts of the Air Force (lampooned in the film) to shoot them down, the idea of UFOs cannot be permanently disproved, and the popular imagination stays tantalizingly alive to them. Spielberg's fantasy is a widely appealing game of What If, played without the menace of the bug-eyed monsters and galactic villains that gave Flash Gordon and Buck Rogers such trouble.

The excitements begin amidst blowing dust in Mexico, where in a remote desert some fighter planes missing since World War II suddenly reappear, engines ready to go at the touch of a switch. François Truffaut as an excitable scientist seems to know what it may mean, but we still don't. Then things go bang in the Indiana night: a boy's electric toys, all the appliances, and manifestations and bright lights and a shaking, rattling and rolling as before the doom. Melinda Dillon is startled, partly by her son's delight at what should be so scary. Teri Garr is alarmed, and her husband (Richard Dreyfuss), a power company worker, has to leave her and try to discover what has blacked out half the state. His van nearly shakes to pieces and goes dead, and mailboxes do a shimmy and there are fireballs arcing across the sky. Dreyfuss and Dillon and a handful of others have been communicated with; they feel it but don't really know it. Except that there is this vision, a dream half remembered, and a sawed-off mountain.

The Spielberg of "Jaws" continues to be a director (and now a writer) of effects rather than characters or relationships. When the script lets Trumbull and his associate Merlins and a platoon of the world's best cinematographers (Vilmos Zsigmond principally, and Bill Fraker, Douglas Slocombe, John Alonzo and Laszlo Kovacs), strut their stuff and the Superdome-sized saucers wheel and hover and turn, it is zowie time at the Bijou.

Then again, a whole sequence in which Dreyfuss builds his dream peak in the living room from mud and shrubbery is so forced and silly it nearly deranges all the rest of the movie. Dillon as another true believer has to cry a lot and Teri Garr has to disbelieve but trust a lot, up to the uprooting of the shrubs.

Although the script has its fun with the pish-tushing bureaucrats, it

does little to give any real credibility to the reactions, governmental, jour-
nalistic or even personal, to the goings-on. A couple of fishermen in Mis-
sissippi (a famous early UFO report) is one thing; half a state and unim-
peachable witnesses is quite another. The mystical pull on Dreyfuss and
the others never becomes quite the parable it was presumably intended
to be. Still, the movie builds toward a time of grandeur that suggests either the opening of the Olympics or Midnight Mass in St. Peter's Square,
and even if Spielberg milks it entirely too long, it is still affecting and uplifting.

John Williams's music is crucial, and once again he seems to work as
effectively when big things are required as anyone now writing. There is a
good deal of sustained and tremulous tone—the quivering hum we have
come to accept as the sound wave of the future, here bridging into the
majesty of Handel's *Messiah* revisted (not literally, of course). It is powerful and hugely contributory.

In terms of bringing off its intentions, "Close Encounters" ranks
somewhat lower on a scale of 10 than either "2001" or "Star Wars." But it
is different from either and may be on to a more popularly intriguing
theme: not Will we find them, but Will they find us? A longer synopsis
would trim the surprises. The mysteries and miracles visited upon
Muncie are bewitching, and at its most effective, "Close Encounters of
the Third Kind" is marvelously clever. Since reviews are now said to be
affecting stock prices, my private Dow-Jones closing might be that I
wouldn't know whether to buy, but I wouldn't sell.

The movie was produced by Julia Phillips and Michael Phillips.

1978

Coming Home

Hollywood made up for lost time in its attentions to Vietnam, the "grunts'" war never better depicted than in Oliver Stone's "Platoon" in 1986, but "Coming Home" remains unique in the intensity of its look at lives forever changed by the war. As I said in the review, it was one of those minefield films that could have self-destructed by putting a foot wrong. It didn't.

IT IS TOO LATE FOR A MOVIE OF ARGUMENT for or against the Vietnam war. Whatever strong feelings may survive, the fact is that a national consensus about that bloody and divisive struggle was finally evolved, a consensus born of anger, despair, disillusion and a weariness in the face of all the costs of the war. But it is not too late for a movie to remind us of what some of those costs were in physical and spiritual terms, or for a movie to dramatize that shift in the national consciousness that made the American withdrawal both possible and inevitable.

The Vietnam movies, avoided by the industry during the conflict (except for "The Green Berets") because there was then no consensus, yet no way for a film *not* to take a point of view, are now emerging. It is hard to believe that any will be more intimate and more moving as a study of the war's impact on individual lives than "Coming Home."

The time is 1968, the place is Los Angeles. Jon Voight is a Marine sergeant who has come back from 'Nam a paraplegic, ferociously embittered to the near edge of madness. There is a long and chaotic sequence in which he careens through the wards, belly down on a wheeled stretcher, propelling himself with a cane, roaring with pain and frustration, and flailing at everyone and everything in reach. It is a wrenching and unforgettable spectacle.

Jane Fonda is the wife of a gung-ho and highly ambitious Marine officer (Bruce Dern), who is just leaving for the war with no illusions that it is a picnic, but no doubts that it is just and every confidence that it is crucial to a good career. Fonda, drawn into hospital volunteer work by a chance acquaintance (Penelope Milford) who is waiting for her own man (Robert Ginty) to come home, discovers in Voight a high school football hero for whom she had led cheers.

Directed by Hal Ashby, "Coming Home" was written by Waldo Salt and Robert C. Jones (who had previously been an editor on several of Ashby's films) from a story by Nancy Dowd. Dowd, who did the script of last year's flawed but well-observed "Slap Shot," had worked on the story with Fonda herself and Bruce Gilbert, the film's associate producer. Whose inputs are whose, it is not possible to say. What matters is that the end result is a difficult but very affecting love story, which stays believable from start to finish because of the accretion of details and the restraint and earnestness of the performances.

"Coming Home" is undeniably a rhetorical film. Voight, although he had gone to Vietnam as gung-ho as Dern, has come back angry and disillusioned if not really radicalized, and as a one-man, one-time protest against the continuing war he chains himself to the gates of the Marine installation. It earns him a brief moment in the headlines and on the eleven o'clock news, and permanent surveillance by the FBI, a reminder of the paranoia that was also a consequence of the war.

Yet the story does not so much fight the old specific battles, or play an empty game of "we told you so," as it does lament the status of the war's long-term casualties, the maimed in body and spirit largely ignored by a society which has gone on to other things. The sense of wasting away of hope, which also figured in "Heroes," is very strong.

"Coming Home" is a passionate antiwar statement—anti all war—and Voight, addressing a high school assembly, provides the movie its most rhetorical passage. And while antiwar sentiments have a history of being used very selectively, depending on who was being aggressed by whom, Voight in his wheelchair in tears is a sitting symbol who cannot be dismissed from conscience.

There are movies which are like minefields, in that they could put a foot wrong at almost every step and blow their intentions sky-high with a scene or an event both gratuitous and beyond all reasonable credibility. "Coming Home" has its chances, but again and again Ashby and his associates seem to choose the right option (which, despite the movie's big events, is most often for restraint). Not invariably. A beery and unattractive homecoming seems almost too gross to be convincing and a suicide is almost too appropriately symbolic of society's inability to reestablish contact with its veterans (and vice versa). The movie's last symbol is also too right-on symbolic.

Yet what is most notable about the movie involving some of the industry's most outspoken talents—Jane Fonda herself, writer Waldo Salt, cinematographer Haskell Wexler among them—is its final sense of resolution, of compassion rather than of rage, and of change.

Dern has played men at the limits of their control so often that preimage works against him here, creating a kind of expectancy which obscures the subtler transformations that go on inside the character. He is a man doubly betrayed and he can't take it, but the result is not craziness but a kind of cold sane seeing which is even crueler. Dern delivers it with his usual high professionalism, if only he and we had not been so near the territory before. For Voight (who ironically was first set to do the Dern role), the part is the grand challenge that has been eluding him ever since his triumphant and astonishing performance in "Midnight Cowboy." In his ragings and then in love and in a calm acceptance of an irrevocable destiny, Voight gives a mature and intelligent portrayal that is acting at its affecting and indelible best.

Jane Fonda is this time the catalyst, the figure who does not so much shape events as set them in motion and who is herself then shaped by those events. The marks of her performance, as of Voight's, are of a particular maturity, of a changed consciousness made visible. She acts with a self-effacing restraint that conceals the craft but suffuses the portrait with earnestness and warmth.

Although it is basically a three-character film, there are very good supporting performances by Robert Carradine (at twenty-three the youngest of his talented family) as a vet who can't get it all back together. Penelope Milford, briefly seen in "Valentino," is very sympathetic as the girl trying to help her brother mend while she waits for her man to come back (and maybe marry her). She is world-wise and realistic but not cynical, and it is a fleeting but dimensional role.

There is a very large supporting cast. The notes list an additional eighty-six names, which could be a record for what is an intimate drama but which may attest to an uncommonly collaborative feeling in the making of "Coming Home." The list includes George Roberts and Bob Ott as FBI men and Stacey Pickren as a hooker who comes to visit Voight. Voight and Fonda have a love scene that is both powerfully erotic and impeccably handled. It leaves no doubt that "Coming Home" is a love story.

The score is a pastiche of the hit records of those times, full of memories and singularly effective.

Ashby has worked with material as different as "The Landlord," "Harold and Maude," "Bound for Glory" and now, "Coming Home."

What I think they have had in common is a feeling of cohesion and control, and a special sensibility for performance. Jerome Hellman, who produced "Midnight Cowboy," was the producer of "Coming Home" and it reflects not least his own meticulous enthusiasm.

Interiors

"Interiors" could qualify as one of the bravest films of the decade, because Allen was deliberately going against the core of his own success to try a film heavily serious and distinctly humorless. The culture shock was too great for audiences and for many critics who found it pretentious and cried, "Bring back the jokes." Even Allen admitted later it might have been a bit dark. But it is brilliantly done on its own terms. Later he would mix light and dark with great success.

IF INGMAR BERGMAN AND Eugene O'Neill had ever collaborated on a movie it might not have been markedly different—in the best sense—from Woody Allen's somber, intense and startling new work, "Interiors." Like Bergman's "Cries and Whispers," in particular, "Interiors" is, among much else, an absolutely masterful use of space, shape and color to convey atmospheres and states of feeling.

Like the greatest of O'Neill's dramas, "Interiors" explores the psyches of a self-centered, self-pitying, self-destructive and mutually lacerating family. It is Allen's achievement that he commands our fascinated attention to a wretched lot of neurotics who are sensitive only to their own needs, but whose sufferings (he makes us see and feel) are real enough and, in one instance, truly pathetic.

It seems, all of it, a startling departure for Allen from the humor that established him. There is nothing like a joke from moody start to moody finish and the humor, such as it is, is seized upon as funnier than it is because it serves as temporary relief to these wrought-up doings. But I don't find the departure so unexpected as it presumes to be. Allen's growing assurance and resourcefulness as a filmmaker have been chartable from the start. He has progressed, in essence, from photographing his verbal jokes to photographing his sight gags to his ambitious if uneven parodies of film style in "Everything You Always Wanted to Know About

Sex" to the more elaborate physical comedy of "Sleeper" to the shadowy and poignant humor of "Annie Hall," in which Allen's serious concerns with love and death and the death of love were more apparent behind the thin mask of jokes than ever before. Now he has dropped the mask of comedy entirely and some of his admirers have already decided that the lack of disguise is not perfect at all.

It must have been a strain. Certainly it is a perilous high-wire act for the artist, because material of this emotional intensity lends itself to unintended parody unless the seriousness is meticulously maintained. This material is specially fraught with peril for Allen because it is full of the self-analytic jargon he has had such sport with in his earlier work. But he has brought it off, in a movie of amazing uncompromised purity. And as a piece of the filmmaker's art, it is thrilling. All of the performances are notable, but the portrayal by Geraldine Page is simply unforgettable. And if the austerely beautiful images by Gordon Willis do not bring him the Academy attention he was denied for "Annie Hall" we should all join Mr. Allen in the pub.

The ocean, gray and heavy and foreboding, under a dark and lowering sky, embraces the whole film, from the reminiscences with which it begins to the kind of exhausted tranquility with which it ends. Miss Page is a designer of interiors, with a taste amounting to obsession for earth tones of grays and beiges, and vast planes of unadorned wall and floor. It has its own austere but perfectly integrated beauty, but in its austerity it is also repressed, joyless, lifeless, puritanical in its frugality (bought at very high decorator prices). Mel Bourne was the mood-making designer.

She has, we learn, put her husband (E. G. Marshall) through law school and seen him into a very rich Manhattan practice. Now that their three daughters are grown, he wants out. His duty's done and he doesn't regret the sacrifices he has had to make (he says with a wondrous smug generosity). But now he needs to breathe. Page, hearing these tidings across the lunch table, dies inside, as we read in her pained and eloquent eyes. It is one of the several moments in "Interiors" when she demonstrates the acting art to all who might have thought they knew it, and confirms that she is one of the finest actresses of her generation.

The three daughters are a trio of ill graces. The lightweight Diane Keaton of "Annie Hall" is now a rather pretentious poet, a successful agonizer who does not, however, seem sensitive or vulnerable enough to be potentially tragic or really good. It is a fine characterization, creating a woman who is too self-aware to feel much else but whose pain is real, and whose spontaneity has disappeared beneath a mannered role-playing which Keaton somehow makes clear is the portrait, not the portrayer. Red-nosed and swollen-eyed from crying, she is a long way from the kooky charm of Annie Hall. She is married to a novelist (Richard Jordan) who is dousing his flame in drink over his bitter awareness (shared by the critics) that he has failed to deliver on his early promise.

Kristin Griffith is a Hollywood actress, bitter about her own inability to be taken more seriously and sniffing her consolation in powdered form. Hers is the least defined of the three parts, and she also seems the least comfortable of the three players.

Mary Beth Hurt is by a narrow margin the most pained of the sisters, the most victimized of them. She gets stuck with Mother but also with her own inability to make a career at something she does well. She is Daddy's favorite, and accordingly his biggest disappointment. On the other hand, she feels most betrayed by his leave-taking and the most hate-filled (and lost) when he returns from a Grecian holiday with a new wife-to-be.

She is Maureen Stapleton, in another matchless display of the acting arts. She is by no mistake in a vivid red dress, the first and only splash of color amid those wastes of embalmed grays, and browns. The symbolism of the dress, like the double-play of the title as suggesting both décor and emotional states, is almost too evident for its own good, but Stapleton, prattling on about steaks and ouzo and beaches and dancing the night away, is vitality personified and, damn, she is a welcome sight.

The menfolk, Jordan and Sam Waterston as a political journalist who patiently keeps company with Ms. Hurt, are amused by her. The daughters can hardly get past their own feelings to hope for old Dad's happiness. Then again, since Allen is orchestrating a symphony of insensitivity, old Dad doesn't really rate a gold star for kindliness. He consoles himself rhetorically that "a dark abyss" yawned beneath the marriage after all those years, but he has abandoned Page to nervous breakdowns and suicide attempts with the anguish he would show donating a suit to the Salvation Army.

The casting of Marshall, with his prior image of heroic respectability and public duty, was inspired. It is an excellent performance. No doubt for a moment that life with Page, with her perfectionist zeal (inner-directed toward her own satisfaction, of course), must have been increasingly a trial. Still, in his pat-on-the-head disregard of her evident acute distress he looks less a victim than a man of stone, hollowed by erosion.

Stapleton, for all her chatter and her card tricks, is no dummy. She catches the vibes at a couple of poisonous family gatherings (the wedding in the old house by the ocean is one) but she is open and direct and spontaneous, a celebrator of life, and imagines (I presume) that she will win all hearts.

What is interesting is that all the circumstantial evidence supplied by Allen suggests that Stapleton, as Pearl, is Jewish. Allen's alter ego in "Annie Hall" was painfully aware of being Jewish and, as such, an odd man out in a WASP society. Looking at this family of bled-out, bred-out devoutly unhappy WASPs, the viewer is bound to suspect that while Allen may not have told a joke, he has delivered a punch line. Like Groucho, he is not sure he wants to join the club, the clubhouse being in such need of repairs and renewal. That does not make "Interiors" a tract, and Allen might be one of the first to agree that unhappy families come in all denominations. But Pearl lends an edge to a film full of edges, all sharp.

Allen's fundamental vision of everything that is absurd and pretentious and hurtful in the world has not altered between the stand-up routines and earlier movies and "Interiors." It is the operative tone of voice that has changed, and you have to cheer the courage it took to move so resolutely and ambitiously away from the principal basis of his earlier success. And, in a period when the prevailing attitude toward the movie audience has seemed to be a calculated cynicism, it is restorative and uplifting to contemplate a film of such great aspiration, such considerable artistry and such emotional impact.

Charlie Chaplin, Buster Keaton and a few other comic masters have moved from jokes to a sentimental consideration of more serious themes. Allen has moved to a serious theme, but his movie is as rich with sentimentality as a traffic ticket. What it has is that amazing power, perplexing even, to make us sympathize with uncommonly selfish and unsympathetic people.

Like "Cries and Whispers," Allen's "Interiors" is, for all the somberness of the material, in the end an affirmation of life and a transcendent piece of art. Film lovers will love it, if joke-seekers do not.

Midnight Express

This film, it has become clear since, was a significant introduction to Oliver Stone, whose first script it was and who revealed in it his gift for generating violent emotional impact on the screen, as he would later reveal in "Born on the Fourth of July" and his other work as writer-director.

BILLY HAYES WAS AN AMERICAN COLLEGIAN, a senior at Marquette, when in the footloose and high-spirited year of 1970 he tried to smuggle some bricks of hashish out of Turkey. He stood to make $3,000, maybe a bit more, selling to his pals. Instead he found himself moving through airport security that was on full alert after a rash of hijackings. In the movie, portrayed by actor Brad Davis, he looks furtive enough to arouse suspicions in a saint. He was caught easily, sentenced to serve four years and then, just short of freedom, was resentenced to thirty years. In the hellhole conditions of his prison, it might as well have been a death sentence.

Hayes's harrowing years in Sagamilcar prison are now the heart of a strong and shocking movie, "Midnight Express" (prison slang for an escape). It was directed by Alan Parker, whose previous feature was unimaginably different—the gangster musical enacted by children, "Bugsy Malone." A first-time film writer, Oliver Stone, did the script from Hayes's book about his ordeal.

Within its fortress walls, the prison seems freeform by American standards, a kind of dank and ratty barracks through which the men wander, a tattered and derelict United Nations of smugglers like Hayes plus the usual local murderers and rapists. Anything can be had for a price. Stabbings and beatings are frequent. Informers are everywhere. Homosexuality is common. The guards are brutal. It is not an advertisement for Turkey.

The movie is violent (although it seems less so than when it was shown, with great success, at this year's Cannes Festival). But it is the feeling of impending violence that is as unnerving as the heartbeat that dominates much of the sound track like a subliminal warning. The latent violence, and the soul-rotting loss of hope, give "Midnight Express" its terrific impact. There is never any suggestion that Hayes is innocent. He was guilty and got caught and was prepared, like any well-taught American boy, to pay the price. But what a price it became. There is at first the awful loneliness: being the subject of torrents of conversation in Turkish, of which he can understand not a word. (No subtitles, intentionally, so the audience shares his uneasy incomprehension.) Then there is the brutality, the sexual frustration. (In a sensual shower scene, Hayes contemplates but declines a homosexual relationship. But the story makes clear that a loving if platonic comradeship was for many of the inmates all that preserved sanity and the thin shreds of hope.)

"Midnight Express" is not an escape movie, although there is a suspenseful, unsuccessful escape attempt through a sewer deep beneath the prison. Hayes, obviously, did escape. It occupies relatively little screen time but it is disproportionately satisfying. Indeed, for all the horrors of the prison scene, "Midnight Express" is in the end exhilarating and affirmative, an object lesson in the joys of freedom and in the value of due process of law.

Made largely on Malta for a remarkably modest $2.5 million, "Midnight Express" is a worthy and engrossing addition to the honored line of prison movies from "I Am a Fugitive from a Chain Gang" through "The Fixer" and "Papillon."

Davis as Hayes reveals rather than tells. He grows gaunt and hollow-eyed and near-mad as we watch nearly six years of hell take their toll. His biggest scene (a diatribe against the court and the country after he has been resentenced) is the weakest in the film, unconvincing as fact (it did not actually happen) and unpersuasively said. Yet Davis's professional naiveté elsewhere is quite effective in suggesting Hayes's own (relative) innocence as a good-time American out of his depth in the lower depths.

The supporting performances are unforgettable, most especially John Hurt as a weak, sensitive, drug-dazed Englishman. Hurt is an even more tragic figure than Davis, chuckling and dreaming and lost. Randy Quaid is excellent as another Yank, longer on rage than brains, and suffering for it. Paul Smith is the bestial chief guard and Paolo Bonicelli the informing trusty with whom Billy has one of the bloodiest man-to-man fights ever filmed. Mike Kellin plays Hayes's hapless, helpless father and Irene Miracle is Hayes's girl, whose visit to the prison is its own superlative—one of the most rending sexual encounters (or non-encounters) ever filmed. Bo Hopkins is a cool American narc and Norbert Weisser is Hayes's closest pal in the prison. Peter Jeffrey has a small, potent role as an old, mad criminal who knows he is defective.

The music of Giorgio Moroder is particularly effective, with a recurrent Turkish motif that suggests the clash of the picturesque and the ghastly. Peter Guber was the executive producer who conceived the project, with David Puttnam and Alan Marshall as the line producers.

"Midnight Express" is, Hayes himself said at Cannes, 80 percent accurate. Characters are composites of several in life; his courtroom speech is what he felt rather than what he said; the escape itself was different from what is shown. But the squalor and the despair and the outrage have not had to be invented, or enhanced, and the lessons of the experience are not distant nor irrelevant. Hash smuggling is a fool's game there or anywhere else, but it is also an item of American faith (inconsistently observed when it comes to drugs) that the punishment ought to fit the crime, as it did not in Hayes's case.

The Deer Hunter

It grew clear in time that "The Deer Hunter" predicted Michael Cimino's impressive strengths, and his weakness. He has bold ideas and a way with dramatic images, but the ideas are compromised or undone with an ultimate lack of control. In the end what his symbol-clogged story was saying remained ambiguous. "Heaven's Gate" was to confirm the talent, the ambition, and the flaw.

"THE DEER HUNTER" is an extremely ambitious and important film on a crucial theme—the impact of the Vietnam war on American lives. In a year in which too few movies have tried to do more than divert and pacify, "The Deer Hunter" aspires to be unique and demands to be measured against the classic uses of the screen to illustrate the way we live and die.

The best passages of Michael Cimino's film are in fact brilliant. The American lives that will be affected by the war are drawn from a Pennsylvania steel mill town, an ethnic (Russian) enclave of gritty streets, hard work, desperate pleasures and tight horizons.

It continues to be an extraordinary year for the camera, and Vilmos Zsigmond has caught the mill town at its late autumn bleakest, the dank streets and matted leaves and warning winds, the semis snarling past and the diesel switchers rumbling by on the elevated tracks above the frame tenements and the saloon whose neon signs are warming beacons in the early darkness. The combat sequences, too, have a numbing authenticity, providing a brief but horrifying taste of the merciless and indiscriminate village warfare, and making My Lai comprehensible and therefore all the more dismaying.

In all its excellences and its aspirations, "The Deer Hunter" chooses to be an extended metaphor, in much the same way that Dalton Trumbo's limbless, eyeless, speechless soldier in "Johnny Got His Gun" was an extended metaphor for the futility of war. "The Deer Hunter," written by Deric Washburn from a story credited to Cimino and Washburn and the team of Louis Garfinkle and Quinn K. Redeker, uses Russian roulette as its metaphor for cruel and random chance by which war picks its victims. Viet Cong roulette it is, actually, since we encounter it as VC guards force their prisoners at gunpoint to play the gunpoint game.

(It is a savagely strong piece of filmmaking, agonizing to watch close-up, as the camera does. The setting is a partly submerged bamboo cage, crawling with river rats, the drunken guards betting and chortling and cursing, the prisoners screaming and dying. It is wrenching stuff.) The game will recur, amid the feverish decadence of collapsing Saigon, back home during a deer hunt in the Alleghenies, and yet again one last tragic time on the last day of Saigon as the helicopters lift off from the embassy roof.

It does not cease to be horrifying, unbearable to watch, but it becomes, I'm afraid, more melodrama than metaphor, creating a movie which at last seems in part curiously at odds with its level of intentions, the poetic realism surrendered to a heavily engineered succession of events and the final statement rendered perplexingly ambiguous and unresolved. Still and beyond the reservations, it is a film of excellences, never more so than in the performances by Robert De Niro and a remarkable supporting cast.

De Niro is Mike, one of the three mill-hand, deer-hunting pals who are going off to 'Nam. Christopher Walken as Nick and John Savage as Steve are the other two. They are leaving after a beery wedding party for Savage and Rutanya Alda, who is pregnant although not necessarily by him, and then a last deer hunt with the other pals, saloonkeeper George Dzundza, John Cazale and bearded Chuck Aspergren. The end of work, the preliminary beer-up at the saloon, the wedding and the hunt are lingered over and have an improvisational feeling (whether or not they were improvised, and I suspect that they were not) that recalls John Cassavetes' "Husbands" in the accuracy of the portrayal of pals together.

For De Niro it is a markedly different characterization from the dark and lethal introvert of "Taxi Driver" or the glib chauvinist of "New York, New York." He is cool, laid-back, a loner who is also a natural leader, a strong and decent realist. It seems at least fairly clear that he is intended to be a symbol within the metaphor, the common man with all the uncommon virtues the national rhetoric gives him, including a pioneer self-reliance and a melting-pot richness of heritage.

Like most palships, these are not without strains. The late and excellent John Cazale as Stan is a quarrelsome, neurotic, pistol-carrying womanizer who requires more tolerance than he gives. To that extent there's one in every crowd. Walken is another moody loner, and a complication because his girl (Meryl Streep) has eyes for De Niro as well, and vice versa. (Actually, there is some uncertainty about where the De Niro character stands sexually, and he catches a taunt from Cazale now and again, but if this was intended as a side theme for exploration, it is not pursued.)

Streep is a welcome discovery, a warm and intelligent actress who somewhat recalls Faye Dunaway, and although she seems almost too good to be marking cans in the grocery store when she could make it OK in Pittsburgh or even Chicago, she is wonderfully sympathetic and understated in the role. It is obvious that she, and a name Raymond Chandler would have loved, will be heard from again.

Like the smuggling episode in "Julia," which works as a drama within the drama, the combat sequence, including the caged captivity, is a suspenseful drama within the larger frame of the movie. There is a daring escape, a rescue and near-rescue and then the pals, saved by De Niro, are separated. It is then, too, that the fabric of the film separates, too, changing from the muscular but artfully controlled naturalism to the far more invented passages, including the appearance of a cynical and opportunistic Frenchman (Pierre Segui) who takes the battled-dazed Walken in tow and seems to have emerged from a different kind of fiction entirely.

Mike comes home alone, for the moment, with his chestful of ribbons and his memories. On home ground again, Cimino the filmmaker also appears more at home, and there is a first-class authenticity about the homecoming, the awkwardness of the greeting, De Niro's sense of isolation, of his permanent difference from anyone who cannot know what he's seen and had to do. He is still the symbol within the metaphor, and a deer-hunting reunion demonstrates that he, for which read the American, cannot be the same again after Vietnam; there has been a loss of innocence (or naiveté) but perhaps a gain of something harder to define. Having created so memorable a hero-figure, "The Deer Hunter" inevitably raises questions about what will become of Mike in a more specific sense. Back to the life as it was? A new life with the excellent Ms. Streep?

But first, there is story as story to be played out: Savage has come home with his own legacy of the struggle, to be resolved. (He is an impressive young actor in this relatively brief but demanding role.) And there is that last trip to Saigon and a lurid confrontation with Walken, set improbably during the fall of the city. The fall has been impressively reconstructed in a clever intercutting of news footage and new shooting, but the private events, gruesomely violent, are closer to hokum than to the steely thoughtfulness of the balance of the film. You wince for the brain pan shattered, and for what is surely a miscalculation that neither heightens the power of the film's statement nor is likely to widen its audience appreciably.

At last the survivors gather over a funeral breakfast and find themselves singing "God Bless America." An affirmation after all? Yes, the studio synopsis suggests helpfully. I wonder, says the viewer, sensing—simply in the context of the movie itself—a bitter irony. Ambiguous, says the verdict: inconclusive either way.

Perhaps the movie is intended to be, as it sees the war to be, a cleansing, a purging of old attitudes, achieved at hideous cost in death, disfigurement, disillusion, but achieved nonetheless and providing a basis for a calm and rational future.

Perhaps.

The movie is long—three minutes over three hours—but like "The Godfather" it is so eventful that you sense time only in the gory delays of the roulette. Peter Zinner was the editor. The effectively unobtrusive music is by Stanley Myers. Ron Hobbs and Kim Swados are the art directors, helping the mill-town realities speak for themselves.

The movie is rated Restricted, with a special additional cautionary note from the studio. The warning is well-taken; the violence is grim and graphic, and abundant. It is a film to be debated and argued over seriously because it is an earnest, serious and impressive work, despite the reservations it is necessary to have about it. "The Deer Hunter" joins a thin company that aspire to greatness.

1979

Norma Rae

*Martin Ritt was one of several directors who came to film out of
live television, in which he both directed and acted. He was one
of few directors drawn to social themes: the lives of black share-
croppers ("Sounder"), blacklisting ("The Front"), the struggle of
miners ("The Molly Maguires") and union organizing in the excellent "Norma Rae." His death in 1990 left a gap which remains to
be filled.*

ANYBODY IN HIS OR HER RIGHT MIND would be bound to say that
as the theme of a major motion picture, labor organizing in the South
falls somewhere between the unlikely and the unthinkable, something
that might have been tried as a bristly and defiant independent venture in
the 30s or 40s and shown in church basements and on the campuses.

But here, by damn, is Martin Ritt's "Norma Rae" and it is a wonderful and—for want of a better word—judicious work. At the heart of it are
beautifully conceived and sustained performances by Sally Field as a textile worker who is just as rural-WASP as she can be, and by Ron Leibman
as a prototypical young New York Jewish lawyer-organizer who comes to
town to tackle the local mill single-handedly. "Norma Rae," written by
Ritt's old friends and frequent collaborators Irving Ravetch and Harriet
Frank, Jr., is another of what I consider minefield movies, which can blow
themselves sky-high by putting a foot wrong at any step. Not here.

These are the 70s, not the 30s, and out of a bloody history the organizer has the protection of a pack of federal laws. The resident fear and
hostility may not have changed much (and it is said that you can still count
the number of unionized textile plants in the South on one spindle), but
the head-whumping goonery is not in fashion the way it used to be. The
subtler pressures and the implicit threats are the same. "Norma Rae"
reflects the new day. It is, in fact, an intimate drama of cultural shock and

of contrasted life-styles illuminated. Labor and management are united only in their deep suspicion of and hostility toward outsiders, Jews most particularly. Leibman has his work all too well defined for him.

The movie carries a message, demonstrated amply. The mill floor is a deafening cacophony, the air thick with lint which makes lung disease common among the workers. The pay is low, hours long, discipline relentless. The management can't be accused of a benevolent paternalism, but the mill is the only employment game in town, and you stagger to work as long as there's breath in you, rather than risk a lay-off. There's no question where the film's sympathies lie.

Sally Field is not a traditional heroine in a bandanna. She takes pleasure where she finds it to make a hard life bearable (although the pleasures, including an intermittent affair with a traveling man, are fairly lousy, too). Her child is not quite legitimate and her worthless husband died in a beer brawl. Her folks, Pat Hingle and Barbara Baxley, also work at the mill and have about all they can do to keep afloat. All of it sounds uninterruptedly grim, but that does not reckon with the extraordinary drive and vitality of Field as Norma Rae. Her resilience, her curiosity, her honesty and her sensitivity are what "Norma Rae" is about, and if the movie is resolutely optimistic, Norma Rae is the carrier of its optimism, and ours.

There are actually two stories in parallel. One is the progress of organizing, which is both suspenseful and interesting in a rather documentary way. (Leibman's lawyer-organizer has been David against Goliath before, and hasn't always won, either. His armor against hostility is a fervent faith in his own cause, masked by a wisecracking humor and imperturbable good cheer.) The other story is the progress of Norma Rae's own life, including the emergence of Beau Bridges as a new suitor and later husband, who then has to share his wife with a new social commitment she has made. Obviously, the two stories are inseparable, but one of the several things which are both useful and unexpected about the construction of the movie is that the two threads are indeed separate and not made one for sentimental effect. The movie continually goes against expectations.

If the sights and sounds captured by Walter Scott Herndon as production designer and cinematographer John A. Alonzo are distinctly of the 70s, the pervasive liberal sentiments are from an earlier and (seemingly) simpler time. The sentiments and the subject matter combine to make "Norma Rae" an astonishment, very pleasant, in 1979. It is as if time had not so much stood still as elected to go in two directions at once.

"Norma Rae" is a further reminder that Fox has lately been the most adventurous of the major studios—betting on artistry to overcome any initial audience resistance to relatively unconventional material. "Star Wars," as obvious an enterprise as it now seems, had been rejected elsewhere first. "Julia," with its focus on the intermittent association of women friends plus its narrative difficulties, including a finally unresolved story, was manifestly chancy. And despite its middle-class romanticism, "The Turning Point," with ballet as its milieu and again the relationship of two women at its center, was a risk. The risks may be relative and at that they may not always pay off. (Robert Altman's cryptic, icy, gloomy and portentous "Quintet" does not appear likely to pay off, but underwriting it was for Fox nothing if not adventurous.) But they are risks.

"Norma Rae" is demonstrably a gamble, yet it could well prove a winner on its artistic excellence and the warm attractiveness of Ms. Field and Leibman, and Beau Bridges in a lesser but crucial role. Hingle and Baxley are splendid at the head of a large supporting cast which notably has Gail Strickland as another of the women in the plant, and Frank McRae (excellent in "Paradise Alley") as a black worker.

Director Ritt has been one of Hollywood's most cogent examiners of the individual in a particular society from his first feature ("Edge of the City") through "Hud," "The Front" and last year's excellent "Casey's Shadow." He is here again a craftsman both solid and sensitive.

David Shire did the effective score. Tamara Asseyev and Alex Rose were the producers.

The China Syndrome

The real-life near-disaster episode at the Three Mile Island nuclear power plant only a few days after "The China Sydrome" opened gave the film a terrible relevance (and the kind of promotion you can't buy, even assuming you'd want to). James Bridges made only a handful of films (also including "Urban Cowboy"). This is his best work and his untimely death cut short a career that promised much.

THE CHINA SYNDROME, it is explained, is the consequence of a nuclear reactor running amok and burning a hole that would theoretically drill straight through the earth to China on the far side—except that the reaction is likelier to vaporize the subterranean water layer, which then spews skyward as a lethally radioactive mushroom cloud extinguishing life over a vast area.

That is a sobering, numbing prospect and "The China Syndrome" is an arresting and skillfully executed What If movie, a tract in the form of a dramatized hypothesis that something *could* go wrong at a nuclear power plant. The accident might or might not put us all aboard a fast cloud to China, but we might not ever know how close we'd come.

Directed by James Bridges (his most expert work by far) and co-authored by Bridges with the team of Mike Gray and T. S. Cook, "The China Syndrome" is that infrequent item, a protest film, an angry caution about the proliferation of nuclear power—not principally because of the problems of nuclear waste, a matter which gets no more than a glance here, but because of the possibility of a major accident of the kind the ads say has not happened, despite the fact there are now seventy-one nuclear power plants on line, generating some 12 percent of U.S. electricity.

The movie "The China Syndrome" most closely evokes is Alan Pakula's What If drama, "The Parallax View," with its all-too-persuasive demonstration that the assassination of a high political figure could be the work of a conspiracy so well hidden that the best efforts of neither government nor a brave loner could bring it to light. In Bridges's truly suspenseful and disturbing film, California and a large hunk of supporting geography teeters at the edge of nuclear catastrophe as the result of a conspiracy not of ideology but of good old non-political greed. But ironically, the movie as story is least convincing when it is shrillest and most doctrinaire in its depiction of the Power Baron and his corrupted toadies engineering cover-ups and murders. The merciless mogul, lacking only a black cape and twirled mustache, is not really a match for the sound-proofed, bulletproofed, many-consoled, many-screened, many-levered, begauged and begraphed control center, a kind of NASA HQ designed to *prevent* blast-offs. That's where the menace is. What lends "The China Syndrome" its real power is not so much the major, cartoony villainy as the minor picayune weaknesses built into men and into their increasingly diabolic machines. The chill is in an old joke updated to say, approximately, How'd you like to live next to a nuclear power plant built by the lowest bidder?

The movie's plot involves a lot of welds on a huge pump that were never checked by X-ray during construction. To cut costs, the OKs were faked. (The power source is new; the plot construction—the cross-cutting, the dials tensely watched, the knotting wait for everything to blow sky-high or China-deep—is as tried and true as any that imperiled Pauline.)

Jane Fonda is a bubbly TV newsperson, covering animal birthdays at the zoo and yearning to taste the hard stuff. She and her cameraman (Michael Douglas, who also produced "The China Syndrome") are doing a gee-whiz feature at a nuclear power plant, gazing down into the control center, when the accident takes place. (My impression was that the accident had been induced by a minor earthquake—a plot element of no minor importance in California—but nobody, I think, says so, and it is never made clear.) Despite the soothing words from James Hampton as a PR man with lethal steel beneath the unctuous charm, it's evident that Jack Lemmon as the chief engineer is in a state of panic and near-collapse. Beyond the mumbo-jumbo, it's obvious, in fact, the nuclear furnace came near to blowing up. Douglas snuck some footage, but the power company is even now involved in sensitive hearings for permission to build another plant at Point Conception. Cover-up is urgent. Hampton has a word with Peter Donat, who owns the channel and knows which side his commercials are buttered on. Douglas is run off, Fonda goes back to the zoo.

Lemmon loves the plant as he might a child and knows it's not right. But the cover-up, and the need for revenue, demand that the plant go back into operation fast. In a performance that equals his portrait of a man in extremis in "Save the Tiger," Lemmon is caught between conscience and duty amidst events that have got beyond him. Following his hunches, he is soon a marked man, trying to escape from the thugs who want to hide the truth but also from Douglas and Fonda who want to tell it.

There are two brief but very effective car sequences which somehow become the more effective because they are handled not as special events, as in the chase movies, but as aspects of the ordinary reality established by the film. Daniel Valdez as an aide to Douglas and then Lemmon himself are the more startled and scared because the pursuits seem so unthinkable, and for the viewers the resulting chases are correspondingly scarier. A melodramatic film builds to an extremely melodramatic climax (through which director Bridges displays a firm hand on big-scale movie logistics).

Special praise is due production designer George Jenkins, who also has "All The President's Men," and its very credible newsroom to his credit. The events of "The China Syndrome" occur partly in a cluttered and chaotic television newsroom of high authenticity, noticeably including the anchor-peoples' closing ad libs carefully printed on the Tele-PrompTer. The "Ventana" power plant is also a masterwork of complexity, mystery and a sort of despotic majesty. How and where it was achieved I've no idea but I've also no doubt the damned thing functions.

The subsidiary casting is of considerable importance here, and one key player is Wilford Brimley as an old power company man, an assistant to Lemmon now but a man who has survived too long to start telling the imprudent truth, even if it's urgent, in a corporation that is forever thirsting for the blood of scapegoats. Scott Brady is the plant superintendent, another company man who knows that "I'm just doing my job" is the unanswerable corporate answer. (It is, as I've said, the minor corruption more than the major villainy that gives "The China Syndrome" its real chill factor.) Richard Herd is the big cheese, conscienceless and amoral, the very model of a captain (Bligh) of industry, seen from the left side. The character seems as much out of touch with current Marxist theory as with current capitalism conceptually, but the problems are not with Herd, who is asked mostly to sneer and bark. Donat is able to be intelligently nasty and credibly unprincipled, and does it well. James Karen is the news director, a good man trying to keep honest despite the pressures.

Some laughable demonstrations dramatize the puniness of the opposition to the expansion of nuclear power. The movie is, obviously, rather a different matter. General Electric, which equips nuclear plants, is reported to have cancelled its sponsorship of a Barbara Walters–Jane Fonda interview because of Ms. Fonda's participation in "The China Syndrome." Fonda is reported to have said, "What are they afraid of? It's only a movie"—a remark whose mocking irony will presumably not be lost on Schenectady.

"The China Syndrome" may be over-weighted, lopsided, wrong-headed, argumentative and loaded. But it is not just a movie; it is a movie with a very strong point of view toward a major current issue, and it is not ignorable. Neither it nor Fonda nor Barbara Walters (whatever she may think about "The China Syndrome") is apt to go away.

Whatever, in fact, anyone thinks about nuclear power plants, the movie demands that the issue be thought about some more. Not so accidentally, the movie can be said to raise questions it does not ask. What *about* a major earthquake, for example? Movies may or may not be able to carry messages, and for all its alarms, "The China Syndrome" cannot reasonably be said to have proved the case against nuclear power (although the attitude of the film is clear enough). But a movie can indeed raise questions, and this one does.

The excellent cinematography was by James Crabe and the editing (to a breathless two hours) was by David Rawlins. Bruce Gilbert, partnered with Fonda on "Coming Home" also, was the executive producer. Fonda's role is, despite some high-tension scenes at the end, less interior than her evolving military wife in "Coming Home." Her change here from self-centered career girl to concerned fighter is an inevitable result of external events, not much sweated over. But she is, as always, commanding and convincing at both ends of the character.

Douglas as the catalyst of events, luring both Lemmon and Fonda to act, is (as seems to have become his specialty) a prototypical free modern man, both concerned and untethered, disestablished but sound, unconventional but moved by old values. Relative to the other roles, it is unshowy to the point of self-effacement, and the more useful for it.

Manhattan

The noisome later revelations attending Woody Allen's private life have subjected his uniquely autobiographical films to fresh speculation. Where does the real Woody Allen begin or end, as if even Allen could say for sure. But if "Annie Hall" is the most poignant of his films in its celebration of love remembered, "Manhattan" was the saddest and the one most critical of its protagonist, in his self-obsession and his matching inability to commit, until it's too late. The subsequent films are still brilliantly surprising in their variety; but they are also more guarded, as if the likeness of the alter egos had come too close for comfort.

THE IDEA TAKES A LITTLE GETTING USED TO, because it is still easier to think of him as the apologetic and deadpan monologuist, coughing nervously and explaining how he bagged a moose at a garden party in Jersey, or as the weird guy ordering 1,200 egg salad sandwiches to go for a revolutionary army in "Bananas."

But the fact has to be faced that Woody Allen, from a sitting start as a teenaged gag writer, has become one of the finest, most thoughtful and individual filmmakers in America. He is an *auteur* who confirms the possibility of that rather controversial theory, and he is a member of that very, very small band of American directors whose works are both inspired and personal in the European tradition of Renoir, Truffaut, Fellini and Bergman.

A forthcoming book on the new Hollywood hotshots does not even include Allen (although the book's theme is the directors' distaste for traditional studio operations, which Allen might be thought to share). Yet Allen's movies reveal a phenomenal growth in both form and content that is not surpassed in the work of any of the trendier filmmakers.

Allen's new comedy, "Manhattan" is even better than his Oscar-sweeping "Annie Hall." It is his masterwork—so far. And beneath its bright and wondrous camouflage of funny lines and razor-edged cross-talk between Allen and Diane Keaton, who is again his costar, "Manhattan" is harder, harsher, crueler, deeper-going, more assertive but in the end no less life-affirming than "Annie Hall."

It is in glorious black and white, which remain absolutely the right colors for recording New York City. "Manhattan" is, among all the things it is, a soul-deep homage to the city. Stunning cityscapes and streetscapes by Gordon Willis bracket the movie fore and aft, and the musical accompaniments, thrillingly appropriate, are the songs of George Gershwin (including the symphonic *Rhapsody in Blue*), performed for the movie by the New York Philharmonic under Zubin Mehta and the Buffalo Philharmonic under Michael Tilson Thomas. In any audience of New York exiles, there won't be a dry eye in the house, even before anybody has heard a word of dialogue. The bridges, the soaring towers, the townhouses and the tenements, the sleazy shops and sleek Bloomingdales are all there and the city in all its teeming clangorous vitality has never had such a valentine since E. B. White wrote an essay on New York in summer a quarter-century ago. The movie commences, indeed, with Allen's voice-over, starting to dictate a novel about the city as a metaphor for our decadent, declining culture (a ploy not deeply pursued).

Within this celebrated city, Allen and his co-scriptwriter Marshall Brickman prove once again that they have been listening at our elbows, eavesdropping on us in crowded saloons, in movie queues and at art galleries, and have invaded the privacy not only of our bedrooms but of our psyches.

Like "Annie Hall," "Manhattan" explores late twentieth-century relationships within what might be called the young professional class, among a sort of inadequately employed intelligentsia, and does so with unsettling accuracy and frequent zingy effect. The difference this time is that the ground has hardened. The nostalgic glow of friendship-after-love in which all of "Annie Hall" was bathed has gone, like color itself, from "Manhattan." Allen is harder on himself, harder on the relationships, more sparing—particularly in the late stages of the story—of the jokes which usually serve as emotional shinguards, or as aspirin. The Allen persona carries forward almost totally intact from "Annie Hall," although he is this time called Isaac Davis, a successful writer of TV comedy for a show that looks vaguely like "Saturday Night Live." (It's hard to tell and doesn't much matter.) He's been married twice, once to a kindergarten teacher we don't meet, then to Meryl Streep (from "The Deer Hunter") by whom he had a son but who has left him for a lesbian relationship and who has written a book telling why. Allen is meantime having an affair with Mariel Hemingway as a very precocious (and heartbreakingly beautiful) seventeen-year-old senior at the Dalton School.

His close pal Michael Murphy, a teacher-writer, is married to Anne Byrne but having a fling with Keaton, a freelance writer out of Radcliffe, with heavy credits in all the heavier magazines. It reads like a résumé of a month's worth of soap opera, but what is interesting is how intimate the focus of "Manhattan" is and how much emotional ground Allen covers in a crisp 106 minutes. Allen says in alarm, "It's beginning to sound like Noël Coward; somebody should be making martinis." The workings of Allen's "La Ronde" (Murphy and Keaton split; Keaton and Allen connect; Keaton and Allen split) are interesting, but even more interesting is the texturing of the lives, the environment, the speech.

If Allen as Isaac Davis is still Alvy Singer and prior persons, Keaton is no longer Annie Hall but an aggressive, hard-talking, iconoclastic woman whose confidence, however, keeps collapsing and revealing an acute shortage of self-esteem. Allen as Davis, is, at that, less exclusively the joker who makes you guess at the pain he's really feeling. In one remarkable scene, Allen, alone on the screen, listens to a chortling recitation of his ex-wife's descriptions of him from the new book. An earlier Allen might have had a line or a gesture; the present Allen looks angry, wounded and very human, and has not a word to say.

The relationship with so young a woman (although it is established that he is not her first affair) is tricky going for the movie. It is handled with a kind of saving accuracy of observation; none of it seems unlikely in the context of the story and in the end it is clear that Allen has very much intended our sympathies to be with her for the good reason that she is a voice of reason. The story is ultimately open-ended, a kind of litmus to test the viewer's imagination (blue for sour, red for optimism, or maybe it's vice versa). But in so different a film as "Cries and Whispers" there was a similar sense of exultation at the end because the power of love had been asserted, demonstrated both by its presence and its absence.

For all the sexual goings-on and the persistence of sex as a major theme in his movies, Allen here reveals himself as a traditionalist (and with, I think, no feeling of irony) who favors commitment and honesty. He blunts the edge with a joke. "You sound like God!" Murphy shouts at him angrily. "You have to pick Somebody for a role model," Allen says. It was possible to get choked up about "Annie Hall" because it dealt with a universal experience—the death of love and a sort of afterlife of memory and affection. And the movie (I realized, seeing it again only the other night) was done with a fine-tuned elegance that does not waste a frame or a line.

"Manhattan" is more profoundly affecting, as if the impulse which produced from Allen so intense and unsmiling a movie as "Interiors" was not a passing fancy. I don't mean to make "Manhattan" sound less amusing than it is; Allen is still the master of the wry line and the contemporary joke. It is just that the jokes have never been more evidently the masks on everything from shyness to emotional scars, and Allen has never been more prepared to let the masks slip to reveal the truth. Thankfully, some of the truth and perhaps the abiding truth is joyous. Nothing that ends with the Manhattan skyline and the music of Gershwin, sumptuously scored, can be all sad. Gordon Willis has earned another Oscar to add to those he has been denied previously, and if he's overlooked again a scandal will have become an outrage. The night shooting and a sequence inside the Hayden Planetarium is, with all else, simply spectacular.

Allen is here more the actor than ever and the other performances are excellent, Murphy in another difficult but rather thankless role (as in "An Unmarried Woman"), Hemingway beautiful and intelligent, Keaton brittle and neurotic ("the Zelda Fitzgerald Award," Allen says of her in the dialogue) and just right. Byrne as Murphy's wife has a minor but sympathetic role and she is first-rate. Streep is briefly but devastatingly seen.

"Manhattan" is a brilliant film, but Allen has long since stopped being only a jokester, and this is a mature work by a very serious filmmaker.

Apocalypse Now

Nothing in Coppola's subsequent work, including "Godfather III," has touched the accomplishment that is "Apocalypse Now," whatever its flaws and whatever feeling a viewer may have that the director never rounded it off to his own complete satisfaction. It is still a bold undertaking, a monumental achievement.

MORE THAN FOUR YEARS AND $30 MILLION LATER, after the travail and tragedy, rumors and reports, delays and distractions, Francis

Ford Coppola's "Apocalypse Now" arrives at last. It arrives in 70mm images and multiple-track sound and without a word's worth of credits at the beginning or at the end of the film, which now runs two hours and thirty-three minutes, about twelve or thirteen minutes longer than the version Coppola showed in competition at the Cannes festival in May. Most of the additional material extends the ending, clarifying the action somewhat but still leaving open the question of moral choice which the character played by Martin Sheen must presumably make and which Coppola said at Cannes was central to his intentions for the film. It is not, in all events, the visually apocalyptic air-strike ending which Coppola also filmed at great cost, and the matter of the alternative endings is likely to haunt Coppola and his viewers for a very long time to come.

But a second viewing of "Apocalypse Now"—even in a 35mm monaural print watched in a jungle-hot and steamy screening room—reinforced and extended the impression from Cannes that Coppola has brought off a landmark in film history, a masterpiece which in its scale, the grandeur of its ambitions and the level of its success demands to be judged with and placed beside the great film works of any time, from "Birth of a Nation" forward.

It is an essay on madness, public and private, and ultimately it deals not with madness clinically witnessed but with madness as experienced. It is, in fact, a carefully and ingeniously orchestrated journey into madness. In the end, when Martin Sheen as an Army-CIA assassin operating in Vietnam has at last found Marlon Brando as the mad Colonel Kurtz, reciting T.S. Eliot's "The Hollow Men" amid severed heads and hanged and rotting bodies in a temple in the Cambodian jungle, the scenes are not of a nightmare fantasy but a reality that has gone unthinkably wrong, a daymare from which there is no awakening.

It is set amid an ugly and violent war and "Apocalypse Now" is frequently ugly and violent, seeming the uglier because it is set amid the green beauty of villages embraced by the geometries of rice paddies and of the forest-banked river winding into the heart of darkness. The Philippines have served for Vietnam and Cambodia, but I would guess that the disguise is perfect.

"Apocalypse Now" is a chipped masterpiece and there are moments—again in the last sequences—when the strain of matching the technique to the emotional intensity of the Sheen-Brando confrontation draws attention to itself, and specifically the play of thin light and thick shadow comes to seem arty rather than artful. At other times Sheen's voice-over narration grows too portentous and threatens to turn grandeur into grandiosity.

Then again, it's almost too easy to pick at "Apocalypse Now." The film's long notoriety, Coppola's public indecision over the ending, the large variations in the film's length, as well as Coppola's occasionally peremptory postures, all invite adversarial attitudes. Those may or may not be balanced off against the bent-knee gratitude of those who are grateful for a high-risk film that tries to be about something.

It is not, that is, an easy film to see coolly. But the evidence on the screen is that this is Coppola, the master storyteller of "The Godfather," at work. Whatever its philosophical or political overlay, "Apocalypse Now" is an unusually suspenseful and unpredictable adventure story, continually aboil with energy and extraordinarily fertile in images and events.

From the opening moments, when Sheen is discovered in Saigon in a fleabag hotel, debauched, hung over and still twitching from his last assignment, Coppola generates a great quantity of excitement on the screen. There follow a whole series of set pieces, first an edgy and clandestine lunch with G.D. Spradlin as a general and Harrison Ford as his aide, setting Brando's fate, and Sheen's. A black-comic assault by helicopter airships (blaring Wagner's "Ride of the Valkyries" to terrify the inhabitants) and napalm-dropping jets, to seize the best surfing beach in 'Nam and only incidentally to launch Sheen's upriver transport, was evidently the heart of the original John Milius script for "Apocalypse" a decade ago. It survives as a dazzling piece of filmmaking, with Robert Duvall as the black-Stetsoned, surf-crazy, death-defying officer in command. By itself, it is a malevolent, absurdist parable on the war. Milius now shares script credit with Coppola.

The voyage upriver toward the near-mythical Kurtz, a Special Forces officer driven mad, apparently by the unique cruelty and appalling complexity of the war, is the core of the film. The journey is indeed into darkness, and it is a journey as well from the modern world toward the more primitive conditions (and horrors) of Brando's jungle fortress.

There are more set pieces en route—a teasing appearance by some Playmates at a supply depot deep in the jungle, a raunchy turn-on that turns into a riot. Most spectacularly, there is a night firefight at a temporary bridge, hallucinatory in its cockeyed brilliance—not least because the leaderless GIs appear drugged-out and crazed by fear equally. The straight-line war narrative merges, of course, into Joseph Conrad's *Heart of Darkness* from another continent, another time.

Whatever the literal borrowings of dialogue and incident from Conrad, "Apocalypse" must work or fail on its own. After one viewing, it seemed to me that the film was weakened by its debt to Conrad and had grown too consciously literary, ambiguous and pretentious—Brando with his Eliot and also his ritual makeup and OUR MOTTO—APOCALYPSE NOW painted in large white letters on the river wall of Brando's temple hideaway.

On a second viewing, I find the film more of a piece, with the coda, so to speak, making the ending less of a philosophical freeze-frame and providing something of the emotional symmetry the story demanded. It is still dazed and protracted stuff, a horror show that works to the degree it does because of the astonishing back pressure Coppola has built up during the voyage. The madness born of unendurable reality is timeless and universal, Coppola is saying at last. "The horror, the horror," Brando murmurs, having generated horrors as great as he inherited.

It may be that only Brando among actors could suggest the grandeur of the mind that is here overthrown. His reading of the role has the calm intensity of the truly mad. ("His mind is clear, it's his soul is mad," Dennis Hopper as a spacy photo-journalist says of him.) But Brando is Brando, carrying the luggage of his own pre-images and setting it aside less effectively, I felt, than he did in "The Godfather."

At last, the impact of "Apocalypse Now" is as unsettling as it is because the viewer has come to feel and grasp the horror that produced the figure, and the response is to the horror rather than to the figure. Sheen goes upriver on a patrol boat, and its crew was excellently cast by Coppola, with Albert Hall as the chief who commands the boat (and who dies by spear, in a modern war). Lawrence Fishburne is a seventeen-year-old black youth, a child at war. Sam Bottoms is a California surfer and Frederic Forrest, a New Orleans chef a long way from home. They are an affecting microcosm of the war.

Sheen's performance, in the course of which he suffered a heart attack, looks as exhausting as it must have been. Kurtz, and not he, is the crucial figure in the story, and it is frustrating not to know anything like as much about the assassinating captain as we know about Kurtz. But his ability to do what he does, never without moral twitches, is perhaps another shade of madness (and intended to be seen as such). His is, by any standards, a portrayal of lean, strong, clenched purposefulness, and you can imagine its having been written differently, not performed better.

The wondrous images, achieved in heroically difficult circumstances, are by the Italian cinematographer Vittorio Storaro. The production design, another heroic achievement, is by Dean Tavoularis. Richard Marks was the supervising editor and Coppola and his father, Carmine Coppola, both had a hand in the pulsing and largely synthesized music, which is atmospheric and at times almost sub-aural rather than intrusive.

No one, I think, who has ever cared about the movies can afford not to see "Apocalypse Now" sooner or later. Some ultimate and flawless perfection may have been narrowly missed. But as a noble use of the medium and as a timeless expression of a national anguish, it towers over anything that has been attempted by an American filmmaker in a very long time, and I include "The Deer Hunter."

All That Jazz

Bob Fosse, who died in 1987 at the age of 60, was one of those extraordinary filmmakers who has never been replaced and will likely never be. In "Cabaret" and "All That Jazz," he created the two best musicals of the decade, revealing what the musical could still achieve. His last film, "Star 80" in 1983, based on the Dorothy Stratten murder, was inventive as usual, but could not transcend its story.

THERE IS OR WAS A SCHOOL CALLED ACTION PAINTING, in which the gesture—bold, spontaneous, personal, direct, uncorrectible—was everything.

Films don't really lend themselves to bold, personal gestures, not with dozens of technicians and performers lurking like spiders and the meter running at $10,000 an hour and up and the gestures having to be transmitted down a longer chain of command than a purchase order in a government bureau. To create the sense of an artfully reckless personal statement in film is a far more testing and improbable achievement than reinventing the past or telling how boy meets girl.

But that's what Bob Fosse has done to a fare-thee-well in "All That Jazz," his superbly spendthrift explosion of energy, imagination, autobiography, choreography, fantasy and all-stops-out celebration of the possibilities of film.

"All That Jazz" has a little (or a lot) of everything, from open heart surgery, very graphic indeed, to the most erotic dance sequence ever filmed north of Tijuana, also very graphic indeed (sensual, not functional). From first to last, it is a *danse macabre* with the idea, the possibility, the imminence of death. Fosse himself was felled by but survived a massive heart attack, and the premonitions and the pain, the flashing back over one's whole life—its fantasies as well as its actualities—invest "All That Jazz" with its furious urgency and its tumultuous piling up of images, including Jessica Lange as a blue-bathed and whorishly sexy Angel of Death, who is also a mocking judge of the hero's life and, too, a teasing, beckoning guide to the afterlife, if any.

Fosse's surrogate is Roy Scheider as Joe Gideon, who started as a kid hoofer spacing the strippers in burlesque clubs and has become, like Fosse, a Broadway director-choreographer who also makes films. Where autobiography stops and invention (or spiritual autobiography) begins is not certain and not really important. The film finally must stand on its own as fiction, and it does, as an engrossing and occasionally overwhelming entertainment whose restless and unceasing invention and quick-shifting moods from dark to light to dark have no exact parallel anywhere in film.

Scheider, showering himself awake (or alive) again, choking down pills to start and sustain the day, commanding himself at the mirror to keep going, an invariable cigarette at the corner of his mouth, is a wonderment, a dancing dynamo whose portrayal of this life-splurging, death-obsessed man poses the Academy voters another mind-boggling decision. Trying out a new, slow balletic dance with a lovely twelve-year-old charmer named Erzebet Foldi as his daughter, Scheider is suddenly both an eloquent dancer and an actor of considerable tenderness.

Scheider/Gideon is elsewhere the compulsive lover, over-endowed with affection, under-gifted with fidelity, somehow, for all his frenzies, retaining the reluctant admiration of his ex-wife (Leland Palmer in a fine characterization, as a woman both embittered and concerned, yet still admiring) and of Ann Reinking (the striking beauty from "Movie-Movie") as the steadiest of his girls.

"All That Jazz" is with all else a lesson on, or at least a glimpse of, the making of dance. Its impressionistic opening sequences, of a stageful of dancers rehearsing, seen from high above and from all over by the agile camera of Guiseppe Rotunno, pull us into the choreographer's world and its unique authorship by dictation and demonstration.

Fosse did the script with the late Robert Alan Aurthur, and its seeming madness is actually never without method and an underlying sense, very strong, of form and progression. Scheider's day-starting shower and pill-taking is, for example, a motif, repeated as in chamber music, with falling and ever more ominous variations.

The film's momentarily bewildering pastiche of reality and fantasy sorts itself out into what is actually a rather orderly remembrance of things past (including a ribald humiliation at the hands of the strip club ladies) and a provocative examination by Gideon of his own motives and betrayals.

Not all of it works well, an allowable shortcoming in so original a film.

Another recurrent fantasy, with Ben Vereen as the glittering host of a su-perspecial variety show, is passable satire on television's incessant good cheer and golden decors. But more than the rest of the film it plays as choreography all too consciously togged out as fantasy. Even so, the final appearance of the Vereen ploy, as a kind of hallucinatory and disintegrat-ing symbol of the transit into the ultimate darkness, develops a weird and nightmarish power.

Most of the film's inventions work brilliantly well. One of these is a film within the film, which Scheider is re-editing even as he prepares a new stage musical. (He is the definitive workaholic, as Fosse himself evi-dently is.) The piece of film, by no coincidence, is a monologue on death, by Cliff Gorman as a nightclub comic with clear resemblances to Lenny Bruce. (Fosse, it will be remembered, directed "Lenny," and Gorman played the title role on Broadway.) The device of the re-editing does double duty or more. It establishes Gideon/Scheider's lifestyle and his compulsive personality; it is on its own terms as a routine raucously and blackly funny; repeated throughout the movie, it becomes another recur-ring motif that, like the morning shower, undergoes down-spiraling varia-tions as Gideon's own dance with death nears a climax.

Movies about death are not sure-fire crowd-pleasers, and "All That Jazz" does not flinch from its subject. But it is impossible to be about death and not to be about life, and "All That Jazz" has more jumpy, gaudy, razzamatazz, fire-sale, jingle-jangle, fandango, sexy vitality than any dozen films about nothing.

It is personal, gestural, intimate, extravagant, original and beautifully executed. It is Fosse's fourth feature and the most innovative film with music since his own "Cabaret." As he has shown in all his work, he is, with all his talent for images and movement, an unusually deft evoker of performances. He and Scheider have collaborated on a masterful portrait of a most marvelously complex and driven man.

The actresses, notably Palmer in a role that must to some extent re-call Fosse's own ex-wife, Gwen Verdon, are each remarkably individual. Lange performs even better without King Kong. Reinking is real and af-fecting as a woman who is reconciled to giving more love than she re-ceives from Gideon, but is not prepared for martyrdom on his behalf. In a brief casting-couch scene during which the caster is unexpectedly can-did, Deborah Geffner is wryly believable. Kathryn Doby is yet another of Gideon's persistent complications. Michael Tolan is his doctor, burdened with bad news and ignored warnings, and Anthony Holland is vivid as usual as a harassed songwriter. Among its several achievements, "All That Jazz" reconfirms anybody's belief in the infinite possibilities of film.

1980

Raging Bull

For once in this collection, I've edited myself. I wrote about "Raging Bull" twice, first in tandem with another film about the Italian-American experience: Taylor Hackford's "The Idolmaker," a well-made film whose only weakness was that it was not about Jake LaMotta. I saw "Raging Bull" a second time and expanded my thoughts about it, and I have here melded the two measurings of Martin Scorsese's darkly unforgettable work.

MARTIN SCORSESE, CONTINUING his intense explorations of his own origins that began with his first feature, "J.R., or Who's That Knocking at My Door," tells in "Raging Bull" the rise and fall and survival of the boxer Jake LaMotta, with a central performance by Robert De Niro that is probably the best of his remarkable career to date.

The aim of the protagonist, as in all the gangster movies from "Little Caesar" to "The Godfather," is to scratch, claw and scuffle an escape route out of the gray poverty and symbolic steerage of the underclass and make it big in all the coinages of American society. LaMotta, like many a sturdy young man of the streets before him and since him, opted for the ring.

"Raging Bull," adapted by Paul Schrader and Mardik Martin, two favored Scorsese collaborators, from LaMotta's candid confessions, published in 1970, is an arduous, unrelenting, rich, densely textured, harshly honest and mesmerizing film, and a disciplined and important achievement that is likely to go unchallenged for a long time as a portrait not only of LaMotta but of a particular segment of the American experience.

"Rocky" it isn't (details to follow), although the producers of "Rocky," Irwin Winkler and Robert Chartoff, produced "Raging Bull" as well. "Rocky" won by gaining a draw. LaMotta, in a sense, lost by winning. He rewrote Sophie Tucker's line about having been rich and having been poor. LaMotta was poor and he was rich and, believe him, it is hard to say which was more trouble.

Only a man with scar tissue around his eyes, ears, nose and soul, a man who had learned the hard way who he was and who he wasn't and made peace with himself, could sit for so unsparing a portrait. Hard times and mean streets may breed the odd saint, but LaMotta wasn't one of them. De Niro's LaMotta is hostile, suspicious, crude, sullen, amoral, insanely jealous and brutal when crossed. He also has an invincible will to win, even if it means dumping a fight to get a better one. I happened to see one of the LaMotta–Sugar Ray Robinson fights in Chicago, a blood-bath of incredible ferocity, and I had no doubts then or now that LaMotta was the most tenacious fighter of them all, a bull indeed.

The accounts of De Niro fattening up to portray the LaMotta of retirement, emceeing at a strip joint in Manhattan and then, round-faced and paunchy, reciting verse and the big scene from "On the Waterfront" in a tuxedo, are well-known. But it is De Niro's lean, hungry, young LaMotta, snarling at his harassed and frustrated first wife (Lori Anne Flax), courting his second (Cathy Moriarty) and fighting all the furies, that will stay in mind.

Scorsese has made "Raging Bull" in black-and-white (except for some blurry color snapshots and home movies of the champ at his short-lived family best) and it is absolutely right for those hard, impervious streets and the dank, stale dressing rooms and the smoke-choked arenas. It is right, black and white, in a larger symbolic way for lives of contrasty and primal feelings—rage, lust, greed, fear, despair.

Michael Chapman ("The Last Waltz") was again Scorsese's cinematographer, and the fight stuff in particular is brutally well done. The sweat glistens and the wounds bleed, the eyes glaze. But there is a difference— no real sentimental cheering for the bull, no orchestrating of suspense in which Rocky, say, cannot be allowed to fail. The reaction to the damage men can do to each other may still be horror, but the onlooking is this time a good deal cooler and more detached. The process, the experience, have become more important than the outcome.

The question for the viewer, and I suppose for the fate of the film itself, is whether the relatively calm fascination one feels for the excellence of De Niro's work and Scorsese's mastery in all areas overrides the fact that LaMotta is indeed not Rocky. He's a man examined so scrupulously as to be a lab specimen, interesting and perhaps even sympathetic in what he doesn't know about living. He is certainly not pitiable (a notion that would renew the rage), but he is a survivor, not a winner, and the deepest wounds are seen to be self-inflicted.

"Raging Bull" is one of the thin handful of superior films of any year. As in a paradox, it is both passionate and bleak, intimate and clinically removed. Scorsese in all his films has revealed a divided attitude toward the New York Italian-American subculture in which he arose: compassion for those who suffer along the mean streets, anger, shaded with despair, for the forces of the past—the paternalistic tradition, the church, the organized crime—that seem to him to stifle the possibilities of the young.

With its still-living real-life model, "Raging Bull" seems to me to be Scorsese's most perfectly shaped film, with none of the conflicting creative tugs that weakened the ending of "Taxi Driver," his previous collaboration with Schrader, and none of the uncertainties of shape and tone that undercut the excellences of "New York, New York," on which co-author Mardik Martin worked.

As always the supporting faces and performances are fresh and right. A newcomer, a model named Cathy Moriarty, is just about perfect as LaMotta's blond, sexy, sloe-voiced, teenaged wife Vicki. In the film she is an ironically ideal match for LaMotta—as much a casualty of the pressures of fame and success as he is and equally a character to be understood and not quite pitied.

Joe Pesci gives a superb performance as LaMotta's brother-manager, who tries long and hard and ultimately fails to save Jack (as he calls him) from his own ruinous self. It is Oscar-level work. [Pesci was nominated, did not win.]

The music, edited by Jim Henrickson, is an artful collage of period recordings, never intrusive, subliminally subtle, not unlike a jukebox you can hear from the tavern next door when there are breaks in the traffic noise.

It struck me the second time around that Scorsese had made significant use of what I can only call semi-slow motion—action slowed almost imperceptibly, just enough to create the impression that the moment means something very special to the protagonist who is observing it. I remember offhand a major story moment, although a minor visual moment, when LaMotta sees the brother from whom he is estranged coming out of a 43rd Street delicatessen. The action is neither frozen nor suspended in time, but it slows as if to register forever on LaMotta's consciousness.

When I saw the film again with a college audience, for all the artistic achievements the students acknowledged, the opinions were briskly divided. "What's the point," someone asked; "what's the justification for doing the movie?"

It's a reasonable question. In comparison to the "Rocky" fairy tale there is hardly anyone to root for. (The brother maybe, a little.) The best you can dredge up for De Niro's LaMotta is a grudging admiration for his stoneheaded if not Stone Age invincible courage and physical stamina. You understand his tears when he throws a fight as the cost of getting a title shot; you are a little less sympathetic when he kicks his downed brother in the belly and gives his wife a belt that would have stunned Sugar Ray. He's a boozer, a chaser, a Grade A, 100-proof vile-tongued male chauvinist consumed with jealousy and touched with paranoia. Other than that, a lovable swell kid and, at a minimum, a survivor.

He's nothing like a standard film hero. But there are any number of answers to the question why make the film. It is an illumination: of a man, a time, a sport, a culture. It is not incumbent on films to give positive moral guidance, but those who demand it can certainly see "Raging Bull" as avoidance therapy for human relations.

But I'm not sure that art requires any justification. Art as expensive as film has become requires some prudent expectation of public interest, and I find "Raging Bull" engrossing if not quite escapist or entertaining in the traditional hedonistic sense. But an artful work "Raging Bull" certainly is, and greatly satisfying in its excellence as craft. It is above all a personal expression that takes its place in a body of work—Scorsese's—that has begun to have the size and coherence of a major novelist's.